PENGUIN BOOKS

BOYS WILL BE BOYS

E. S. Turner was born in Liverpool in 1909 and educated in Shrewsbury and Newcastle under Lyme. During the 1930s he worked on newspapers in Glasgow as a reporter, sub-editor and columnist. After serving in the Royal Artillery he was editor of the War Office magazine *Soldier* from 1946 to 1957. He is now a well-known freelance writer, has been a regular contributor to *Punch* since 1933 and is a member of the *Punch* Table. He has had articles published in over seventy different publications, writing widely but in particular on travel.

Among his previous publications are *The Shocking History of Advertising* (1965, Penguin), *Roads to Ruin* (1966, Penguin), *A History of Courting, The Court of St James's, What the Butler Saw, All Heaven in a Race* and *May it Please Your Lordship*. His novels include *The Third Pip* (as Rupert Lang) and *Hemlock Lane*. His most recent book is *Amazing Grace: The Great Days of Dukes* (1975).

E. S. Turner is married and lives in Richmond-on-Thames. He was awarded the O.B.E. in 1953.

THE ALDINE ROMANCE OF INVENTION, TRAVEL, & ADVENTURE

JULES VERNE OUTDONE !!!] [LIBRARY.

FRANK READE JR., WITH HIS NEW STEAM HORSE AMONG THE COWBOYS; OR, THE LEAGUE OF THE PLAINS.

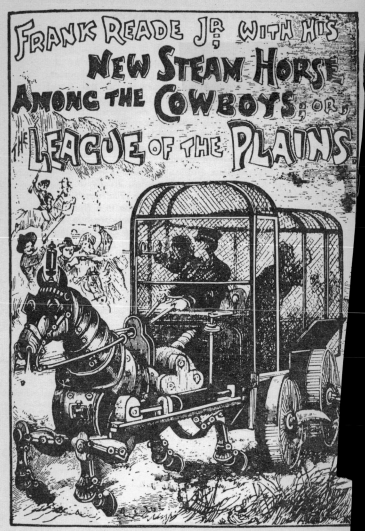

No. 8] While Frank manipulated the reins, Barney and Pomp kept up a steady [1d
fire upon the foe. The Cowboys lashed their horses, and tried
to overtake the Steam Horse.

E. S. TURNER

BOYS WILL BE BOYS

THE STORY OF SWEENEY TODD,
DEADWOOD DICK, SEXTON BLAKE,
BILLY BUNTER, DICK BARTON,
et al.

PENGUIN BOOKS

Penguin Books Ltd, Harmondsworth, Middlesex, England
Penguin Books Inc., 7110 Ambassador Road, Baltimore, Maryland 21207, U.S.A.
Penguin Books Australia Ltd, Ringwood, Victoria, Australia
Penguin Books Canada Ltd, 41 Steelcase Road West, Markham, Ontario, Canada
Penguin Books (N.Z.) Ltd, 182–190 Wairau Road, Auckland 10, New Zealand

—

First published by Michael Joseph Ltd 1948
Second edition 1957
Third edition 1975
Published in Penguin Books 1976

—

Copyright © E. S. Turner, 1948, 1957, 1975

—

Made and printed in Great Britain
by Richard Clay (The Chaucer Press) Ltd,
Bungay, Suffolk
Set in Linotype Baskerville

CONTENTS

ACKNOWLEDGEMENTS

I AM indebted to the late Philip Youngman Carter for the idea of this book, and for his help and encouragement.

Permission to reproduce extracts and illustrations was generously given by the Directors of the Amalgamated Press (now absorbed in the International Publishing Corporation), the Directors of Messrs D. C. Thomson and Co., the Editors and Publishers of *The Tatler* and *Horizon* and the late George Orwell.

I am grateful to Mr W. Howard Baker, of the Howard Baker Press, for helping me to bring up to date, for this third edition, the saga of Sexton Blake.

NOTE TO THIRD EDITION

Boys Will Be Boys was first published in 1948, when the juvenile idol of the day was the BBC's Dick Barton. It was revised and extended in 1957, after the Parliamentary battle over 'horror comics'. By that time the picture-strip was well on the way to ousting the printed story. The theory was (and is) that youth reared on television are capable of assimilating print only if it is accompanied and sustained by pictures.

In the space of a generation the cry has changed from 'Yaroooh!' to 'Aaaaargh!' The boys of Greyfriars are not entirely lost to the bookstalls, but they appear in handsome facsimile volumes of the *Magnet* tailored for the nostalgia trade. 'Frank Richards', otherwise Charles Hamilton, creator of Billy Bunter and Harry Wharton and Co., died on Christmas Eve, 1961, in his eighty-sixth year. A biography of this Grand Old Man, whose early life remains something of an enigma, is being written by a relative. He may be the first man to have achieved an entry in *Who's Who* under an alias. His white-haired admirers still meet to discuss and analyse his writings.

The *Boy's Own Paper* died in 1967. It had long fought the good clean fight, but if its fans ever met for readings from the works of Talbot Baines Reed they kept their sessions secret.

Sexton Blake, when this book was last revised, had just shaken off sixty years' asceticism and had introduced provocative young women into his entourage. Older readers dared not think what changes might follow the dissolution of the Baker Street monastery. Their worst apprehensions were unfounded. It was a shock when, in 1963, the old *Sexton Blake Library* came to an end, with Blake apparently retired to a foreign strand; but soon afterwards he

escaped into hard covers (see Chapter VIII). He was a
tougher and worldlier man than the middle-aged moralizer
who fell from a balloon into the English Channel in the
Marvel of 1893.

Even more hard-nosed and worldly is Nick Carter, the
American investigator who will soon be a centenarian.
Like Blake he has moved 'up market'. Instead of having
his own weekly he has his paperback series. A recent
chronicler attributes to him 'a face that might have belonged to a Renaissance princeling', a sensual mouth and,
like Blake, a quizzical eyebrow. We are invited to admire
his sexual prowess.

The name Marvel is now worn by a group of comics,
American in origin but English in imprint, whose ultra-
fantastic characters are compounded of ice, fire, smoke,
rubber, sand and builders' rubble. They are touched on
in the last chapter.

The Dundee boys' papers battle on, as predictably unpredictable as ever. It is rare for a paper to be merged
with another and then fight its way free again, as the
Wizard did. In a recent issue it carried a picture-strip
feature based on R. M. Ballantyne's 'Coral Island', as if
to show that nothing is too old-fashioned for the jet age.
The beefed-up hearties of this group still fight the world
wars over again, not to mention earlier imperial wars.
Every now and then a Member of Parliament is shocked
to find that these papers carry recruiting advertisements
for the armed forces. The Dundee publishers declined –
wisely, one feels – to lend any material or encouragement
to a 'celebration of comics' organized in 1970 by the
Institute of Contemporary Arts. It was entitled, inevitably, 'Aaaaargh!' The *Sunday Times Magazine* of 29
July 1973 published two alarming, full-page, grainy, dark
blue photographs of the 'mystery men' behind the *Wizard*
and *Beano*; the cover showed a third mystery man pacing
through a graveyard. It is hard to believe that such sombre,
even sinister-looking, men have been guilty of providing
so much innocent enjoyment.

This edition has been revised and brought up to date where necessary, but the list of 'births, marriages and deaths' among boys' papers in recent years is so long that no attempt has been made to log them all.

PREFACE

Literature is a luxury; fiction is a necessity.
— G. K. CHESTERTON

IN this book the reader is invited to take a backward plunge into the new mythology – the mythology of Sexton Blake and Deadwood Dick, of Jack Sheppard, Jack Harkaway and Billy Bunter; of all the idols of boyhood from Dick Turpin down to Dan Dare.

It should not be necessary to do as Alfred Harmsworth did in 1894 when he launched *Union Jack*, and assure the reader: YOU NEED NOT BE ASHAMED TO BE SEEN READING THIS!

Of the adult population of these islands, it is doubtful whether half of one per cent could truthfully claim that they had never dipped in their youth into what undiscriminating parents used to call 'bloods'. The writer's hope is that many will welcome the opportunity to look back, if not sentimentally, then critically or even shudderingly, at the he-men, the super-men and the bird-men whose adventures they followed under cover of Hall and Knight's Algebra or in the precarious privacy of bed.

It was a pity that this type of reading had to be associated with a feeling of guilt, though it may well be that this went to heighten the reader's appreciation. Probably there is no product of the human brain which has been the object of such remorseless and misconceived abuse as the boy's thriller. On no theme have magistrates, clergymen and schoolmasters talked more prejudice to the reported inch.

G. K. Chesterton in *The Defendant* (1901) brought down a withering fire on the critics who were branding 'penny dreadfuls' as criminal and degraded in outlook. He had grown impatient with the thesis that a boy who could not read stole an apple because he liked the taste of apple, but that a boy who could read stole an apple because his mind was aflame with a story about Dick Turpin. No less muddle-minded, he pointed out, were the critics who charged the authors of 'penny dreadfuls' with romanticizing outlaws, and yet praised the works of Scott, Stevenson and even Wordsworth who had done the same thing in the name of literature. Any reader who wished to revel in corruption, Chesterton pointed out, could do so by buying a full-length novel by a fashionable author. Such literature could not be bought at one penny, for if it were published at that price the police would seize it.

Critics had also urged, said Chesterton, that 'penny dreadfuls' ought to be suppressed because they were 'ignorant in a literary sense', which was like complaining that a novel was ignorant in the chemical sense, or in the economic sense, He said:

The simple need for some kind of ideal world in which fictitious persons play an unhampered part is infinitely deeper and older than the rules of good art, and much more important.

Robert Louis Stevenson, an addict in youth of 'penny dreadfuls', has told how little he cared about their literary qualities: 'Eloquence and thought, character and conversation, were but obstacles to brush aside as we dug blithely after a certain kind of incident, like a pig for truffles.'

The Times has been sensibly tolerant on the theme of boys' fiction. In 1918 the *Literary Supplement* deplored the parental policy of foisting on schoolboys 'pietistic powder concealed in jam':

Boys of school age have not yet arrived at writing books for themselves; but at least as the instinct of self-protection asserts itself they can kick; and the kick is the conscious healthy protest of youth that its mind shall not be pauperized by well-meaning seniors.

The same leading article was critical of four boys' writers hitherto regarded as unimpeachable: W. H. G. Kingston, for 'the curse of condescension' which sometimes afflicted him; R. M. Ballantyne, who 'sank to insufferable goody-goody'; Fenimore Cooper, whose *The Last of the Mohicans* only just passed muster because realistic-minded schoolboys knew him to be the author also of the notorious *The Pilot*, which was a regular prize at dames' schools; and Captain Marryat – 'To palm *Masterman Ready* upon a child and to hold *Peter Simple* up your sleeve was no better than a trick.' *The Times Literary Supplement* had a weak corner for 'penny dreadfuls'. There was a leader in 1941 regretting that the famous collection of the late Barry Ono – which that hospitable collector was so proud to display to his friends – was henceforth to be hidden away in the caverns of the British Museum.[1]

It was left to George Orwell, in *Horizon*, to lay waste the field of boys' thrillers on the ground that they are 'sodden in the worst political illusions of 1910'. At first thought, he admits, the idea of a left-wing boys' paper makes one slightly sick; no normal boy would look at it. Then he remembers that in Spain of pre-Franco days there were some successful examples of adventure fiction with a leftist slant. Even if this example cannot be copied here, he says, there is no reason why every boys' paper should be guilty of snobbishness and gutter patriotism. (For Orwell's blast and Charles Hamilton's counter-blast, see Chapter XIII.)

It may be that as the reader scans the ensuing chapters he will begin guiltily to try to assess how much of his present-day outlook was conditioned by the peculiar codes of the bravos of his boyhood, or to what extent his class

1. This collection of early 'penny dreadfuls' was quarried with excellent results by Louis James in his *Fiction for the Working Man, 1830–50* (O.U.P. 1963).

prejudices were sharpened by the tales of Greyfriars or St Frank's, or whether he voted Conservative because he was pretty sure that was how Sexton Blake voted in 'The Great Election Mystery'. If this kind of self-examination distresses him, he should lay the blame on George Orwell, who brought the question up.

This book, it must be emphasized, is purely a refresher course. It has no other object than to transport the sentimental reader back to that agreeable period when steam men puffed across the prairie trampling Indians underfoot; when the elect of Britain's boarding schools set off every other week by balloon or submarine to discover a lost city or a vanishing island; when almost every Northcliffe boys' paper carried a serial describing the invasion of Britain by Germans, French or Russians; when wellnigh every tramp, ice-cream vendor, organ grinder or muffin man turned out to be Sexton Blake; and when every self-respecting football team had its mysterious masked centre-forward.

The writer, researching through back numbers, found that memories were powerfully evoked by the advertisements alone: the coveted Daisy air rifle; the monster watch – 'yours for sixpence, chain free'; the singing scarf pins, shocking coils, multiplying billiard balls, solaphones, plurascopes, cella-phones, tubogliders, stink bombs and pocket picture palaces of a pre-atomic generation. By no means all the advertisements were aimed at boys. Stop blushing – yes. Watch yourself grow – yes. Learn ventriloquism – yes. Join our Christmas Chocolate Club – yes. But who was the advertiser getting at when he promised 'Red noses completely cured', when he urged 'Banish hair poverty', or undertook to cure the smoking habit in three days? Alongside an appeal for recruits to the armed Forces would appear the exhortation: 'Write to the Editor of *Answers* if you are not getting your right pension.' It would seem that the readers covered all the ages of man from childhood to second childhood, from pimples to rheumatism. And somewhere in this span – it is not certain where – were the readers who were expected to apply for the secret of making their hair curl ('Mine curled at once,' writes Major).

It may be that some readers will look through these pages in vain for any mention of their favourite hero or journal. The writer can only plead the vastness of the field. Take detectives alone. Then take only those detectives who, like Sherlock Holmes, had one-syllable surnames and two-syllable Christian names (with the accent on the first syllable): Sexton Blake, Nelson Lee, Falcon Swift, Ferrers Locke, Dixon Hawke, Martin Track and a dozen others. It is impossible to give a chapter on each. The best plan seemed to be to concentrate on Blake, the doyen of them all, and to lump the others together. This is perhaps hard on Nelson Lee, whose peculiar fate it was to become a detective-schoolmaster, and on Nick Carter, who was sufficient of an individualist to have a one-syllable first name and a two-syllable surname. Regretfully but firmly one had to omit the *Jester*'s tireless Hawkshaw, who saved so many buxom somnambulists from ghastly deaths.

The *Jester* and the other 'comics' have been touched on only lightly. Some day a thesis-writer will probably attempt to assess the social significance of the Bruin Boys and Weary Willie and Tired Tim.

It would have been easy to fill this volume with an account of Victorian 'penny dreadfuls' alone. The temptation has been resisted, partly because the number of readers who can remember following the adventures of Spring-Heeled Jack and Jack Sheppard must by now be limited. But it is important, as well as oddly fascinating, to examine the kind of literature from which the later boys' thrillers sprang. Whatever its faults, the 'penny dreadful' was a work of vivid imagination, as Wells and Barrie have testified. And if the shockers of those days seem altogether grimmer and gorier, it must be remembered that our grandfathers were that much nearer to an age of crude violence and crude superstition, of dwarfs and misshapen things, of legalized atrocity.

It would have been easy, too, to have written more about the *Boy's Own Paper, Chums* and *The Captain*, which were the kind of journals that parents wanted their sons to read. Many lads, however, preferred to put off perusal of these until they had acquired, at half price, from the boy next door all the journals they knew their parents did not want them to read.

It may surprise the reader, though not the reader of *Exchange and Mart*, to know that for many years there has been a busy trade in old boys' papers. It has been fostered by a number of amateur publications some of which are themselves collectors' items: *Collector's Miscellany* (no longer published); *Collectors Digest*, founded by Herbert Leckenby and edited latterly by Eric Fayne, an outstanding authority on Charles Hamilton; and the *Story Paper Collector*, published by William Gander from Transcona, Manitoba. In the unashamedly nostalgic pages of these magazines new discoveries about Jack Harkaway, Sexton Blake and Billy Bunter have been eagerly passed on; long-concealed identities hidden behind pen-names have been triumphantly revealed; the passing of well-loved publications has been mourned; and readers have been invited to test their memories on questions like: 'What was the title of the first school story in the *Boys' Realm* and who wrote it?' and 'Name the Eskimo who was a prominent character in several *Boys' Friend* serials.' Here and there dwindling groups of enthusiasts meet in each other's houses to exchange new lore and old copies, and to shake their heads over a generation which has lost Nelson Lee and gained the Incredible Hulk.

Some day perhaps there will be a book about boys' papers from the inside. No doubt it will be highly disillusioning. It will contain the real reason why such-and-such a magazine was killed, why such-and-such a character was slain in his apparent prime, to be replaced by a son indistinguishable from the father. It will describe angry battles by authors to retain exclusive rights over the characters they created and nurtured. It will give details about the working habits and private lives, if any, of those prodigies who, adapting the battery-hen system to literature, took on contracts to write 50,000 words a week *and upwards*, and fulfilled them, without benefit of 'ghosts' or dictaphones or even secretaries. It will describe the editorial conferences at which story policy was decided, at which old taboos were discarded or new ones introduced; at which the circulation staff made their periodic demand that a popular character should be made to undergo adventures in Birmingham, Liverpool, Glasgow or Leeds; at which the decision was made to put someone on to dusting off old plots and giving them a new lease of life; and at which everyone, from general manager to office boy, was invited to suggest ways of injecting adrenalin into a flagging serial. They were shrewd men who ran the fiction factories both north and south of the Tweed. They did not make many mistakes, and when they did they passed them off as triumphs. Was there ever a boys' paper which was discontinued on the ground that it lacked support? Two weeks before a journal was due to be pole-axed would come the warning 'Watch for a Sensational Surprise!' In the last issue would appear a dozen warnings – 'Don't ask for So-and-So next week, ask for Such-and-Such!' The reason given was that So-and-So had proved so popular that it had been decided to extend it and include in it a variety of features never before assembled in any magazine. In the thrill of this news nobody bothered to ask why the title was being changed. Perhaps it is too much to hope for a behind-the-scenes book. There are too many tricks of the trade which it would be impolitic to give away.

Meanwhile, let us do the best we can without access to the innermost secrets.

Summon up the blood!

CHAPTER I

GOTHIC HANGOVER

CHARLES ADDAMS, the macabre-minded artist of *The New Yorker*, has a sketch of a sinister-looking building which bears a notice: 'Beware of the Thing'. That notice is a fair expression of the Gothic mood in which the boys' 'blood' was born, more than a hundred years ago.

Popular fiction of the early nineteenth century was steeped in darkness and diablerie. Spectres gliding in a green phosphorescence, hags picking over the bones of charnel houses, deathsheads in closets, heirs to great estates chained in dungeons, forests stuffed with robbers and werewolves, graves creaking open in the moonlight to let the vampires out – these were the stock-in-trade of the Gothic, and bogus Gothic, novelist. The vogue for these romantic horrors had been set by Horace Walpole (*The Castle of Otranto*), Anne Radcliffe (*The Mysteries of Udolpho*) and Matthew Gregory Lewis (*The Monk*): and there were plenty of pens ready to imitate, translate, paraphrase or purloin for the benefit of the literate fringe of the working classes. In rising spate, and at ever cheaper cost, came romances set in clammy castles in the German forests or in convents ruled by degenerate nuns who wielded the knout upon their novices. The atmosphere of all of them was oppressive. Neither indoors nor outdoors was there a stirring of fresh air. In the turrets of castles censers smoked before unholy altars; no one opened a window, unless to jump from it. Out of doors the air was foul with the reek of gibbets.

There was one basic plot running through the Gothic thrillers. Indeed it grew to be the basic plot of the nineteenth century. It was that of the young and rightful heir deprived of his birthright by evil-scheming relatives or guardians. So that the reader might be sure that he was

receiving the familiar prescription, the plot was frequently
outlined at length in the sub-title of the story. For example:

Lovel Castle, or the Rightful Heir Restored, a Gothic Tale;
Narrating how a Young Man, the supposed son of a Peasant,
by a Train of Unparalleled Circumstances, not only discovers
who were his Real Parents, but that they came to Untimely
Deaths; with his Adventures in the Haunted Apartment,
Discovery of the Fatal Closet, and Appearance of the Ghost of
his murdered Father; relating also how the Murderer was
brought to Justice, with his Confession and the restoration to
the Injured Orphan of his title and estates.

This plot was gratefully taken up in the thirties and
forties by the popular low-priced magazines which began
to compete for the pence of the masses, and by the publishers of penny parts – to be known all too soon as 'penny
dreadfuls' – which for the next half-century were to provide sorely needed escapism in humble homes.

The first 'penny dreadfuls' were not aimed at the juvenile market, but the scalp-tingling subject-matter readily
seduced the young from their lukewarm loyalty to *Robinson Crusoe* and *Quentin Durward*. Edward Lloyd, founder
of *Lloyd's Newspaper*, who put out a wide range of penny-
a-week Gothic shockers during the forties, was not sufficiently hypocritical to pretend that he was publishing for
adults only. It has been put on record by Thomas Frost
(*Forty Years' Recollections*, 1860) that Lloyd, if in doubt
whether a manuscript held the elements of popular appeal, would deliberately 'try it out on the office boy'. The
procedure was explained to Frost, who was hoping to sell
a story for publication in penny parts, by Lloyd's manager
– 'a stout gentleman of sleek costume and urbane manners':

'Our publications circulate among a class so different in
education and social position from the readers of three-volume
novels that we sometimes distrust our own judgement and
place the manuscript in the hands of an illiterate person – a

servant, or machine boy, for instance. If they pronounce favourably upon it, we think it will do.'

Lloyd, who operated from Salisbury Square, off Fleet Street, surrounded himself by a small group of writers of demoniac imagination, prodigious output and an engaging lack of scruple. Outstanding among them was Thomas Peckett Prest, supposedly a relative of a Dean of Durham, who for all his industry rates no mention in the reference books of today. His chief claims to notice are that he was the creator of Sweeney Todd, a legend destined to span the generations (see next chapter); and that he was almost certainly the head of the group who, at Lloyd's behest, plagiarized the works of Dickens as fast as they came out. The law of the day offered friendly shelter to literary pirates, and Lloyd was able to make the nucleus of his fortune by putting out the *Penny Pickwick, Oliver Twiss, Nickelas Nicklebery, Martin Guzzlewit* and others as thinly disguised. Enthusiasm for Dickens was so great and uncritical that it readily embraced all his imitators. 'Bos' was the pseudonym under which Prest and his associates laboured. According to Montague Summers,[1] the original idea had been to ascribe the piracies to 'Boaz', but this name was ruled out on the peculiar ground that it was more dangerously close to Dickens's 'Boz' than was 'Bos'; and also on the ground that it was too Biblical.[2]

Before he took on the mantle of 'Bos', Prest had edited *The Calendar of Horrors*, which included a story called *Geralda the Demon Nun*. He continued to write many tales in the same vein for Lloyd. The grand catalogue of

1. *A Gothic Bibliography.*
2. Dickens fulminated in vain, not only against Lloyd but against dramatists like Stirling and Moncrieff who produced complete stage versions of his novels before he himself was in sight of the last chapter. His threat to hang his imitators 'on gibbets so lofty and enduring that their remains shall be a monument to our just vengeance to all succeeding ages' was greeted with derision. He took some of the pirates to court, but, in his own words, 'I was treated as if I were the robber instead of the robbed.'

his works contains such inviting titles as *The Maniac Father, or The Victims of Seduction*, and *Vice and Its Victims, or Phoebe the Peasant's Daughter*.

A characteristic of Prest and all Lloyd's writers was that they could turn their pen to any kind of fiction. Most of their stories were published anonymously and in consequence it is almost impossible to distinguish one man's work from that of another; bibliographies are sadly contradictory. Between them these writers who constituted the Salisbury Square School piled up a library of Gothic delights which included *The Black Monk, or The Secret of the Grey Turret*; *Almira's Curse, or The Black Tower of Bransdorf*; *The Ranger of the Tomb, or The Gypsy's Prophesy*; and *The Castle Fiend*. But Lloyd's most ghoulish and goriest publication was probably *Varney the Vampire*, which preceded Bram Stoker's *Dracula* by nearly half a century. The British Museum attributes this work to the astonishing James Malcolm Rymer, who was reputed to keep ten serials running at the same time. He also wrote under the name of Errym; a further anagram yields Merry, which may or may not have been his real name.

Varney the Vampire had as its alternative title *The Feast of Blood*, which was if anything an understatement; the story was an unmitigated shocker. According to the author's preface, the death of a real-life Sir Francis Varney 'made a great noise in the public prints for the year 1713', but the stories in the public prints of that period were hardly distinguished for their authenticity. The opening illustration showed a buck-toothed horror sinking its jaws deep in the throat of a fair young woman lying prostrate over her bed; in the background was a portrait of a saturnine cavalier who surveyed the scene with relish. Here is an excerpt from the first chapter:

The figure turns half round, and the light falls upon its face. It is perfectly white – perfectly bloodless. The eyes look like polished tin; the lips are drawn back, and the principal feature next to those dreadful eyes is the teeth – projecting like those of some wild animal, hideously, glaringly white and fang-like.

It approaches the bed with a strange gliding movement. It clashes together its long nails that literally appear to hang from the finger ends. No sound comes from its lips . . .

The storm has ceased – all is still. The winds are hushed; the church clock proclaims the hour of one; a hissing sound comes from the throat of the hideous being and he raises his long gaunt arms – the lips move. He advances. The girl places one small foot from the bed on the floor. She is unconsciously dragging the clothing with her. The door of the room is in that direction – can she reach it?

With a sudden rush that could not be foreseen – with a strange howling cry that was enough to awaken terror in every breast, the figure seized the long tresses of her hair and twining them round his bony hands he held her to the bed. Then she screamed – Heaven granted her then the power to scream. Shriek followed shriek in rapid succession. The bed clothes fell in a heap by the side of the bed – she was dragged by her long silken hair completely on to it again. Her beautiful rounded limbs quivered with the agony of her soul. The glassy horrible eyes of the figure ran over the angelic form with a hideous satisfaction – horrible profanation. He drags her head to the bed's edge. He forces it back by the long hair still entwined in his grasp. With a plunge he seizes her neck in his fang-like teeth – a gush of blood and a hideous sucking noise follows. *The girl has swooned and the vampire is at his hideous repast!*

The incomparable Rymer kept his tale going for 220 chapters. He gloated on the lustrous eyes and rosy cheeks of the happy, well-fed vampire; on the shot vampire reviving in the first rays of moonlight; on the impaling of suspected corpses of young women with a wooden stake (an illustration shows a spectator with a fine sense of fitness raising his hat during this proceeding); on a covey of vampires dragging a new corpse into the moonlight and inciting it to deeds of mischief; and on a couple of gibbering resurrectionists fleeing from an opening casket in the vaults of a church. At length came the written confession of Sir Francis Varney, that unhappy miscreant perpetually deprived of what the author called 'the downy freshness of Heaven's bounty'. In other words, although he had died several times Sir Francis could not lie down. 'I have a keen remembrance of being hunted through the streets of London in the reign of King Henry IV,' he wrote. His second 'death' was suffered at the hands of Charles II and Rochester, who wanted no surviving witnesses to one of their whoring expeditions in Pimlico. A postcript to the story recorded the visit to Naples of an ugly, wealthy Englishman, who asked for a guide to Vesuvius. Briefing this guide amid the poisonous odours of the volcano, the stranger said:

'You will say that you accompanied Varney the Vampire to the crater of Mount Vesuvius, and that, tired and disgusted with a life of horror, he flung himself in to prevent the possibility of a reanimation of his remains.'

Before the guide could utter anything but a shriek Varney took one tremendous leap and disappeared into the burning mouth of the mountain.

The only light relief in these 828 closely printed pages was that provided by fire, shipwreck, cliff falls, collapse of great buildings and fantastic thunderstorms. But from the length of the story it is obvious that it had an insatiable following. At the end of a preface to the reprinted work in 1847 Rymer said: 'To the whole of the Metropolitan Press for their laudatory notices the author is peculiarly obliged.' Evidently there were publications which did not disdain to assess the merits of 'penny dreadfuls', though the writer has not come across one.

Rymer is credited with being the author of *Ada, the Betrayed, or the Murder at the Old Smithy*. Some of his works defy classification; for instance, *The Unspeakable, or The Life and Adventures of a Stammerer*.

Edward Lloyd also published a number of domestic romances with titles like *Fatherless Fanny, or The Mysterious Orphan*, and *Alice Horne, or the Revenge of the Blighted One*, full of go-and-never-darken-this-door-again and dead-dead-and-never-called-me-mother. Prest and Rymer turned these out with accomplished ease.

Nor did Lloyd overlook the historical romance. Here, however, he had the field by no means to himself. Pierce

Egan, for instance, rarely lacked a publisher for his ponderous and bloodthirsty romances. Historians accuse him of a contempt for fact and a predilection for scenes of cruelty and slaughter, but acquit him of any 'immoral or irreligious' tendencies. The editor of the *London Journal* sought to dispense with Egan's gory romances in 1859 and began printing the works of Sir Walter Scott, but had to recall Egan hurriedly; not the first or the last time that Scott was soundly defeated in the lists of popular fiction.

Egan's style was floridly prolix. His characters would stand and apostrophize each other in melodramatic metaphor for columns on end. Here is an extract from *Quintin Matsys, the Blacksmith of Antwerp*, which introduced a band of German vigilantes known as the *Fehm-gerichte*:

'To Satan with thee! thou croaking frog – thou blot on our 'scutcheon – thou canker in our flower – thou worm upon a green leaf. I hate to look on thee, thou ugly weed in our garden! Thou ever comest as a blight. I know whenever I see thy sneaking, paleface visage that I must pray the devil for help, for there is some cursed disaster sure to follow thy appearance. Out of my sight, thou venom-jawed reptile, or I may forget thou'rt my brother and strangle thee.

'Degenerate descendant of a family that had no stain upon its character until thou hast placed it there; unworthy follower of an art itself so elevated that its votaries should be the soul of honour! Base, unmanly, evil-minded knave! who hast crawled into the bosom of my peaceful home to void that poison on all within thy influence, quit my sight and never let my eyes suffer the disgrace of gazing on one so false and vicious!'

In spasmodic demand from the forties onward was the sea story – usually a tale of buccaneers or smugglers. There was precious little ozone or salt spray in the earlier stories, however. One of Lloyd's titles was *The Death Ship, or The Pirate's Bride and the Maniac of the Deep*. The seas were cluttered with spectral barks and gallows ships (with men hanging from every available spar from the yardarms to the flying jib boom). When the hero, cheated of his inheritance, put to sea there were hags in the hold and hunchbacks in the rigging. The pirate chief would prove to be a giant Negro, glittering with jewels as big as pigeons' eggs, whose whim it was to dine in his saloon with half a dozen skeletons, all that remained of the masters and midshipmen of His Majesty's sloops sent to take him. Setting up skeletons for the captain's table was only one of a score of gruesome tasks for the ship's surgeon under the Skull and Crossbones; he had to be an anatomist of no mean attainments.

The writers of these tormented sea stories made no strong claims to nautical knowledge. They were happiest when they could bring the hero ashore to a sorceress's cabin where snakes curled above altars laden with skulls and the word 'Death' was embroidered menacingly on the altar drop. The pirates' cavern was another favourite haunt. Here, surrounded by the loot of the seven seas, the robbers would stage spectacular carousals. Tired of swilling rare wines down their gullets, they would crave something more exciting:

'Fill up your glass,' cries the Captain, '*and this time we will drink it in flames*!'

All the lights are extinguished, splinters of wood are kindled, and the flaming goblets set fire to and quaffed by the whole band at a single gulp.

That there were certain dangers in this practice is seen by an extract from the innocently titled story *The Darling of Our Crew* which appeared under the imprint of Edwin Brett in 1880 (even at that date popular fiction was often hag-ridden):

She (Mother Shebear) made her way to a keg which stood before the fire.

From this she took a pint of raw brandy and put it over the fire, until it seemed on the point of exploding, and a blue lambent flame floated on the top.

Chuckling fiendishly as she regarded this, she blew out the flame and drank half of it at a draught.

Now madness glared in her eyes unmistakably.

She drank off the remainder of the fearful potion and danced.

Her face assumed a frightful colour.

She stretched forth her long talons, yelling in the fierce grip of delirium tremens, as she advanced to where Jack was, to fling him into the flames, shrieking –

'Now, boy, you shall be my victim. Ha! Ha! Ha!'

Hitherto he had stood horrified and fascinated.

But the instinct of self-preservation was strong within him.

He stepped back and drew his pistol to fire.

But there was no necessity for him to use his pistols.

A sight which no pen can adequately describe greeted him.

The hag paused in her rush and pressed her hand over her breast.

Then the fearful sounds she was uttering came forth no more.

Their place was taken by a bluish lambent flame that came forth from her mouth and curled in fearful fantastic wreaths about her face.

The boy covered his face with his hands.

He could gaze no more.

The sight was too awful.

Moments passed.

Centuries they seemed to him.

Again he ventured to look up.

She was still standing there but another change had come over her.

Now the features that had likened her to humanity had disappeared.

She was an incandescent mass of matter like a statue, burning and glowing like the centre of a fire.

He sprang forward.

There was some water in a bucket.

He seized it and poured it over what had once been a woman.

The water turned at once to steam and flew off.

But it had no perceptible effect in quenching the burning mass.

Again and again he tried.

The result was the same.

Water had no power to put out the burning mass!

He sat down in sheer despair.

The fearful effluvia cast off by the burning body made him ill.

And so he sat there sick with horror and watched the mass turn from red to dull blue and finally go out altogether.

Some of the writers of 'penny dreadfuls' had axes to grind. The redoubtable G. W. M. Reynolds, Chartist sympathizer and founder of *Reynolds' Weekly Newspaper* (1850), used every opportunity to play up the violent contrast between Wealth and Poverty. His marathon work, *The Mysteries of London*, inspired by Eugene Sue's *The Mysteries of Paris*, ran for the best part of a decade, though after the first two volumes other pens took over. It professed to be an exposure of voluntary vice in high places and involuntary vice in low places, of the system by which 'the daughter of a peer is nursed in enjoyments and passes through an uninterrupted avenue of felicity from the cradle to the tomb; while the daughter of poverty opens her eyes at her birth upon destitution in all its most appalling shapes and at length sells her virtue for a loaf of bread'.

Reynolds left little to his readers' imaginations. His slums were incestuous, pox-ridden hells in which pigs ate the bodies of newly-dead babes and hardened undertakers' men fainted at the sights which met their eyes. Hump-backed dwarfs, harridans and grave-robbers groped past against a background of workhouses, jails, execution yards, thieves' kitchens and cemeteries. His readers could depend on him to bring in the theme of maiden virtue rudely strumpeted as often as possible. The downfall of one daughter of the poor began when she 'sold her face' – that is, allowed masks to be made from it, even though these were for the modelling of Madonnas in Catholic chapels. She next sold her likeness to an artist; then her bosom to a sculptor (he is pictured poised over her naked torso with a pair of callipers); and finally her whole form to a photographer (French). At a later stage her wealthy protector asked her why she was *distraite* in his house. The reason was that it contained reminders of most of the steps in her downfall: a plaster of paris Diana in a staircase recess was the work of the man who had bought her face; a portrait of Venus rising from the waves was the work of the artist who had bought her likeness; and a female bust was the work of the man who had bought her bosom. As for her virtue, she reminded her protector, he himself had bought that. But what, asked Reynolds, was the girl's alternative to selling herself piecemeal? To work for a farthing and a half per hour at embroidering flowers, or to earn twopence-halfpenny a time stitching 'dissecting trousers' for sale to anatomy students.

When his indignation grew too much for him Reynolds would reproduce workhouse dietary tables or introduce diagrams of this kind:

The Sovereign

The Aristocracy

The Clergy

The Middle Classes

The Industrious Class

Declared the author:

The lowest step in the ladder is occupied by the class which is the most numerous, the most useful, and which ought to be the most influential.

The average annual incomes of the individuals of each class are as follows:

Sovereign £500,000
The Member of the Aristocracy . . . £30,000
The Priest £7,500
The Member of the Middle Class . . . £300
The Member of the Industrious Class . . £20

Is this reasonable? Is this just? Is this even consistent with common sense?

Then he went on:

It was New Year's Day, 1839.

The rich man sat down to a table crowded with every luxury; the pauper in the workhouse had not enough to eat. The contrast may be represented:

Turtle, venison, turkey, hare, pheasant, perigord pie, plum pudding, mince pies, jellies, blanc-mange, trifles, preserves, cakes, fruits of all kinds, wines of every description.	half-pound bread, four ozs. bacon, half-pound potatoes, one and a half-pints of gruel.

And it was New Year's Day, 1839. But to proceed ...

And to give him credit, when he did proceed Reynolds left few dull passages, though sometimes half a column was taken up with a glossary of thieves' slang. He also persuaded his artist to provide, in addition to the customary illustration every eight pages, incidental illustrations showing the secrets of card-sharping and of dice manipulation. No one could say that Reynolds did not give value for money.

For those pre-typewriter days, his output was high. Once, fired perhaps by the achievements of Rymer, he took on, and won, a bet that he would write simultaneously four romances each involving an eight-page weekly instalment.[1] Among his chronicles of erring womankind were *Pope Joan, Lives of the Harem* and *Mary Price, or the Memoirs of a Servant Maid*. He died a respectable churchwarden.

Statistics about the sales of early 'penny dreadfuls' are hard to come by, but there is no doubt that these ill-printed sheets formed the basis of many a publisher's fortune. The successful romances went on for years, then after an interval were republished under the same or different titles, or were appropriated by rivals and purged or made

1. To many a latter-day writer for boys, a feat like that would seem unremarkable.

bloodier according to taste. Penny parts were rarely dated, and not all bore a publisher's imprint. It was a common custom, in launching a new 'penny dreadful', to announce 'Numbers Two and Three Given Away With Number One.' Often 'beautiful chromo pictures' were presented open-handedly during the early chapters, then more frugally as the story caught on. Some publishing houses made a habit of presenting with alternate issues sets of scenes and cut-out characters for use in toy theatres – the 'penny plain, two-pence coloured' models beloved by Robert Louis Stevenson – along with an offer of a book of words, price one penny.

'Penny dreadfuls' were sold, not only by newsagents, but by all kinds of small shopkeepers – tobacconists, sweet sellers, chandlers – who were attracted by the high rate of discount allowed by the publishers. James Greenwood in *The Wilds of London* gave a glimpse of the economics of publishing penny parts in the sixties, and it is likely that Lloyd's publications were marketed on very similar terms. First, Greenwood pointed out that each penny part weighed a mere quarter-ounce against the two ounces afforded by such meritorious publications as *Leisure Hour* and the *Family Herald*. He declared: 'It is the infinitesimal quantity of trash that may be palmed off for a penny that serves as the carrier bait to attract towards it the blow-flies of the book trade.' The ordinary trade discount, he said, was 25 per cent, but the publishers of penny parts were able to pay twice that and more. A dealer could buy them at fivepence a dozen and later exchange unsold copies for an equal number of the latest instalment.

According to Thomas Catling in *My Life's Pilgrimage* the practice in Lloyd's Salisbury Square was to plan each story eight weeks in advance. For each instalment of eight book-size pages the author received ten shillings. It was small wonder, in view of these sweated rates, that many writers found it easier and more profitable to plagiarize stories from across the Atlantic. If contemporary evidence is to be believed, their working day was spent, not disagreeably, in eliminating Americanisms, changing Saratoga to Brighton, Senator to Duke and 'brown-stone mansion on Fifth Avenue' to 'stately edifice in Belgravia'. It was a two-way traffic, for the Americans were pirating British publications at the same time.[1]

The task of editing and proof-reading 'penny dreadfuls' would appear to have been discharged light-heartedly. There was no attempt to make an instalment end at a logical pause in the narrative. Rarely was there any attempt to build up a climax, in order to stimulate the reader to buy the next number. Possibly such a device would have been considered meretricious by the peculiar standards of the time; it is more likely that editor and author just could not be bothered. As it was, an instalment frequently ended in the middle of a sentence of dull explanation, and there was no 'summary of what has gone before' in the next instalment. It was by no means rare for the illustrations to refer to a previous part, or to a future part; occasionally they bore no relation to the story whatever. Spelling mistakes were nearly as copious as grammatical mistakes, and they were legion. Few of the writers of penny parts seemed to be happy about their moods or tenses. Any entry into the field of the conditional or the subjunctive was usually doomed to failure. Gradually extreme simplicity of style came to be cultivated – that *pizzicato*, short-sentence style of which a glimpse has already been seen in the extract from *The Darling of Our Crew*. The old school of writers despised this literary adulteration, pointing out that some columns of narrative contained more white space than black. Each

1. The *Quarterly Review* (1890) describes how an English author complained that he had found on an English bookstall a plagiarized version of one of his books. It turned out that his original work had been pirated in America. This in turn had been pirated in Britain, and 'translated' back into English (though not quite the same English as the original) by a firm which was ignorant of its English origin. This firm, however, was able to escape the consequences by showing that the plot had originally been lifted from a German source.

paragraph consisted of but a single sentence, and five out of six sentences were strangled at birth. Quite a number of sentences, indeed, contained one noun, one verb and nothing more. Sometimes they did not contain even a verb. All affectations like colons and semi-colons were ruthlessly purged, but exclamation marks were used profusely. Simplification – presumably for the benefit of the only-just-literate public and not (as some averred) for the convenience of only-just-literate authors – was carried to a pitch never seen before or since. Two possibilities cannot be ruled out: that short-sentence style was a deliberate economy of effort by writers earning considerably less than a penny a line; and that sometimes the extreme brevity of the paragraphs may have been a desperate editorial device to spin out copy which had fallen short of the space allotted.

Here is a characteristic short-weight passage from *The Young Apprentice, or The Watchwords of Old London*:

She could see every now and then glimpses of the road and the solitary windmill, whose phantom-like sails moved slowly some quarter of a mile away.

This was all.

No human being seemed here.

Not even a wild animal disturbed the stillness by leaping from its lair.

Yet presently, as I have said, footsteps seemed following her.

She stopped and listened.

All was still.

Then again she advanced.

The steps went on once more.

She became alarmed.

Should she go back?

Or should she hide herself?

The latter idea she soon dismissed.

It would be useless.

If followed in the way she imagined, the one who followed could see her and would find her at once.

So she hurried on more quickly.

'I shall soon see Max,' she thought, 'and he will protect me.'

Suddenly she started back in horror.
A man was hanging from the tree.
It was the Alsatian.
She shrieked aloud.

With all their editorial infelicities the 'penny dreadfuls'
prospered. Some, like *Tyburn Dick*, came out twice a
week, on Tuesdays and Fridays. It was very rare for them
to carry advertisements, unless of romances published by
the same house, hence a healthy circulation was essential
for profit-making. A flagging story would be knocked on
the head, without compunction, no matter how far the
plot had progressed; a successful one had to be kept going
at all costs. The author might have made his plans to
finish the story in, say, a score of instalments, but would
find himself forced to spin it out for fifty, or a hundred.

Thomas Catling tells of one of Lloyd's woman writers
who unexpectedly sent in the last instalment of a serial
which had looked like running for a long time. Lloyd sent
round a trusted representative to find out what was the
trouble. The answer was that the lady was imminently
expecting a baby. Tactfully, they persuade her to write as
much as possible in the fortnight which remained. A few
chapters came in, then the supply stopped abruptly. As
the printers' deadline grew uncomfortably close Lloyd put
one of his own writers on the job of improvising an instalment. This conscienceless deputy skimmed through
the previous chapter without bothering to read the earlier
ones, and dashed off enough copy to placate the printer.
When the authoress was able to sit up she grew most indignant over the interpolation; but on being pressed to
supply twelve more chapters her displeasure abated.[1]

1. There is a delightful story, attributed to more than one publishing house, of the serial writer who disappears in the middle of
a story. As he shows no sign of turning up, it is decided to carry on
without him. Unfortunately he has left his hero bound to a stake,
with lions circling him, and an avalanche about to fall for good
measure (or some such situation). Relays of writers try to think of a
way out, and give it up. Then at the eleventh hour the missing

THE YOUNG APPRENTICE

OR, THE WATCHWORDS OF OLD LONDON

"NELLY STARTED BACK IN HORROR."

"Well, Max," he said, "you must go your way. My daughter can never wed one who is so utterly an enemy to his king and his country also. Return to me in a week, and let me hear that your ideas are changed. Otherwise, Nelly can never be more to you than she is."

"May I not bid her farewell?" asked Max, sorrowfully.

Typical title page to a popular Victorian 'penny dreadful'

(Clare Leighton in her book *Tempestuous Petticoat* tells
how the *accouchements* of her mother, Marie Connor
Leighton, who wrote 'powerful' serials for Northcliffe,
caused dismay among her editors. Northcliffe did not
share their fears, asserting that not even triplets would
prevent Mrs Leighton from completing her instalments.)

One of the risks of publishing penny parts was that an
author might develop a grievance and summarily dispatch
his characters in their prime. Rymer, at one stage in his
career, is said to have adopted this course, placing all his
rogues in a boat and sending it to the bottom of the
Thames. He was, it seems, following a precedent set by
another writer on receiving a better offer from a rival publisher.[1] In such an event, the killing-off instalment could
be thrown away and the story handed over to another
writer.

Many stories have accumulated about Lloyd. In the
course of a restless youth George Augustus Sala was ap-
prenticed for a short spell to a Mr Calvert, who cut – 'or
rather chopped' – the illustrations for Lloyd's penny publications. Sala in his *Life and Adventures* claims to have
received from Lloyd a letter asking for more blood –
much more blood, spouting blood in fact, and more prominent eyes. Illustrations, supposedly the work of Sala, from
The Heads of the Headless suggest that he did his best to
follow instructions. In later life, Sala resented suggestions
that he had written 'penny dreadfuls' for Lloyd. In 1871
he collected £500 damages from an author who alleged,
inter alia, that he was the author of *Ada, the Betrayed*
and *Sweeney Todd*.

Lloyd's romances were among those sternly criticized by
a fellow publisher, Charles Knight, in *Passages of a Working Life* (1865). Knight spoke of the mortification inspired

---

author returns. He takes the briefest look at the previous instalment
and then, without a moment's hesitation, writes: 'With one bound
Jack was free.'

1. See 'Claude Duval in Literature', by W. Roberts, *National
Review*, June 1925.

by much of the literature of the forties in 'those who, like myself, had formed an over-sanguine estimate of the benefit that was likely to result from the general diffusion of the ability to read'. He went on to cite 'manufactories ... where large bodies of children are employed to arrange types, at the wages of shirt makers, from copy furnished by the most ignorant, at the wages of scavengers'. It is not clear just whose sweat-shops these were. Certainly Knight's charge of 'diffusing a moral miasma through the land' would be hard to substantiate against Lloyd, who was by no means without his standards. In one of his journals Lloyd claimed that all his stories went to show that 'the wild turbulence of vice' could bring 'nothing but evil fruits and deep vexation of spirit'. His publications in no way contributed to the outcry which produced the Obscene Publications Bill in the fifties.

In later life, when he had acquired *The Daily Chronicle* and was a publisher of power and prosperity, Lloyd preferred not to be reminded of the penny parts which he put out in the forties. He lived to be a member of the Political Committee of the Reform Club, a citizen of the utmost respectability. When he died the newspapers forbore to dwell on his early publishing activities. If the obituarist of *The Times* knew that this worthy old gentleman was the first sponsor of Sweeney Todd he held his peace.

CHAPTER II

THE DEMON BARBER

A LEADER writer in *The Times Literary Supplement* has advanced the theory that it was the astonishing popularity of the Sweeney Todd legend in early and mid-Victorian times that caused a good old English word to lapse into disrepute among respectable people. In the late nineties when the public 'sacrificed almost anything to be genteel', Sweeney Todd 'both on the stage and in print was considered so vulgar the word "barber" was considered vulgar too'. Hence arrived the word 'hairdresser'.

Probably a psychologist could be found to assert that the macabre relish with which successive generations have devoured the stories, stage plays and even radio plays and films of Sweeney Todd, the Demon Barber, springs from a desire deep down in every man's heart to know what his neighbour tastes like. Whatever the reason, dealers in 'bloods' today know that in Sweeney Todd they have one of their best-selling lines, and raise their prices accordingly.

There has been much argument about whether a real-life model for Sweeney Todd ever existed. Such evidence as there is suggests that the story was imported from France. The researcher can take his pick of two French Figaros, both Parisians. One supposedly flourished in the fourteenth century in the Rue des Marmouzets. According to *Les Rues de Paris* (1844): 'Le temps n'effacera pas le souvenir du patissier homicide qui sert encore d'épouvantail aux petits enfants de la Rue des Marmouzets.' The better-documented of these monsters – his record is detailed in Fouché's *Archives of the Police* – operated in a barber's shop in the Rue de la Harpe, Paris, in the first flush of Liberty, Equality and Fraternity. One day two hurried travellers, accompanied by a dog, arrived at the

perruquier's, and asked to be shaved. While one sat in the
chair the other slipped round the corner to make some
inquiry, only to find when he returned that his friend had
disappeared. According to the barber the traveller had
paid his money and left as soon as he had been shaved.
This seemed odd, but odder still was the presence and behaviour of the dog outside, impatiently awaiting the re-
appearance of its master. Presently the dog began to shiver
and howl and no entreaties could move it from the spot.
The suspicions of the second traveller were aroused. He
rallied a crowd, told his story and led them in an assault on
the now-locked shop. When the door was breached the dog
flew at the barber's throat and nearly killed him. Then it
nosed its way to the basement, where it sniffed around and
set up an anguished howl. In the basement wall was found
an aperture leading to the next house, and in the adjacent
basement was found the body of the missing traveller. The
owner of the building was a pie-maker, whose wares were
the most-sought-after in Paris. Then neighbours remembered that they had never seen meat going into the shop
and a search revealed 300 skulls on the premises. For their
unseemly enterprise the barber and the pie-maker were
executed on the rack, and the law directed that the
property should be pulled down and the site left vacant
evermore as a reminder of great wickedness.

Newspapers and magazines on both sides of the Channel
made much of this story. It was left to Thomas Peckett
Prest, the wayward virtuoso of Salisbury Square, to revive
the tale, with the *locale* changed to Fleet Street. Edward
Lloyd published it about 1840 under the strangely restrained title *The String of Pearls (A Romance)*.[1] It was an
excellent story, in the wordy fashion of its time, and the
suspense was well kept. To the unsuspecting readers of
that day the confirmation of their mounting suspicions
must have come as a first-class shock. So far as is known no

1. Oddly enough a pie shop used to flourish in the quarter where
Prest located his story, in spite of, or perhaps because of, the unfortunate association.

one attacked the publishers on the ground that the story
was likely to drive unbalanced persons to practise canni-
balism.

Two years later a stage version of Sweeney Todd by
George Dibdin Pitt was produced at the Brittania Saloon,
Hoxton. It was a theme which was readily adapted to the
theatre, and stage carpenters were to be busy for the next
hundred years constructing disappearing chairs. In 1843
appeared Dickens's *Martin Chuzzlewit,* in which Tom
Pinch was made to express the hope that, because he had
stayed out late, no one would suppose that he had been
murdered and made into meat pies. Obviously Prest and
Pitt, between them, had furnished the public with a welcome new joke. In 1846 the story was again run by Lloyd
in his *People's Periodical and Family Library,* a weekly
magazine which contained, among other attractions, articles entitled 'Confessions of a Deformed Lunatic' and 'The
Madhouse of Palermo'. Despite the extreme thinness of
the paper and the trying type-face the story sent new
joyous waves of horripilation through the respectable
families who read it.

The String of Pearls set the general pattern for all
Sweeney Todd stories. Todd usually had a terrified boy
assistant whom he ill-used, and sent out of the shop on
some errand when a likely customer was about to be dispatched. The chair was dropped through the floor by the
pulling of a bolt in a back room. Victims were usually
strangers to the town, wealthy drovers who boasted of
their profits at market, or seafarers back from long voy-
ages. The proprietor of the pie shop was usually a woman,
and the actual pie-maker a wretch imprisoned in the basement. There was commonly a hat found hanging in the
shop after the customer had departed, and of course a dog
which sat outside the shop and howled. A curious detail in
Prest's version was that while this dog turned 'with loath-
ing' from bits of pie thrown to it, a newly bereaved widow
showed no instinctive dislike of a pie containing portions
of her late partner in marriage.

SWEENEY TODD,

THE
DEMON BARBER OF FLEET STREET.

"STOP THE DOG! STOP THE DOG!" ALMOST SHRIEKED SWEENEY TODD.

A grim *double entendre* was a feature of Prest's narrative, and was copied, not always so successfully, by those who later took over the torch. The barber would assure his customers that there was not a shop in London which could polish off a customer as quickly as he could; or he would advise a waiting customer to go round the corner to watch the animated clock of St Dunstan's striking the hour 'while I finish this gentleman'. Once he extracted himself from a tedious discussion by saying 'I have another subject to dissect.' Not always was the double talk a deliberate jest by the speaker. When the boy Tobias, having newly applied for the job, was advised not to 'repeat a word of what passes in this shop, or dare to make any supposition, or draw any conclusion from anything you see or hear, or fancy you see or hear', he replied: 'Yes, sir, I won't say anything. I wish, sir, as I may be made into veal pies at Lovett's in Bell Yard if I as much as says a word.' It was not surprising that Sweeney Todd looked at him for a minute or two in silence. On another occasion an apprentice eating one of Mrs Lovett's pies exclaimed to his friend, 'Lord bless ye, I'd eat my mother if she was a pork chop!'

The artist who illustrated 'The String of Pearls' in the *People's Periodical* hardly did justice to the author's description:

The barber himself was a long low-jointed, ill-put-together sort of fellow, with an immense mouth, and such huge hands and feet that he was, in his way, quite a natural curiosity; and what was more wonderful considering his trade, there never was such a head of hair as Sweeney Todd's. We know not what to compare it to; probably it came close to what one may suppose to be the appearance of a thick-set hedge in which a quantity of small wire had got entangled. In truth it was a most terrific head of hair; and as Sweeney Todd kept all his combs in it – some people said his scissors likewise – when he put his head out of the shop door to see what sort of weather it was he might have been mistaken for some Indian warrior with a very remarkable head-dress.

Later it appeared that he 'squinted a little to add to his

charms', and his short, hyena-like laugh (described as a 'cachinnatory effusion') was such that 'people had been known to look up to the ceiling, then on the floor and all around them, to know from whence it had come, scarcely supposing it possible that it proceeded from mortal lips.'

Prest never lost an opportunity of discoursing on the merits of Mrs Lovett's pies. The arrival of each fresh batch from the bakehouse was the signal for a near-riot in Bell's Yard. Lawyers and their clerks and apprentices were the principal consumers.

And well did they deserve their reputation, those delicious pies! There was about them a flavour never surpassed and rarely equalled; the paste was of the most delicate construction and impregnated with the aroma of a delicious gravy that defied description. Then the small portions of meat which they contained were so tender, and the fat and lean so artistically mixed up that to eat one of Lovett's pies was such a provocative to eat another that many persons who came to lunch stayed to dine, wasting more than an hour of precious time and endangering (who knows to the contrary?) the success of some law-suit thereby.

Although he had been promised that his throat would be slit from ear to ear if he did not mind his own business, the boy Tobias could not help noticing curious incidents. It was strange that a customer should depart and leave his hat, and not come back for it. And then there was the mystery of why the barber's chair was securely screwed to the floor. One day Tobias broke into Sweeney Todd's private apartments. Here he found a large number of walking-sticks, more than a hundred umbrellas, a collection of swords and some pairs of shoes, and finally, a large desk stuffed with jewellery. His unlawful entry was detected; but instead of cutting the boy's throat the barber decided to have him shut away in the madhouse at Peckham Rye, confident that if the lad began to voice his suspicions of what went on in the barber's shop his statements would be accepted as proof of insanity. The madhouse keeper was an understanding fellow and knew that

Sweeney Todd would not want to pay the expenses of Tobias's incarceration indefinitely. A previous lad whom Todd had committed to his care for a year died conveniently at the end of the paid-up period.

Now the author found something else on which to let his fancy roam:

About this time and while these incidents of our most strange and eventful narrative were talking place, the pious frequenters of old St Dunstan's began to perceive a strange and most abominable odour throughout the sacred edifice.

It was in vain that old women who came to hear the sermons, although they were too deaf to catch a third part of them, brought smelling bottles and other means of stifling their noses; still the dreadful charnel-house sort of smell would make itself most painfully and most disagreeably apparent.

The beadle, whose function it was to cuff small boys who dared to look at the bishop, began to go about with a key in one hand and a vinegar cloth in the other, as was the fashion during the Great Plague. When the bishop arrived to take confirmation classes he was so overwhelmed by the odour that 'the people found themselves confirmed almost before they knew where they were'. The bishop then stalked out to his carriage, ignoring the cold collation which had been set out for him (and which, for once, did not contain any of Mrs Lovett's pies). At this stage the church authorities decided, a little belatedly, to explore their mephitic vaults in an effort to trace the nuisance. It could not have been caused by the corpses in their racks, they decided, because these had been dead too long to vex the atmosphere.

Meanwhile an anxious pieman was becoming dissatisfied with his conditions of labour in Mrs Lovett's underground bakehouse. It had seemed like a good job at first – he was allowed to eat unlimited quantities of pies, which he did until he was glutted. But he was not allowed to leave his underground chamber. He even had to sleep there; and while he slept a fresh supply of meat would arrive on the shelves at the other end of the room, ready for the next day's bake.

This mysterious arrival of the meat puzzled the pieman. He began to search the far end of the vault. Lightly pencilled on the wall was this disturbing message:

'Whatever unhappy wretch reads these lines may bid adieu to the world and all hope, for he is a doomed man! He will never emerge from these vaults with life, for there is a secret connected with them so awful and so hideous that to write it makes one's blood curdle and the flesh to creep upon your bones. The secret is this – and you may be assured, whoever is reading these lines, that I write the truth, and that it is impossible to make the awful truth worse by exaggeration, as it would be by a candle at midday to attempt to add any lustre to the sunbeams.'

If the unknown author had thought less of his literary style and more of his duty to society he might have been able to get his message across. As it was the communiqué broke off at the word 'sunbeams' with an ominous scrawl which suggested that the author had been forcibly interrupted. While pondering the possible implications of this warning, the pieman noticed a clean sheet of paper on the floor. It bore a written message:

You are getting dissatisfied, and therefore it becomes necessary to explain to you your real position, which is simply this: you are a prisoner and were such from the first moment that you set foot where you now are ... it is sufficient to inform you that so long as you continue to make pies you will be safe, but if you refuse, then the first time you are caught sleeping your throat will be cut.

Then, as if to drive the message right home, the trapdoor in the roof opened and Sweeney Todd's evil face appeared.

'Make pies,' advised Todd. 'Eat them and be happy. How many a man would envy your position – withdrawn from the struggles of existence, amply provided with board and lodging, and engaged in a pleasant and delightful occupation; it is astonishing how you can be dissatisfied.'

But not all these warnings could keep the prisoner from trying to find out where the supplies of meat came from. With the aid of an iron bar he forced the hidden communicating hatch at the end of the vault and stepped through, bearing a torch. There he found his answer.

With a cry of horror he fell backwards, extinguishing the torch in his fall, and he lay for fully a quarter of an hour insensible upon the floor. What dreadful sight had he seen that had so chilled his young blood and frozen up the springs of life?

By now Sweeney Todd, who had spent such of his time as was not passed in slaying and dissecting in trying to sell his victims' property, had made enough money to retire, and was preparing to poison Mrs Lovett in order that she should be in no position to betray him. But the net was closing in.

In reply to the notice Todd put in his window after Tobias's departure – 'Wanted, a lad; one of strong religious principles preferred. Apply within' – he received an application from a strikingly good-looking youth, whom he engaged. This was Johanna, the heroine of the story, who had volunteered to play an undercover role in an endeavour to find out what had happened to her seafaring lover, missing after a visit to Sweeney Todd's. Two gentlemen of the town had also undertaken to visit Todd's shop as customers. These were exciting hours for Johanna – and for the reader. One thing which gave Johanna food for thought was that a gash in the arm of the chair caused by her carelessness with a razor had vanished completely a few minutes after her return to the shop from an errand.

The *dénouement* was as exciting as could be hoped. One of Johanna's gentlemen was seated in the chair, the other was concealed in a cupboard. Johanna herself, sent on another errand, was watching obliquely through the window. After the usual double-talk the barber made his excuses to go to the back shop. Smartly, and none too soon, the intended victim jumped out of the chair. With a clank and a thud the chair on its trapdoor dropped through the floor and a duplicate swung up in its place. The 'victim' sat down in the seat again. When Todd reappeared he went rigid with fright, thinking that the dead man had returned to confront him. At that point he was arrested.

The climax in Bell's Yard was equally satisfactory. A fresh batch of pies was due up at nine o'clock.

One, two, three, four, five, six, seven, eight, nine! Yes, it was nine at last. It strikes by old St Dunstan's Church clock, and in weaker strains the chronometrical machine at the pie shop echoes the sound. What excitement there is now to get at the pies when they shall come! Mrs Lovett lets down the square moveable platform that goes on pullies into the cellar; some machinery which only requires a handle being turned brings up a hundred pies on a tray. These are eagerly seized by parties who have previously paid, and such a smacking of lips ensues as was never known. Down goes the platform for the next hundred and a gentleman says:

'Let me work the handle, Mrs Lovett, if you please. It is too much for you, I am sure.'

'Sir, you are very kind, but I never allow anybody on this side of the counter but my own people, sir. I can turn the handle myself, sir, if you please, with the assistance of this girl. Keep your distance, sir. Nobody wants your help.'

How the waggish young lawyers' clerks laughed as they smacked their lips and sucked in all the golopshious gravy of the pies, which by-the-way appeared to be all delicious veal that time, and Mrs Lovett worked the handle of the machine all the more vigorously that she was a little angered with the officious stranger. What an unusual trouble it seemed to be to wind up those forthcoming hundred pies! How she toiled and how the people waited, but at length there came up the savoury steam and then the tops of the pies were visible.

They came up upon a large tray about six feet square, and at that moment Mrs Lovett ceased turning the handle and let a catch fall that prevented the platform receding again, to the astonishment and terror of everyone away flew all the pies, tray and all, and a man who was lying crouched in an exceedingly flat state under the tray sprang to his feet.

Mrs Lovett shrieked, as well she might, and then she stood trembling and looking as pale as death itself. It was the young cook from the cellar who had adopted this mode of escape.

The throng of persons in the shop looked petrified, and after Mrs Lovett's shriek there was an awful silence for about a minute and then the young man who officiated as cook spoke.

'Ladies and gentlemen, I fear that what I am going to say will spoil your appetites; but truth is beautiful at all times, and I have to state that Mrs Lovett's pies are made of *human flesh!*'

*

How the throng of persons recoiled – what a roar of agony and dismay there was! How frightfully sick about forty lawyers' clerks became all at once, and how they spat out the gelatinous clinging portions of the rich pies they had been devouring ...

The exclamations of the consumers, once they could find tongue, were strangely anti-climatic, consisting of 'Good Gracious!' 'Oh, the pies!' and 'Confound it!'

Mrs Lovett collapsed and died from the mingled effects of shock and the poison with which Sweeney Todd had already laced her brandy. The barber himself was removed to Newgate and in due course hanged. By a happy coincidence the pieman turned out to be Johanna's missing lover.

Concluded the author:

The youths who visited Lovett's pie shop and there luxuriated upon those delicacies are youths no longer. Indeed the grave has closed over all but one and he is very, very old, but even now as he thinks of how many pies he ate and how he enjoyed the flavour of the 'veal' he shudders and has to take a drop of brandy.

Beneath the old church of St Dunstan's were found the head and bones of Todd's victims. As little as possible was said by the authorities about it, but it was supposed that some hundreds of persons must have perished in the frightful manner we have detailed.

It is unnecessary to follow Sweeney Todd through all the vicissitudes of penny publication. A generation after Edward Lloyd had launched him, Charles Fox took over and gave the barber a new run under the best-known title – Sweeney Todd, the Demon Barber of Fleet Street'.

Sweeney Todd also made appearances in quite unexpected quarters. In 1883 a story called 'The Link Boy of Old London' began in Fox's *Boy's Standard*. After a few chapters of old-fashioned Gothic, with a highwayman or two for good measure, the Demon Barber made his appearance. There were certain variations. Instead of the victims falling on to their heads twenty feet below the trapdoor, as in Prest's story, this author had them falling on to iron spikes. A suspicious constable was introduced. Failing to get any evidence on Todd he would go round the corner and solace himself with half a dozen pies from Mrs Darkman. Instead of having his assistant put away in a madhouse, the Barber knifed him in the back after a particularly crimson battle with two customers. Wiping his hands at the end, Todd observed, 'Well, well, Mrs Darkman can't complain of the supply tonight.'

This barber was sufficient of a sentimentalist to fall in love with the wife of one of his customers. He dispatched the husband in the usual way, but knowing that he could not marry the widow unless she had proof of her husband's death he forebore to have the corpse made into pies and arranged for it to be discovered mutilated in the street.

In this version Todd was finally spitted through by a constable in a fight in the cellars of his shop. Mrs Darkman died by poison. 'A good riddance of two wretches,' said the head officer, 'for there is no death devised by law except burning which is bad enough for them.'

Not all publishers are sensationalists. The cover of the Mellifont Press *Sweeney Todd* (1936) was a lurid affair in colour, showing a victim being dropped through the trap-door; but only in one shocked sentence near the end was there any suggestion of dirty work below stairs:

It was never made quite clear how Todd got rid of the bodies of his various victims, the men whom he had murdered and robbed. There was one horrible rumour which grew into a legend in the neighbourhood that Mrs Lovett's pie shop had disposed of them, but such a thing is too terrible to contemplate.

A good companion to this work would have been the story of Dracula with all references to blood-sucking omitted.

CHAPTER III
ROGUES AND VAGABONDS

'The highwayman was my favourite dish.'
— ROBERT LOUIS STEVENSON

AMONG the Victorian 'penny dreadfuls' which earned the greatest condemnation and the greatest circulation were those which invested with knightly qualities the knaves of the *Newgate Calendar, or Malefactors' Bloody Register*: highwaymen, jail-breakers, house-breakers, all the incorrigible free-lances who haunted the thieves' kitchens of the Great Wen and ended their days at Tyburn with the bells of St Sepulchre's tolling in their ears, if they still had any ears.

James Catnach, of Monmouth Court, found an ever-expanding public in the years following Waterloo for his 'last sorrowful lamentations' of criminals, and is credited with selling more than a million copies of Corder's confession in the Red Barn murder. To him is due in no small degree the consuming curiosity of that generation in the exploits of criminals. Catnach can hardly be blamed, however, for the nineteenth century's persistent ennobling of the highwayman; the man on whom the major responsibility must be laid is Harrison Ainsworth.

It was in 1834 that Ainsworth published his *Rookwood*, with its famous description of Dick Turpin's ride to York (he is said to have written the equivalent of 100 printed pages in 24 hours, in a flush of inspiration). Dick Turpin, it is perhaps superfluous to say, performed no such ride. *Rookwood* was a landmark of popular literature and there is not the least doubt that it directly inspired the scores of highwayman 'penny dreadfuls' which fascinated the next two generations. Equally there is no doubt that

Ainsworth's life of Jack Sheppard, serialized in *Bentley's Miscellany* in 1839–40, stimulated an excessive popular interest in that slippery rogue, who had already been indulgently treated by Daniel Defoe. Ainsworth was subjected to much censure for his choice of heroes, but the real anger was reserved for those who dared to put out similar tales in penny numbers.

In a day when masked raiders no longer ranged Finchley and Hammersmith, the public were ready to see the highwayman romanticized. They wanted him depicted, if not as an out-and-out hero, then as a dashing rogue with a Robin Hood streak in him. If Rob Roy, a pioneer of what a later age has called the 'protection racket', could be passed off as an heroic chieftain, there seemed no reason why gentlemanly and gallant instincts should not be attributed to his contemporary, Dick Turpin.

Wage slaves had no intention of spending their scanty leisure reading about wage slaves. Their spirit craved more powerful stimulus. They wanted to read about fiery individualists, men of spirit who defied harsh laws and oppressive officialdom, even though they finished at the end of a hempen rope. The public were prepared to be especially tolerant towards any malefactors who could be shown to have been forced into wrong-doing through deprivation of parents, miscarriages of justice, or the activities of oppressive guardians, grinding employers, rascally landlords and lecherous squires. The author of Hogarth House's *The Blue Dwarf* (*c.* 1870) disposed of the moral and ethical problems involved as follows:

The sum realized by some highwaymen in those days was something fabulous. The money spent in riot and debauchery in a week would often have provided for fifty families.

'Light come light go' had always been the motto of those whose money came to them in a nefarious way.

But many modern ways of making money are infinitely more nefarious than taking it by force.

The cheating done by lawyers and brokers whose clients trust them, the hundred and one ways of levying blackmail by men in power and with influence in any place of trust, the disgraceful sweating exercised in professions where such mean tricks were never supposed to have been heard of, are infinitely more despicable than highway robbery.

At all events, the man risked his neck, and was always amenable to the laws of his country.

But for the mean, crawling thieves we speak of there is no punishment – not even that of their consciences, for they have none.

There were scores of highwayman stories, in both penny and halfpenny parts: *Dick Turpin, Tom Turpin, Captain MacHeath, Captain Midnight, Moonlight Jack, Gentleman Jack, Black Hawk, Black Wolf, Black Highwayman, Sixteen-String Jack, Turnpike Dick* and *Tyburn Dick*, to name but a few; and, on the distaff side, *May Turpin, Starlight Nell* and *Nan Darrell*. Consistently the most favoured character was Dick Turpin. Any similarity between the facts of his life and the fancies of his chroniclers was purely coincidental; and the liberties the authors took with the facts of Turpin's career (even his schooldays became a theme for high-flown adventure) were as nothing compared with the liberties they took with time and space.

The industrious author of *The Blue Dwarf* made Turpin the tool of his terrifying blue-spotted homunculus, Sapathwa. The Dwarf was supposedly the heir to ancient estates, but was prevented by his revolting appearance from assuming his inheritance. He and the loyal highwayman used to rescue each other from calamity in turn. After one narrow squeak the Dwarf gave this instruction to Turpin and Tom King ('the modern Damon and Pythias', as the author liked to call them):

'Hold yourselves in readiness within ten days to leave the country. We must go no matter where, so we be out of their reach – Scotland, Ireland, even America, if need be.'

And go they did. The author of *The Blue Dwarf* had to throw in not only Scots clansmen, Irish banditti and

Red Indians, but a great deal else before his tale of Turpin had run its course.

The biggest monument to Turpin was that produced by Edward Viles, whose *Black Bess, or The Knight of the Road*, published by E. Harrison of Salisbury Court, ran to 254 weekly parts, a total of 2,028 pages – believed to be the longest 'penny dreadful' by one author on record. The total number of words, allowing for illustrations, is something like two and a half million.

On the title page of the bound work, published in 1868, is a quotation from Henry Fielding's *Tom Jones*:

'Some of the author's friends cry'd – "Look'ee, the man is a villain: but it is Nature for all that." And all the young critics of the age, the clerks, apprentices, etc., called it low and fell agroaning.'

Supporting this is a defensive preface:

The author of *Black Bess, or The Knight of the Road*, has one request to make:

It is that those who have, unread, condemned the present work will take the trouble to peruse it. And an entire change of opinion will be the result, because in no place will vice be commended or virtue sneered at; nor will any pandering to sensuality, suggestion of impure thoughts or direct encouragement of crime be discovered; neither are there details of seduction, bigamy, adultery and domestic poisoning, such as are indispensable ingredients of our popular three-volume novels. On the contrary, the work will be found full of exciting personal adventures such as can never be re-enacted until the railways are swept away and the stage coaches replaced on our highways – until, in fine, the present state of things is changed to what it was a century and a half ago. If anyone is weak-minded enough to be carried away by the idea that a highwayman's career as depicted in these pages can be equalled in reality at the present day he must be imbecile indeed. Let not the 'Life of Robin Hood' fall into the hands of such a one, or, sure as fate, Sherwood Forest would be his destination, with bow and arrows for his stock in trade.

The Blue Dwarf to the rescue ...

DICK TURPIN AND HIS FAIR COMPANION ARE PURSUED BY THE POLICE.

An illustration from Edward Vile's Black Bess,
which ran for 254 weeks

There were four heroes in *Black Bess*: Dick Turpin,
Claude Duval, Tom King and Jack Rann (Sixteen-String
Jack); or five including the horse. To disarm any pedants
who might have pointed out that Turpin lived from
1706 to 1739 and Duval from 1643 to 1670, the author
wrote: 'the Claude Duval of whom we are about to speak
was not the one who came to an ignominious end in the
reign of the second Charles, but his nephew. The two
have often been ignorantly confounded.' The author does
not appear to have considered it necessary to explain how
Turpin came to rescue the Young Pretender at Cull-
oden in 1746.

The story opened with Turpin, single-handed, robbing
the stage coach containing London's Lord Mayor, who
was clutching to his fat belly a massive silver cup on
which were 'set forth at length the suppositious talents

of Lord Mayor Funge. Such was his euphonious appellation. Ezekiel Funge.' In the remaining 1,135 chapters, Turpin spent his time shaking off bloodhounds and police spies, rescuing oppressed damsels, cutting down the bodies of his less fortunate comrades, exploring haunted houses, escaping from Newgate, following the Pretender and resuscitating Claude Duval, who was for ever being picked up 'dead' after some bloody encounter and escaping live burial at the last minute. Among the highlights were a battle on the deck of a smuggler's vessel, an encounter with dragoons amid the monoliths of Stonehenge, and Dick's marriage to Maud Gouldman, performed under duress by a kidnapped parson standing on a powder barrel with a train of explosive running to it.

Long before the end Turpin knew he was a doomed man. He mourned at the death-bed of his wife, and he mourned at the death-bed of Black Bess. The horse he buried personally at dead of night – a feat which can be appreciated only by someone who has tried to bury a horse single-handed. Then came his final capture and trial, at which the judge found him 'guilty of innumerable crimes all of which are punishable by death ... may Heaven extend that forgiveness towards you which the Law will not allow us to show on earth'.

There was an illustration depicting Turpin on the scaffold, but the text showed a certain reticence:

It would be too painful to linger over the last moments of the hero whose career we have followed for so long with such deep interest.

Viles's Turpin was drugged before execution to prevent him making a last-minute attempt at escape. But he was able to deprive the executioner of the pleasure of pushing him off the ladder, electing to jump of his own free will.

The 2,028th page was the only short-weight page of them all; it contained seven-eights blank space. With the penultimate instalment came the announcement:

OBSERVE! With next week's number, No. 254, will be given away No. 1 of *The Black Highwayman*, being the second series of *Black Bess*.

Edward Viles had not yet shot his bolt.

Nor had his conscientious illustrator, who had seen Turpin through all his scrapes (frequently, and perhaps deliberately, anticipating the event by several chapters), with an occasional large folding picture thrown in. But *Black Bess* did not depend on give-aways; it earned its 'unexampled favour' on its own merits.

An assortment of highwayman 'penny dreadfuls' examined by James Greenwood in *The Wilds of London* included *Blueskin* (of which there were many versions, one supposedly by Viles); *Claude Duval, the Dashing Highwayman*; *The Boy King of the Highwaymen*; and *The Knight of the Road*. Greenwood was scandalized by the drinking song which the author of *Tyburn Tree* put into the mouths of his desperadoes:

> Let the asses who choose drive the plough or the spade,
> Let the noodles of commerce get guineas by trade,
> Let the sailor for wealth skim the wild, raging sea,
> I envy not either – the high road for me!
>
> And if, boys, at Tyburn our exit we make,
> A curse on the sneak who shall peach, or shall shake,
> Let's swear to be faithful, if such our end be,
> And manfully drop, like ripe fruit, from the tree!

Yet, the reader may wonder, what kind of moral song would James Greenwood have put in the mouths of highwaymen, or pirates, or any kind of fictional villain?

Greenwood described a personal meeting with the author of *Blueskin*, a rum-loving hack whom he styled Mr Haddick. 'His faded, threadbare coat was buttoned high at the throat, either to conceal the dirtiness of his linen or the naked fact that his solitary possession in that material was at that moment undergoing the process of washing.' This may or may not have been Edward Viles.

Perhaps it was not strictly necessary in these highwayman stories to show Runners and dragoons as so often corruptible, dull-witted and cowardly, the occupants of stage coaches as invariably pompous and crapulous, and to describe the robbers as 'our gallant and adventurous friends', or to give them fine-sounding names like Victor St George, Gallant Tom, Dashing Ralph or Devil Duke. Highwaymen of fiction were always attentive to their horses and womenfolk, and generous to their ostlers, as well they might be; they also had a wholesome and proper contempt for the frog-eating Papists across the Channel. The *Quarterly Review* on a later occasion complained that highwaymen always got the pick of the women – 'lovely and persecuted damsels whose physical charms and voluptuous embraces are dilated upon with exceeding unction'. And again: '... their mistresses are queens of beauty and romance, whose venal caresses are the rightful guerdon of skill, daring and dash'. The love scenes, in the opinion of the *Quarterly*, were 'almost as offensive in their way as the performances of certain young lady novelists of higher rank'.

There were some critics who were prepared to wink at the romanticizing of highwaymen of a bygone age but who strongly deplored the lavishing of sympathy on such ruffians as Jack Sheppard, the robber and jail-breaker, and Charles Peace, the burglar. Plain robbery and burglary were too easy to imitate, they felt. A witness before the Select Committee on Public Libraries, in mid-century, expressed the opinion that the chronicles of robbers had 'perhaps a worse tendency than the positively indecent or immoral'. Much of the affection felt by the public for Jack Sheppard sprang from the fact that he was usually matched against the infamous Jonathan Wild. Opposed to this self-styled thief-taker, who was himself an organizer of thieves, receiver, blackmailer, brothel-keeper and murderer – possibly the blackest rogue England has produced – any adversary was apt to look like the embodiment of justice in arms, a daring knight errant fighting against a corrupt confederacy of crime.

Charles Peace, the most successful burglar of Victorian times, hardly rivalled Sheppard in popularity, but he had his admiring public. Starting in crime as a Manchester porch robber, Peace shot a policeman and confessed only just in time to save another man from the gallows. Later he shot another man, and then disappeared. Not for a long time did anyone suspect that the respectable Mr Thompson of Evelina Road, Peckham, was Charles Peace, or that he was carrying out lucrative burglaries almost every night. Eventually he was hanged for the second murder.

One of the 'penny dreadfuls' which took Peace for hero, *Charles Peace, or the Adventures of a Notorious Burglar*, is a literary curiosity by virtue of the columns of staggering irrelevancies with which the author eked it out. He was incapable of mentioning an inquest without discussing at great length whether inquests served a useful purpose or not, and the behaviour of people who attend them. He could not mention a jail without describing the operation of a treadmill, which 'must be terrible work for a fat man. It is possible for such a one to lose three stone in as many months.' At the end of one such lengthy digression he naïvely explained:

Happily for Peace he was spared this dreadful infliction, as the jail in which he was confined did not at that time contain a treadmill ...

But that digression was trifling compared to the one which occurred in Chapter LIX, entitled 'Mysterious Murders'. The author described a vain search for a murderer, and then went on to say that it was most extraordinary how many crimes of this kind went undetected. As proof he cited for the next 3,600 words a series of notorious unsolved crimes, including murders (mostly of prostitutes) by mutilation, dismemberment, garrotting, throat-slitting and clubbing. Many of the facts were taken from newspaper reports of inquests and were scarcely

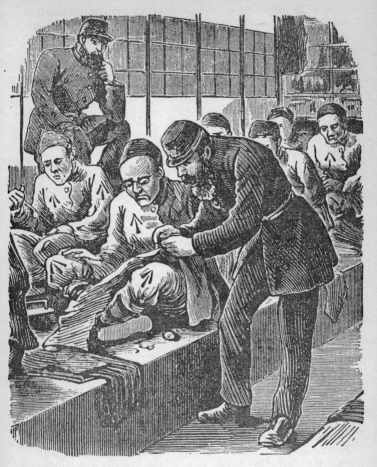

Charlie Peace in the tailor's shop

paraphrased. Other passages read like rehashed editorials
denouncing the wickedness of the age.

The author finished his long digression with:

Some alteration in the mode of administering justice will

have to be made, as we are going on at present. The evil is beginning to assume gigantic proportions, and nobody's life will be safe.

He then persuaded himself to tackle the next chapter of the narrative, in which again there was not the slightest reference to Charles Peace.

Soon he steered the story round to a mention of witch-craft, which gave him an excuse to recapitulate the his-toric cases of witch-hunting in England and elsewhere; not omitting references to capsie-claws, pilliewinks and tor-ture-boots. This occupied the author, if not the reader, for 2,400 words.

In the next chapter, describing the last hours of a con-demned man (not Charles Peace), he discussed for 1,300 words whether capital punishment was a good thing or not, and decided that it was. He did at least mention Peace in passing:

Peace often declared that he never took human life if there was any means left open for him to escape without having recourse to such a dreadful alternative.

He was, perhaps, the most reckless scoundrel of modern times, but 'fired wide', as he termed it, to frighten his pursuer, whose life he had no desire to take.

The hanging of the malefactor, in the next chapter, in-spired 1,100 words of discussion on the best method of dispatching a condemned man; with notes on strangling as practised by 'our estimable ally, the Turk, and despotic Russia', the Spanish garrotte, the German sword, the French guillotine and the Jack Ketch technique in which the hangman perched astride the suspended victim's shoulders to ensure the breaking of his neck. The next chapter, promisingly entitled 'Charles Peace Leaves Dart-moor', described chiefly the unsatisfactory treatment of discharged prisoners, and deplored the stupidity of hand-cuffing men on their way to discharge.

The author was really a leader writer *manqué*; it is clear

that he preferred airing his views and knowledge to telling a story which he must have realized was stale.

Sheppard and his cronies inspired a variety of fictional characters who traded on their names.[1] Most notorious of them all was Charley Wag, described variously as 'the new Jack Sheppard' and 'the Boy Burglar', whose adventures appeared about 1860. The authorship is in some doubt. According to the publishers, the writer had spent two years collecting background material, and his 'intensely exciting real-life romance' was not a product of the 'wild imaginings of the novelist's brain', but a story rendered 'in stern truthful language by one who has studied in all its blackest enormity the doings of secret crime'. It is more probable that the writer had spent his two years studying G. W. M. Reynolds. He reproduced in his narrative the same familiar dietary tables from workhouses and incorporated admiring references to the *Mysteries of the Court*, one of his characters claiming that aristocrats were in the habit of borrowing the penny parts from their footmen.

The creator of Charley Wag seems to have derived great pleasure from shocking the righteous, mixing sex, scandal and a crude form of socialism freely. 'A thoroughly depraved, unprincipled, godless, servile, blasphemous, lecherous old wretch' was his description of an aristocrat introduced as an ex-Premier of England. This skinny old goblin was said to bathe daily in beef tea to strengthen his satyr's appetites, with a bath of rosewater afterwards as a freshener. He dined with six demireps and took pleasure in seducing virtuous country spitcats.

A magistrate who entered the story was said to give, like most of his kind, 'a daily recurring exhibition of besotted ignorance, sickening vulgarity and bad taste'. Clergymen turned out to be Tarquins one and all. The author tackled protests as they came:

1. Cartouche, the legendary French criminal, was introduced to English readers as 'the French Jack Sheppard'.

I left Lucinda in very bad company, although that company was chiefly composed of reverend gentlemen.

Since I had the misfortune in a luckless moment to introduce these clerical parties into my story a terrific volley of letters from unknown correspondents has been fired at my offended head.

It seems, if I am to believe these ladies and gentlemen, that there really are no naughty parsons in existence, and even if there were it is not the proper thing to represent them in their natural colours. There are a great many people in the world who do not like to hear the truth, and a great many who do not like truth to be told ...

The author went on to protest that while he portrayed wickedness he did not encourage his young readers to practise the sins he showed up. If they did so, all they could expect was tears and anguish, and the Devil's pitchfork.

Always, however, he declined to give his readers any hint whether the boy Charley was to be 'comfortably hanged' or made a Lord Mayor of London. 'You do not imagine I am going to tell you what it is to be, do you?'

As an unwanted babe, Charley was thrown into the Thames in the first sentence of the story. His mother, retreating up Villiers Street, remarked a little prematurely, 'There goes the record of my sin and folly.' Charley was rescued, offered to the workhouse of Saint-Starver-cum-Bag-o'-Bones and rejected, and then left on the doorstep of – inevitably – an elderly spinster. He grew up high-spirited and uncontrollable, a cigar smoker at thirteen.

The author described Charley thus:

He is pugnacious, great at punching heads and bunging up eyes, and gave the youth of Slogger's Alley one of those heavy taps upon the nasal organ which is, I believe, in the language of the prize ring denominated a 'smeller'.

Add to this, he is a regular rascal where a pretty girl is concerned.

Half a dozen times at least I have begun a sentence in which I was going to dress the young gentleman's jacket. I have a small collection of moral remarks about things in general, all nicely cut and dried, and when I am at a loss to fill my chapter I stick one or two in to make my incidents go a little further. You do not blame me, do you? We all have little tricks. Have we not, brother tradesmen?

I will not upon this occasion inflict upon you any of the moral philosophy to which I have referred. I am at a loss to tell what I ought to say about a young fellow who is too general in his love-making. Why are so many of you young ladies so pretty? It is very hard to choose among you. I should feel much obliged if one out of my thousands of fair readers would write and tell me what she thinks of Master Charley's conduct, and I could put her opinion into the next part.

It was the insincerity of these protestations which doubtless infuriated the 'unco guid'. But the first number had sold 40,000 copies and the author of *Charley Wag* thumbed his nose at Society as cheerfully as Charley thumbed his at the magistrate. A provocative cover showed the boy burglar fleeing confidently down the street with a stolen goose and two bottles of rum. His dog scampering beside him was also in possession of a stolen goose. In the background a policeman brandished a truncheon. A notice on the wall offered £500 for the apprehension of Charley Wag.

From small-scale crimes the boy burglar worked his way up till very soon he was breaking into the Bank of England. Justice, panting, caught up with him from time to time but incarceration often had its compensations – such as flocks of frangipani-scented French ladies coming to gaze enraptured on him. And soon he was back at the old round of breaking into bank and boudoir.

The fate which the author had in store for Charley Wag proved to be an uncommonly lenient one. He was arrested for murder but was pardoned through the intercession of his mother, who was, of course, a duchess. Fortunately he had the grace to retire from the Park Lane high life which he was then adorning and to spend the remainder of his days abroad in strict retirement. Less fortunate was his mother, the duchess, who was strangled by her mad husband in a charnel house.

The fiercest 'penny dreadfuls' of mid-century were not the highwayman or burglar stories but the 'wild boys' series and the uncommonly lurid products of the Newsagents Publishing Company, founded by Edwin J. Brett. In the sixties the 'penny dreadful' seemed to go out of its way to live up to its nickname. It is difficult to defend the extreme examples, but even the worst compare favourably with the 'horror comics' which were to cause an outcry in the nineteen-fifties.

The 'wild boys' stories bore titles like *The Wild Boys of London, or The Children of Night*; *The Wild Boys of Paris, or The Secrets of the Vaults of Death*; *the Poor Boys of London, or A Life Story for the People;* and *The Boys of London and New York* (published, rather surprisingly, from Wigan).

The precocious young pariahs whose adventures were related in *The Wild Boys of London* (1866) used to hatch their mischief 'round a fire in their haunt beneath the sewers of London' (an odd place, it may be thought, to find a friendly fire). Splashing about in the city's effluent, they fought off ruffians, salvaged corpses and trafficked in stolen goods. On their ventures above ground they came to grips with thieves, murderers, kidnappers, child-stealers and grave-robbers, not to mention bumbling 'peelites'. Yet they never lost their high spirits. Illustrations show them swinging mischievously on an Oriental gentleman's pigtails and belabouring a Jew whom they have suspended upside down on a rope. At times the scene shifted to a mutinous convict ship, or to the Australian bush, but sooner or later the writer would return, nostalgically, to the sewers of London. The distinctive *bouquet* of *The Wild Boys of London* is perhaps best conveyed in that passage which begins with a beautiful young girl throwing herself from a bridge into the Thames. A rescuer plunges in but fails to find her, for the excellent reason that she has already been pulled ashore by body-snatchers. After taking her to their hide-out and gloating over her bust, they offer her unconscious body to a doctor for twenty guineas (twice the fee normally payable for a corpse). The would-be rescuer has meanwhile suffered an unpleasant fate in a pit, and his body also is offered to the doctor, who judges it to be worth only three guineas. Alone with the girl, the doctor checks that her heart is still beating;

'She lives,' he murmured in evident pleasure as he approached the door and locked it. 'She *shall* live on as my mistress. When I am tired of her she can die and prove to my school the greatest triumph of anatomical beauty.'

Ravishment and Murder! exclaimed the author, in case he had not made himself clear.

Like the writers of highwayman stories, the author of *The Wild Boys of London* was at pains to impute wickedness to those of high degree. After getting a titled character into trouble, he wrote:

> The facts were not to be disguised.
> He had murdered his opponent.
> Yet like other aristocrats he knew he had a privilege.
> In this land there is justice.
> What does it mean?
> One law for the rich and another for the poor.

From piracy to lynching, *The Wild Boys of London* ran the gamut of crime. Once, the artist was emboldened to draw a girl, bare to the waist, being flogged by her uncle. It became increasingly difficult to match the performance of the author with his opening pledge: 'Boys themselves, the young of every community and class, will read our book and it will tell them all they have to do and what can be done by honesty, steadfast purpose, industry and truth.'

How many thousands mourned when *The Wild Boys of London* ended we do not know; but when the story was reissued a few years later it came to a sudden stop. On the last page of the bound volume in the Barry Ono Collection is pencilled a note: 'This work was suppressed by the police after this number. No more published.'

It would be difficult to argue that the suppression of *The Wild Boys of London* by the long-suffering 'peelites' was a serious interference with the liberty of the press. The publisher was F. Farrah, of the Strand; doubtless he lost no time in launching a new title. The identity of the author remains obscure. Whoever it was, he was a characteristically tongue-in-cheek moralist, with a tendency to laboured facetiousness. Thus, having written 'a bright idea suddenly struck the boy', he put an asterisk after 'boy' and explained in a footnote: 'It may be as well to inform the reader that the boy did not strike it back again.' Like many of his kind, he used footnotes in an effort to support his more preposterous flights of imagination. After introducing gangs of fashionable young men called the Grey Brethren, the Companions of the Silver Dagger and the Companions of the Iron League, he explained: 'That such leagues are in existence is no fiction ... the Freemasons and their brotherhoods are proof of this.'

A fair example of the products of the Newsagents' Publishing Company is *The Skeleton Crew, or Wildfire Ned*. One chapter tells how the lights go out suddenly in the servants' quarters at Darlington Hall. When they come on again a well-armed skeleton is standing behind everybody's chair. The Skeleton Crew, Scourge of the Seas, are on a recruiting mission. They incite those present to fight each other to the death, and the survivors are signed on or hanged on the spot, at the chief's whim. 'It was a terrible feast of blood,' says the author, apologetically. When the floor is awash with gore and the rafters suitably weighted with dangling men, the 'best-looking of the females' are carried off, bound and gagged, to suffer a fate denoted by asterisks. The less good-looking ones are hanged 'without mercy', which is probably preferable to being hanged with mercy.

Later the author introduces into his narrative, appropriately enough, Colonel Blood. Later still he has King Charles climbing into the boudoir of the heroine, who is guarded by a Nubian eunuch. As if the Nubian had not suffered enough deprivation, the King makes to slash off his head, but is dissuaded by the heroine.

Another ferocious 'blood' put out by the Newsagents' Publishing Company was *The Dance of Death, or The Hangman's Plot*. The authors were said to be Detective Brownlow and the admirably named Monsieur Tuevoleur, Sergeant of the French Police. More interesting than the subject matter were the promotional methods used by the publishers. Readers were invited to take part in a draw for £250 worth of prizes. Among these were 'six splendid guns', 'sixteen costly stilettos as used by the brigands in Italy', and twenty volumes entitled 'Lives of Notorious French Criminals'. These delights were counterpoised by the offer of eight sets of 'cricketing implements' and twelve concertinas.

Given away with one of the first numbers was a large folding drawing entitled 'The Deadly Affray on the Rooftops'. It was a highly moral drawing in the sense that almost every character who was about to stab, shoot, club or cleave another was himself about to be stabbed, shot, clubbed or cleft by a third party. Only one lucky assassin was being allowed to stab his adversary in peace (doubtless with one of those costly Italian stilettos).

In these 'bloods' of the Newsagents' Publishing Company the authors gloated much over the scantily dressed bodies of the heroines, driven by economic pressure into evil company. The author of *The Dance of Death* broke off reluctantly from one such episode to exclaim: 'Add your voice to that of John Stuart Mill, M.P., the greatest thinker of the age; swell the ranks of the reformers and see whether our monopolizing manufacturers cannot be made to pay a better price for labour ...'

If the nature of these lurid 'bloods' of the sixties had to be summed up in one sentence, the following, from *The Wild Boys of London*, would serve:

In the doorway, in her nightdress, which revealed all the beauties of her buxom form, stood Mary Kelly, a pistol in each hand.

One character who must not be omitted from this chap-

SPRING-HEELED JACK,

THE TERROR OF LONDON.

"SIR ROLAND," SAID SPRING HEELED JACK, "THIS IS A MERRY NIGHT FOR US TO MEET."

ter is Spring-Heeled Jack. Whether there was ever any solid substance to his legend is doubtful. In 1907 the resourceful readers of *Notes and Queries* contributed all the information they knew about this bogeyman. One said that a Spring-Heeled Jack had been active in the Midlands in the 1850s. Another described how a coal merchant's son had terrorized country folk in Warwickshire twenty years earlier – 'his shoes were fitted with powerful and noiseless springs enabling him to leap hedgerows with ease'. Yet another said that thirty years previously a Spring-Heeled Jack had harried sentries at South Camp, Aldershot, leaping across the canal and then pouncing on their shoulders; this marauder, however, was thought to have been 'a lively officer of the Rifles'. Two other correspondents were of the opinion that the original Spring-Heeled Jack was an eccentric Marquess of Waterford; if so, his eccentricity has not qualified him for admission to the *Dictionary of National Biography*. All that really emerges from this correspondence is that Spring-Heeled Jack, whoever he was, inspired a number of emulators. The dictionary says of Spring-Heeled Jack:

A name given to a person who from his great activity in running or jumping, especially in order to rob or frighten people, was supposed to have springs in the heels of his boots. *dial.* a highwayman.

The Spring-Heeled Jack of the 'penny dreadfuls' traversed the countryside in giant bounds, as a man might do on the moon; he could clear stage-coaches, haystacks or cottages with contemptuous ease. As if this was insufficient to unnerve wayfarers, his appearances were often accompanied by horrific displays of thunder and lightning. In *Spring-Heeled Jack, the Terror of London* (published in the 1870s) the 'weird being', as he was usually described, wore a skin-tight glossy crimson suit, with bat-style wings, lion's mane, devil's horns, talon hands, cloven hoofs and a 'sulphurous-breathing mouth'. Sometimes his emanations were such as to set everyone choking in the vicinity.

Though his aspect was undeniably Mephistophelian, his intentions were honourable. He was the friend of the weak and downtrodden, which makes it the more regrettable that so often, by his appearance, he drove them shrieking and gibbering from his path. Once he burst through the windows of a church where a marriage was about to be solemnized, crying, 'Constance Marfield! Consent not to this unholy service! Parson, close your sacred books and leave this den of infamy!' He leapt from trees to separate duellists, he seized the reins of coaches and drove the horses in suicidal gallop, he stuffed an interfering police-man head first down a chimney, and he broke into a tor-ture chamber crying, 'Hold, monsters in the form of men!' It turned out that Spring-Heeled Jack was a man in the form of a monster, for when stripped of his clothes (or, as the author would prefer, denuded of his habiliments) he stood revealed as just another cheated heir. Inside his suits, which were made of best chamois, were steel rods coupled with springs in such a way that when he stooped the springs were compressed sufficiently to propel him smartly through the air, aided by his bats' wings. How the sul-phurous breath was contrived the author omitted to men-tion.

Not every Spring-Heeled Jack dressed like this one, or had as his objective the terrorizing of usurping baronets. One at least was a waggish fellow whose idea of a jest was to drag an old maid by her nightgown into the bedroom of a shy bachelor. There was a Spring-Heeled Jack series running, under the Aldine imprint, as late as 1904, the author being Charlton Lea, famous for his highwayman stories. Although the coloured covers were luridly mag-nificent, the series did not run long. Perhaps the younger generation were growing just that little more sophisti-cated. As far as the present writer can discover, Charlton Lea's 'weird being' was that most intransigent of mortals – a cashiered officer with a grievance.

CHAPTER IV

BRAVEALLS AND FEARNOTS

FROM mid-century onwards, the 'penny dreadful' had been aimed more specifically at the juvenile market than in Edward Lloyd's day. The heroes now ranged from 'wild boys' to boy apprentices, link boys, trace boys, call boys, boy gypsies, boy sailors, boy soldiers, boy crusoes. Those adults who remained convinced that a boy was a creature to be sent up a chimney or down a mine continued to deplore this unnecessary widening of the horizons of youth. What worried middle-class moralists was that for every *gamin* of the 'penny dreadfuls' who became a lord mayor perhaps a dozen became knights of the road or smuggler kings.

In 1855 appeared the first (so its publisher claimed) of a long string of boys' magazines hopefully designed to wean the young from 'unhealthy' reading. It was the *Boy's Own Magazine* of Samuel Orchart Beeton, a rising publisher who had done singularly well out of the pirating of *Uncle Tom's Cabin*. While drawing up plans for his new venture he was courting the young woman who, after their marriage, compiled the immortal cookery book.

The adult reaction to the *Boy's Own Magazine* is best told in Beeton's own words, in the preface to his first annual volume. '"This won't do," we heard on all sides. "It is too *high*, too *solid*, too good!" They were not boys who said so and we waited till we heard what would be said by the boys.' According to Beeton, they fell over each other to buy the paper, thus demonstrating that it was not necessary when writing for boys to descend to words of one syllable. 'We then pitched the tone of the magazine a little higher; and more boys – more thousands of boys – rushed to buy.'

This reads all very well, but Beeton over the years had

to give away a great many watches, umbrellas and chemistry chests to stimulate interest in his earnest little monthly. It specialized in historical fiction – serials with titles like 'How I Won My Spurs; or A Boy's Adventures in the Barons' Wars' and 'Cressy and Poitiers; or The Story of the Black Prince's Page'. More popular, perhaps, were stories by Captain Mayne Reid ('that cheerful, ingenious, romantic soul', as Robert Louis Stevenson called him), notably 'The Scalp Hunters'. The *Boy's Own Magazine* contained a high proportion of articles on 'manly exercises' and 'physical prowess', on nature study and science. Nor was the editor afraid to throw in a poem by Wordsworth. Readers were continually being urged to write 'papers' on topics like 'Fortification and Military Architecture', 'Lighthouses and Their Builders', and 'The Story of Milton's *Paradise Lost*'. Then, magisterially, Beeton would criticize his readers' efforts, rebuking them for slipshod grammar and orthography, prolixity, juvenility, priggishness and plagiarism.

By 1862 Beeton claimed a circulation of 40,000, a creditable enough total but one unlikely to cause grave anxiety to the publishers of 'penny dreadfuls'. Indeed, it was Beeton who was now worried by competition from better-class imitators – 'if we were not the best-tempered fellow in the world we should here break into a grumble'.

In 1866 the Rev. J. Erskine Clark published his *Chatterbox* at a halfpenny, in a bold effort to undercut the 'penny dreadfuls'. Sir James Barrie, who was an eager consumer of sensational literature in his young days, admits that he was side-tracked on to *Chatterbox*, which broke him of the 'penny dreadful' habit, though not before he had tried to write one or two himself. But the real publishing event of 1866 was the launching of Edwin J. Brett's famous *Boys of England*.

Brett has already been encountered as the founder of the Newsagents' Publishing Company, which specialized in fierce 'bloods'. In his youth he had been an associate of G. W. M. Reynolds and Fergus O'Connor, and (according to *The Biograph*) had been a speaker at radical meetings; however, he had realized just in time 'how easily the people can be led by a few unprincipled men who have more eloquence than the people they address'. With the change in his political opinions came a change in his publishing policy.

Boys of England, the journal in which Jack Harkaway first saw the light, was the beginning of a new era in boys' reading. Less bloodthirsty than Brett's earlier publications, but still far from anaemic, it was to run until 1899, absorbing many shorter-lived magazines. 'Our aim is to enthral you by wild and wonderful but healthy fiction,' said the first number, promising that the journal would be 'a hearty, free and trusty companion'.

Brett advertised his first issue widely, even in the gory pages of *The Skeleton Crew*. The prizes he offered put Beeton in the shade: 2 Shetland ponies, 6 Newfoundland dogs, 50 spaniels and other fancy dogs, 50 pairs of pigeons, 50 pairs of ducks, 50 pairs of rabbits, 50 cricket sets, 50 watches, 50 volumes of Shakespeare, 100 concertinas and a great deal else. As a result, the first issue was an instant and splendid success. It was obvious, moreover, that it was going to be bought for more than its dogs and ducks.

One who devoured *Boys of England* in his youth was H. G. Wells. In *Tono-Bungay* its stories are classed as 'ripping stuff'. Edgar Jepson tells in *Memories of a Victorian* how he read the groom's copies and was inspired to scour the countryside for back numbers. He found a set of bound volumes in the house of a widow 'whose only son that weekly had sent to sea', and bore them home in triumph to the hay loft (the journal was under the parental ban). Periodically the volumes were buried under fresh loads of hay, and a 'laborious mining operation' was necessary to recover them.

Havelock Ellis was another who surrendered to the powerful fascination of *Boys of England*. It held him (he told in *My Life*) in a 'kind of fever ... it was an excitement

which overwhelmed all ordinary considerations. My
mother forbade me to read these things, but, though I
usually obeyed her, in this matter I was disobedient without compunction. But the fever subsided as suddenly as it
arose – probably it only lasted a few weeks – and left not
a trace behind. It is an experience which enables me to
realize how helpless we are in this matter. If this is the
literature a boy needs, nothing will keep him away from
it; if he needs more than ever it can give it will leave no
mark on him. So far as I remember *Boys of England* was
innocent enough, though full of wild and extravagant action. It is doubtless in its appeal to the latent motor
energies of developing youth that its fascination lies.'

Later issues of *Boys of England* carried this boast under
the title:

'Subscribed to by H.R.H. Prince Arthur, the Prince Imperial
of France[1] and Count William Bernstorff.'

The *Quarterly Review*, which missed nothing, professed
to be at a loss to understand why these gentlemen should
give the journal their patronage. It was an improvement
over 'penny dreadfuls' admittedly; but, with insufferable
smugness, the *Review* added: 'It may be doubted whether
the time spent over [such journals] would not be infinitely
more usefully employed in cricket and football or some
lighter games.'

There followed a fierce competition – none the less
fierce for being on occasions farcical – with W. L. Emmett,
who had also published full-blooded 'penny dreadfuls'.
Emmett's counter to *Boys of England* was the *Young
Gentleman's Journal*, published in 1867. Brett retorted
next year with *Young Men of Great Britain*, and the same
year Emmett capped this with *Young Gentlemen of
Britain*. The climax came when on the same day in 1872
Brett issued *Rovers of the Sea*, and Emmett put out
Rover's Log. In his *History of Old Boys' Books*, which

1. Then an exile in England.

records the Brett-Emmett rivalry, Ralph Rollington[1] gives no clue as to how this unfortunate 'double' occurred.

It is not surprising that there was no love lost between the two firms. One of the Emmett family – there were five of them – upset Brett by making fun of his collection of arms and armour. Brett was left to find satisfaction in the fact that his periodicals were usually the more successful. Both houses put out numerous other titles like *Sons of Britannia*, *The Young Briton*, *The Young Englishman* (Emmett) and *Boys of the Empire* (Brett) which the youth of the day must have found almost impossible to distinguish one from the other. Brett also had a *Boy's Comic Journal*, which was noticeably more sensational than comic.

In his own good time Charles Fox, another 'penny dreadful' impresario, who took over many of Lloyd's titles, including *Sweeney Todd*, decided to bring out a boys' magazine. His *Boys' Standard*, raised in 1875, ran for twenty years and enjoyed a circulation comparable to that of *Boys of England*. Fox also put out a *Boy's Champion* and a *Boy's Leisure Hour*.

Often the stories in the Brett, Emmett and Fox boys' magazines did not greatly differ from the type of story put out as 'penny dreadfuls'. They were written, as often as not, in the short-breath, short-sentence style. Gothic influences were by no means extinct. The tales were still bloodthirsty to a degree, notably those in Fox's *Boys' Standard* (a typical cover picture of which shows a Spartan holding up the decapitated head of his adversary in the arena). There was a high proportion of historical tales, featuring heroic apprentices or real-life characters ranging from Rob Roy to Taffy ap Morgan, from Guy Fawkes to Drake. Probably the Roundheads versus Cavaliers period was as popular as any; and there were any number of tales about Colonel Blood and the 'bravos of Alsatia', the swash-

1. His real name was Allingham – an uncle of Herbert Allingham who wrote popular serials of prodigious length in the *Jester* and many other boys' journals. Rollington published *Boys' World*, *Our Boys' Paper* and *Boys' Pocket Library*.

buckling rogues who found sanctuary from creditors and other persecutors in their own disreputable corner of London, where they elected their own 'ruler'.

There were also tales of ancient Greece and Rome, of the Saxon kings and even of the German and Scandinavian gods. It was the day of hairy, deep-chested characters with names like Zar and Zek, which made for confused reading. One story featured a character called Clek, another called Clek-Clek, and a third called Clek-Clek-Clek. No matter what the period of the story all characters tended to talk in that peculiar jargon which is reserved for persons who lived and died before 1800. These historical romances seem to have been genuinely popular. The reaction against historical fiction did not set in until our own century, when the plea that boys 'learned too much history at school' was the usual editorial excuse. It is at least doubtful whether twentieth-century schoolboys were primed with as much history as nineteenth-century schoolboys; but tales of the tilt yard could hardly hope to compete against tales of aerial dog fights. It was Excalibur against the death ray, and the death ray won.

The *Boys' Standard* launched a popular Celestial called Ching-Ching, whose adventures, linked with those of Handsome Harry of the Fighting Belvedere, enjoyed a vogue almost rivalling that for Jack Harkaway. The creator was E. Harcourt Burrage. There was no malice, but a great deal of cunning, in Ching-Ching. His antecedents were vague and the wily youth told many improbable tales of his early days and illustrious forbears in Pekin. He spoke in a pidgin dialect which to the modern reader is rather trying, and must have been still more trying to the proof-reader. Ching-Ching was a fellow of infinite resource and inextinguishable cheerfulness. He would tackle a rogue on the highroad with the same insouciance as he sought to tackle that secret society, based on South America, which was in the happy position of being able to give orders to the Nihilists in Russia, the Socialists in Germany and the Communists in France (the

THE BOYS COMIC JOURNAL

STORIES OF FUN, ADVENTURE, AND ROMANCE

No. 545.—VOL. XXII.)   EDITED BY EDWIN J. BRETT.   [PRICE ONE PENNY.

"LUTTRELL WAS ABOUT TO REPEAT THE COWARDLY BLOW."

UNMASKED;
OR,
THE DAY OF RECKONING

CHAPTER VI.—(continued.)

THE girl's beautiful blue eyes betrayed no signs of fear as Luttrell entered.

"I am here once more, Alice Melville," he said.

"So I perceive."

"And, as usual, a warm welcome awaits me," he sarcastically added.

"I can have no welcome for the man who,

To the week ending AUGUST 19, 1892.

A companion to Edwin Brett's 'Boys of England' – notably more sensational than comic

date of this story was 1881). There were several series of Ching-Ching tales, with titles like 'Cheerful Ching-Ching', 'Daring Ching-Ching', and 'Wonderful Ching-Ching'. There was even a *Ching-Ching's Own* in 1888.

It was the fashion about this time for heroes to be saddled with names which proclaimed to the world their dash and daring – Ben Braveall, Frank Fearnot, Frank Fearless, Dick Dare, Tom Tearaway and Tom Wildrake; names recalling those of the young heroes and heroines of the chapbooks – Jemmy Studious, Johnny Dawdle, Betsy Algood and Nancy Careful. This tendency was especially marked in school stories which were now becoming a firm fashion. There were schoolboy Ned Nimbles, Tom Torments, Rattlin' Toms and Jolly Jacks by the score. Schoolmasters – handicapped by such names as the Rev. Theophilus Wagjaw, or Mr Hackchild – were commonly represented as pompous, cretinous and bibulous. Swishing was the recognized cure for high spirits – every other academy had a name like Bircham or Scarum or Stingboys.

The comedy in most of the school stories in the late Victorian years was fairly crude. The height of humour was for a boy to impregnate his trousers with snuff or pepper before a beating. One writer was even able to fill several columns describing how an offender sought to mitigate his punishment by lining his trousers with books.

The boys of a school featured in *Boys of England* had fun at the expense of one of their number with a 'probang' which was described as 'a flat board with a hole in the centre. This was used for forcing between the jaws of a cow who might swallow too large a piece of turnip. The other portion, the ramrod to wit, was then forced down her throat through the little hole in the centre.'

Among the most celebrated schoolboy characters were: Hogarth House's Tom Wildrake, who, when his classroom adventures were exhausted, was pitchforked into the Indian Mutiny and then packed off to Australia; and the redoubtable Jack Harkaway, whose adventures require a chapter to themselves.

CHAPTER V

JACK HARKAWAY

To rub one's grandfather the wrong way, it used to be enough to make a disparaging reference to Jack Harkaway. Vehemently, he would proclaim there never was a lad like Jack ... high-spirited, of course, but nothing vicious about him. If only the present generation had been reared on Harkaway, how much manlier they would be for it. And so on.

Yet what a ruthless fellow was this idol of the youth of the seventies, eighties and nineties. He was too much for M. Willson Disher, who in *Pilot Papers* (March, 1947) quoted the first part of a Harkaway passage describing the torture of a Red Indian brave, and then, sickened by the smell of burning flesh, said:

Honestly, for your sake even more than mine, I think I had better leave off. It is, without exaggeration, dreadful. And there is a great deal more of it. Grand Guignol is soon outdone. How on earth schoolboys could read it without vomiting can only be understood by clinging to a belief that they had acquired the horrid taste gradually. My father, who forbade me to read the harmless Dick Turpins and Robin Hoods of the reign of Edward VII, brought himself up on this hardy diet. I have a still greater admiration for his stoic ideals of life now I know how they began. The incidents I have spared you are more trying than anything in the pages of the most admired of unflinching realists.

For the defence, there is Sir John Hammerton, who, writing of the boys' stories read by him in his youth (*Books and Myself*) says: 'It pleases me to think that these stories – notably the Jack Harkaway series in which a robust humour was an ingredient – wrought not one per cent of the harm to their boy readers that the gangster films have done to the boys of the last quarter of a century.'

And George Sampson, well known for his *Concise Cambridge History of Literature*, admits in *Seven Essays* that he devoured Jack Harkaway along with Sweeney Todd and Spring-Heeled Jack, and comments: 'There was no harm in any of them.'

The creator of Jack Harkaway was Bracebridge Hemyng, barrister of the Middle Temple, who found that turning out fiction was vastly more profitable than sitting around waiting for briefs. He threw all he had into Harkaway – adventure, humour, sentiment, sadism, out-of-the-way knowledge, even a dash of religion. To what extent Harkaway was read for (or in spite of) the author's descriptions of torture is anybody's guess. Children nourished on Grimm's Fairy Tales, with their wealth of decapitation and burning alive, probably took Harkaway comfortably in their stride. It is more likely that the Harkaway stories succeeded because the central character was likeable, fearless and full-blooded, a lad with an eye for a practical joke who took the whole world for his oyster and remained aggressively English. There was nothing Gothic about the Harkaway stories. There may have been a strong smell of blood, but not of the charnel-house. There may have been some uncommonly ruthless characters, like Magog Brand, who cut off one brigand's head and threw it at another, but there were no secret, black and midnight hags. Here at last were stories which were free of the aura of the *Newgate Calendar*.

The Jack Harkaway stories began in 1871 in Edwin J. Brett's *Boys of England*, the journal for which newsagents had fought in the streets when it was first published five years earlier. Promptly the stories were pirated in America, appearing in *The Boys and Girls Weekly*. The publisher of this, Frank Leslie, offered Hemyng an exceptionally generous contract if he would break with Brett. Hemyng did so and journeyed to America, where he wrote a number of Harkaway romances.

The Harkaway titles (which came out in penny parts as well as magazines) include:

Jack Harkaway's Schooldays.
Jack Harkaway After Schooldays.
Jack Harkaway at Oxford.
Jack Harkaway's Adventures Round the World.
Jack Harkaway in Search of the Mountain of Gold.
Jack Harkaway in Search of his Father.
Jack Harkaway Among the Pirates.
Jack Harkaway on the Prairie.
Jack Harkaway Out West Among the Indians.
Jack Harkaway and his Father at the Haunt of the Pirates.
Jack Harkaway in Australia.
Jack Harkaway and his Son's Adventures in China.
Jack Harkaway and his Son's Adventures in Greece.
Jack Harkaway and his Boy Tinker.
Jack Harkaway at School in America.
Jack Harkaway at the Isle of Palms.
Jack Harkaway in the Transvaal.
Jack Harkaway's War Scouts.

It is said that there was another Harkaway story, 'Jack Harkaway in Search of Wealth', which was proofed but never published. From the list it will be seen that there was a Harkaway *père* and a Harkaway *fils*. There were in fact three Harkaways. In Brett's short-lived *Jack Harkaway's Journal for Boys* (1893) appeared Harkaway the Third, 'son of the second of that name and the grandson of the first who was now well up in years but still hale and hearty as of yore'. All the Harkaways conformed to the same pattern of behaviour.

The first Harkaway, who studied (after a fashion) at Pomona House School, was a lad of uncertain parentage, which prompted the school bully to chant:

> 'He never had a father
> And he never had a mother
> He never had a sister
> And he never had a brother,
> He was nobody's child.'

The first fight between Harkaway and the bully Hunston was notable in so far as it revealed the author's ignorance of, or contempt for, the Queensberry Rules.

The fight began after Jack had kicked the bully's crony for talking out of turn.

He [Hunston] made a rush at Jack but failed to hit him, whereupon Jack feinted with his left and struck him in the stomach with his right.

'Oh!' ejaculated Hunston, doubling himself up. Jack followed this advantage by dealing his opponent two heavy blows one after the other in the face, and Hunston rolled over.

Excusably, perhaps, the bully thought he would try some dirt now. He tripped Jack by 'a trick learned at Porto Rico'. Jack quickly recovered, and caught Hunston round the neck with his left arm 'in an iron-like grip'.

Then he dealt him blow after blow in the face until he fell from his hold and lay like a log on the ground.

'Bravo, Jack! Well done, Harkaway!'

There was a pause while Hunston was slapped on the back, for he was in danger of choking on a half-swallowed tooth. One of his eyes was closed, the other was of little use. But the fight went on:

Hunston senior now tried what in France is known as the *savate*.

This is a sharp and quick kick in the face which is not allowed in fair English fighting. Unprepared for this, Jack was struck under the chin by the toe of his opponent's boot in a way that made his teeth rattle like castanets, and cut his tongue.

'Shame! Shame!' cried half a dozen voices.

While these belated shouts were still ringing, Hunston tried the *savate* a second time, but Jack caught his up-raised foot and made him hop about while he battered him senseless.

Fighting apart, there was little to do at Pomona House School except rag as graceless a set of pedagogues as ever gathered under one roof. Jack, being a ventriloquist, had a head and shoulders start over the others. By causing Mr Mole to say 'Frogs!' and 'Waterloo!' to M. Bolivant, the

French master, he succeeded in making these excitable gentlemen fight in front of the class. Then the Head, Mr Crawcour, entered, and the fun really started:

'What is this?' exclaimed Mr Crawcour. 'Mr Mole with his fists clenched and M. Bolivant on his back. Disgraceful! How can you expect boys to be orderly when they have such a bad example. Gentlemen, I am ashamed of you!'

'Shut up,' said Jack, making his voice come from the senior master.

'Mr Mole!' exclaimed the Principal in astonishment.

'I said nothing, sir,' replied the senior master. 'My opinion is the place is bewitched; I shall go out, and then perhaps you will get at the bottom of it.'

'It wouldn't be the first time. He's caned a good many.'

This time Jack made Mr Pumpleton speak.

'Mr Pumpleton,' said the Principal. 'Did that remark emanate from you?'

'No, sir, it did not, on my honour.'

'Don't believe him,' said Jack.

This time it was Mr Stonor.

'Mr Stonor, are you too forgetting yourself? It seems to me I shall have to change my staff.'

'Go it, old cock,' said Jack, making M. Bolivant the speaker this time ...

And so on and so on. Jack was detected and punished, but the masters of Pomona House School never learned by experience. A few chapters later Jack had them at each other's throats again, by the same means.

When it came to punishment Jack was a realist. A panel of his fellows found him guilty (for the Head was a believer in the jury system), and the sentence was that he be sent to Coventry for a week. Many a young hero of fiction would have preferred a whipping; not this one.

Jack thought he had got off very well as he infinitely preferred the silent system to being soundly birched, and congratulated himself on his good luck.

He knew he had been wrong and had sense enough to know that order could not reign in the school if the boys did not obey their masters.

'I mean to run away,' said Jack Harkaway, 'will you help me?'

Another pupil who might have preferred seven days in Coventry was the sneak whom Jack punished by forcing him to eat, raw, a soot-covered carp which had died in the course of a prank.

Though Jack was a realist in not relishing corporal punishment he nevertheless allowed himself to be birched in front of the school on a framed-up charge rather than tell the truth and incriminate Little Emily, the girl on whom he was 'spoony'. Emily had broken open her money-box, and sent him the money he was accused of stealing.

Those who were brought up on Jack Harkaway doubtless shook their heads over the play *Young Woodley*, regarding it as sloppiness at the best and decadence at the worst. But there was a time when Jack was in grave danger of becoming 'spoony' over his headmaster's wife, who had nursed him through an illness.

She put her arm round his neck and kissed his forehead, while she smoothed back his curly, chestnut hair from his temples.

'How would you like to have me for a mama?' she asked.

'I would rather have you – for – for –'

He hesitated.

'Well, dear, for what? Speak out,' said Mrs Crawcour in an encouraging tone.

'I was going to say for a sweetheart, ma'am.'

'But you have one. The little girl who sent you the money is your sweetheart, is she not?'

'I like her very much, but not nearly as much as I do you, ma'am. You are so very lovely,' replied Jack.

'Am I lovely?' Mrs Crawcour repeated, looking at her handsome and majestic figure in the glass with some satisfaction.

The hot blood mounted to Jack's face and made it burn.

'How you blush! Why do you blush so?' she said.

'I don't know, ma'am. It comes to me talking to you, I think.'

'But you cannot have me for a sweetheart. I am your schoolmistress and your master's wife.'

'Still, I may love you quietly and at a distance, ma'am. You cannot help people loving you.'

'You funny boy,' she exclaimed, kissing him again.

However, it was not because of this perilous trend in his affections that Jack had to leave Pomona House. There had been too many pranks, and one of them had led to the school catching fire. It was noteworthy that no pupils thought of trying to extinguish the flames until they were dragooned into so doing. Reverence for the Old School was not yet a feature of schoolboy stories.

It was decided to send Jack to sea. He received the news with equanimity, pausing only at the last to write a couple of letters, the first of which he did not scruple to pen in the fist of the beautiful if foolish Mrs Crawcour:

To Mr Burroughs, Undertaker, Lillie Bridge:

Sir, will you oblige me by coming up tomorrow about three o'clock to Pomona House to measure my unfortunate husband for a coffin as, I regret to say, he has died suddenly.

The other was to the editor of the *Hertfordshire Mercury*:

A gentleman residing at Pomona House, Lillie Bridge, feels

that he has hitherto been wanting in the divine attribute of charity which should distinguish all mankind and wishes to make amends for his deficiency. Therefore this is to say that he will present every woman who calls on Friday at the above address between the hours of ten and twelve with the sum of half-a-crown.

Jack's life henceforth was one of voyage, shipwreck and travel in strange lands. Not the least peculiar experience to befall him occurred on the banks of a river in Italy. A bandit slipped up behind him and snapped a thick india-rubber ring round him, pinioning his arms, then tossed him in the river. This incident was too much for Edgar Jepson, who recalls it in his *Memories of a Victorian*. 'You could not get away with that ring to-day, not on the neo-Georgian boy,' he says. Obviously, Mr Jepson had never studied *The Wizard*.

On some of Jack's expeditions he was accompanied by his friend Harvey, and other characters from Pomona House cropped up on one pretext or another, including Mr Mole who had a tea garden left to him in China. It was the fate of the hapless Mr Mole to lose one limb after another and to be bastinadoed, stuck with stilettos. plucked half bald and otherwise maltreated in Jack's service. For this he received such dubious compensations as being awarded a plurality of native wives. Jack allowed the bully Hunston to be tattoed all over in bizarre patterns by a tribe of cannibals. This was considered to be a not unfitting punishment for the trouble he had caused. He was lucky not to have suffered the fate of the man whom Jack watched being eaten alive. Explained Mr Hemyng:

The parts of the human body which are esteemed the greatest delicacies by these cannibals are first the palms of the hands and then the eyes.
When the chief has gratified his choice the others are entitled in turn to advance and cut out bits.
The savage feast proceeded quickly and the victim's shrieks and moans were pitiful to hear. Jack ground his teeth with

rage, but on looking to his rifle found that he had lost the percussion cap off the nipple and had not another with him. Beside, the man might have been a criminal for what he knew.

It was important not to be too sentimental about the fate of criminals. Jack's friend Harvey had both strong principles and a strong stomach. When Jack was betrayed into captivity by a native girl Harvey wanted her put to death. The other natives preferred to torture her for more information. Harvey was not in favour of this, but did not feel strongly enough to make an issue of it.

Nuratella was dragged to another part and her cries were soon heard at intervals.
She was beaten with bamboos.
Fire was placed under her feet.
Red-hot stones were applied to various parts of her body and a band of twisted reeds was tied so tightly round her forehead that her eyes threatened to burst from their sockets.
At length her fortitude, great though it was, gave way.

One can guess how differently the heroes of the *Boy's Own Paper* would have reacted in these circumstances ...
After one of his adventures Jack came home to Emily. (Hunston, tattooed as he was, had beaten him to the first kiss, and not even her plea that it was like the touch of a snake quite reassured Jack.) He was prepared now to become a soldier if someone would buy him a commission. But first it was agreed that he should go to university. He chose Oxford because it was 'more swell than Cambridge'. All too soon he was the object of proctorial interest. He took part in a very spirited battle between Town and Gown, going out of his way to assault one townsman on the sole grounds that he was a bargee. Jack's real trouble at Oxford was that he was always being tricked into gambling with shady types. But he was a disconcerting adversary to cheat at cards. Once he startled the assembly by suddenly pinning his opponent's hand to the table with a table fork. When this was extracted, not without difficulty,

a card was found underneath the palm; though bloody, it was recognizable as the ace of clubs.

After losing £500 at dice, Jack called 'double or quits' and lost. This debt was due to be paid to Moses Manasses, a Jewish money-lender whose daughter Jack had providently saved from drowning in the Cherwell. In the circumstances it did not seem likely that Jack would be pressed for payment. But there was no gratitude in the Tents of Israel. The moneylender was anxious to marry off his daughter to Jack, who, he claimed, had gone out of his way to encourage the girl by turning over the pages of her music. Some of his friends thought it would be a good thing for Jack to marry the moneylender's daughter. One of them, knowledgeable in these matters, assured him that she was 'as fine a spoon as there is in Oxford'.

But Jack still cherished an obstinate affection for Emily. She for her part must have been deeply in love with him, otherwise she would hardly have co-operated with him in such episodes as the punishment of one Davis, who had been detected making a pass at her. Jack first had the offender bound hand and foot and rolled him under the sofa where he and Emily were sitting. Davis still showed sufficient spirit to bite Jack in the ankle, for which he was threatened with a kick in the face. But Jack thought of a better punishment:

Jack put his arm round Emily's waist and looking at Davis said –

'You wanted a kiss, just now, from the best girl that ever lived?'

Davis made no answer.

Jack got up and kicked him in the ribs.

'Answer when you are spoken to, or it will be the worse for you,' he exclaimed.

'If I did, what then?' asked Davis, with some of his old independent manner.

'Just this. See me kiss her. That's all, old boy. That's your share.'

Jack drew Emily to him as he spoke and she let her head fall on his breast while he bent down and kissed her as he liked.

When he had done, he said –

'How do you like that? Nice, isn't it?'

Nor was that the end of Davis's (or Emily's) discomfiture. In a lordly way Jack ordered a number of fowls to be killed and plucked, and sent someone else for a barrel of tar. Emily was then obliged to witness the disfiguring of the man who had been rash enough to desire her.

Poor Emily! It was no fun being in love with a Harkaway. It must have been both a disappointment and a relief for her when Jack went on his travels again, though she was often to meet him in the most unlikely places.

Powerfully as he appealed to his readers' spirit of adventure, Bracebridge Hemyng periodically went out of his way to preach old-fashioned prudence. For instance, when Jack had been on the point of running away from school, he said:

His wish was to get away, at all hazards, from the tyranny under which he groaned, and when we remember that he was friendless and persecuted, perhaps some excuse can be made for him.

Let us not be misunderstood.

We are no advocates for running away; boys who run away from school generally turn out scamps in after life.

They show an independence of action and a strong self-will, in which it is very injurious for the young to indulge.

Or could that have been the cautious hand of the publisher Brett, who often in his correspondence columns gave out such advice as:

A boy must have his parents' consent before he enters the merchant service, and no boy with good intentions and hoping to get on in the world would dream of going to sea without the permission of those who have loved him and provided for his comforts from infancy.

In his more sententious moments Hemyng could lay it on thick. This kind of passage, describing Harkaway's friendship with a boy dying of tuberculosis, reads oddly from the same pen which so heartlessly described the choking of a sneak with a sooty carp, or the frying of a Red Indian:

Of books he [the sick boy] had a large store, but he did not like travels and biographies, unless they related to missionaries and good men.

Fisher's eyes would glisten still more brightly, and an expression of almost divine enthusiasm cross his eloquent features, as he listened with greedy ears.

'Ah!' he would say with a sigh, 'that is what I should like to have done.'

'You will be able to do it when you grow up,' said Jack.

Fisher shook his head sadly.

'Gladly would I give up everything for my Saviour,' he answered. 'But I fear I shall be called away before long.'

'Oh, no, you won't. You are ill, and feel weak. You'll soon be strong and on your legs again,' Jack said.

'Do you really think so?' asked the invalid thoughtfully. 'I wish I could, and yet I don't know why I should wish it. It is nice to die young, Jack – I mean before one has been exposed to any great temptation. It is very hard to try and keep steadfast in the faith.'

'The doctor thinks you will get better,' said Jack, passing the back of his hand over his eyes.

'Whether I do or not, I shall never forget you. Will you read to me now? Take the New Testament; open it anywhere, you are sure to find something comforting. It is only when we are ill, Jack, that we know the value of the Bible.'

'Have something more lively,' suggested Jack. 'Robinson Crusoe now.'

'To me there is nothing so interesting as the Bible. You are strong, and well, and perhaps don't think as I do. The boys say you did not know your mother. Oh! Jack, if you had a mother like mine, you would – but you seem pained. Have I said anything to hurt you?'

Any admirers of Harkaway the First, who, twenty years later, chanced to read the adventures of Harkaway the Third, might pardonably, if anachronistically, have said, 'This is where I came in.' Young Jack and his chum arrived at Plato House, which also was served by an over-

Enter Jack Harkaway: his forcibly tattooed opponent is held to the ground by Harvey

indulgent Head and by masters over-indulgent in liquor. The boys made their snobbish tutor drunk the first night by pretending to be titled Etonians, but no disciplinary action was taken.

Young Jack took exception to a fellow pupil of foreign appearance.

'You're not a true Englishman,' he said. 'There's a touch of the tarbrush about you which shows you are not a white man.'

Later occurred this dialogue:

'There is some of the bandit blood in you.'
'That is my misfortune, not my fault, even if it is true.'
'Fellows like you require to be kept down and have some of the cur knocked out of them.'
'Do you call me that?'
'Yes, a half-bred Spanish cur,' answered Jack.

The 'gipsy' decided that these were fighting words.

They fought. Jack licked him (no kicking this time), but the fellow chose an unfair revenge:

To go behind a man and hit him on the head with a cricket bat, exerting all your strength, was not English.

This the Platonians, as they called themselves, knew full well.

Jack Harkaway had fought a fair fight and won it in a handsome British manner. Why should he be attacked in this disgraceful manner? And by a youth who could only boast of half-English blood?

All were inclined to cry, 'Out upon the dastard who has brought this blood upon the school!'

It was Harkaway the Third who fought against the Boers in 1899. The stories 'Jack Harkaway in the Transvaal, or Fighting for the Flag', and 'Jack Harkaway's War Scouts' appeared in *Up-to-Date Boys*, a Brett publication which lasted a little longer than *Jack Harkaway's Journal for Boys*. Harkaway was a captain of Hussars, leading a 'private army' which had a spiritual affinity with some of the irregular units of World War Two. He had an exhilarating time, rescuing daughters of the veldt from death or dishonour, and making Boers chant 'Rule Britannia' at the point of the sword. His keenest displeasure was visited upon an unfortunate Frenchman whose part in the war effort was obscure but whose designs on the fair Gretchen were all too clear. Annoyed at being interrupted by this impertinent Hussar, the Frenchman sought to run him through with his sword. Jack announced that to teach him a lesson he would cut off one of his ears and give him a flesh wound in the arm.

Harkaway was an expert swordsman.

The weapon flashed twice in the air with the rapidity of lightning.

At the first stroke the Frenchman lost his left ear, which was sliced off close to the head; the second wounded him in the right arm above the elbow, and he sank to the ground bewailing his fate.

Jack tore a piece of stuff from his tunic and bound up his

wound, but the little man collapsed and fainted away like a woman.

Gretchen did not faint. She entirely approved of the proceedings, smiled on Jack and handed him his rifle when he had finished. They were beautiful but tough, those Harkaway heroines.

Not every authority agrees that Bracebridge Hemyng wrote all the Harkaway stories. Brett liked to pretend to a proprietorial right in them, and gave the name of Harkaway House to his publishing offices in West Harding Street, off Fetter Lane. This was probably intended as a slap at Hogarth House which also published a number of Harkaway stories. There is no doubt that Jack Harkaway materially contributed to Brett's £76,538 fortune. What Hemyng made out of his hero is not recorded.

Hemyng launched many other characters, such as Hal Harkforward and Tom Tallyho, but it is by Harkaway alone that he is remembered. Indeed, it was as Jack Harkaway that he liked to refer to himself, and as such that many of his friends thought of him. Nor was he the only writer of romances to masquerade as his fictional creation.

CHAPTER VI

NOT SO CALLOW

THE magazines of Brett, Emmett and Fox did not commend themselves to squeamish Victorian parents; but the most fastidious father could hardly fault the new paper which came out in 1879: the *Boy's Own Paper*. Was it not published by the Religious Tract Society, and edited by James Macaulay, M.A., M.D.? Did it not carry fiction by clergymen, headmasters, baronets, officers of field rank, titled ladies, the worthy Mr Ballantyne and gentlemen with M.A. and F.R.S. after their names? Were not the stories written in decent English, and the drawings executed by persons who had been to art school? This obviously was a journal which could safely be allowed in the home.

Some younger readers were more cautious. Because an author put after his name the letters C.M., M.D., R.N. (as Gordon Stables did), or 'Late Professor and Crown Examiner at Moscow' (like J. F. Hodgetts, author of 'Edric the Norseman'), did that make him any the better story-teller? And who was Lady Broome, that she should pretend to be a boy and write a first-person adventure story? Again, the editor of the *Boy's Own Paper* had a good deal to learn when it came to thinking out a lively title; witness 'Frank Harding; or From Torrid Zones to Regions of Perpetual Snow'. He was partial also to headings like 'For England, Home and Beauty'. (In 1882, when *Punch* ran a series of skits on the *Boy's Own Paper*, one parodied tale was entitled 'Wet Bob, or The Adventures of a Little Eton Boy Amongst the Hotwhata Cannibals', by the Author of 'The Three Young Benchers and How They All Got the Woolsack', 'From Back Bench to Yard-Arm', etc.)

But the *Boy's Own Paper*, with discreet parental encouragement, was quick to prosper. At certain schools boys were paraded and handed copies of the new weekly to read, a bold approach which might have prejudiced them against it for good, but the new paper in the buff cover was not easily thrown aside. In its early years its readership was in the region of a quarter of a million. *Boys of England* had boasted the patronage of Prince Arthur and the Prince Imperial; the new journal claimed the allegiance not only of Prince Arthur but of Prince George (later King George V).

Although the titular editor was Dr James Macaulay, the real editor was George Andrew Hutchinson, who conducted it as a weekly from the first issue until 1912, when he died in harness. A well-loved character, Hutchinson kept the standard high while insisting that the magazine must be written for boys and not for their grandmothers. He encouraged many brilliant new contributors and recruited old hands like R. M. Ballantyne, G. A. Henty and W. H. G. Kingston. The roll of his writers includes Conan Doyle, Jules Verne, Algernon Blackwood, Gunby Hadath, H. de Vere Stacpoole and, of course, Hutchinson's greatest find, Talbot Baines Reed. *Boy's Own Paper* serials by Reed include 'The Adventures of a Three-Guinea Watch', 'The Fifth Form at St Dominic's', 'A Dog With a Bad Name', 'The Master of the Shell' and the 'Cock-House of Fellsgarth' – all reprinted many times as schoolboy classics. Reed incidentally never went to a public school. Jules Verne's *Boy's Own Paper* serials included 'The Clipper of the Clouds' and 'Twenty Thousand Leagues Under the Sea', both of which were drawn upon lavishly by lesser journals.

Not the least popular feature of the *Boy's Own Paper* was the splendid folding colour-plate given away with the monthly edition. It made the free chromographs of the 'penny dreadfuls' look remarkably shoddy by comparison. Famous artists associated with the *Boy's Own Paper* were R. Caton Woodville, who excelled at military subjects, and Stanley L. Wood.

The *Boy's Own Paper* stood above the blood and thunder class, but it certainly did not offer milk and water. D. B. Wyndham-Lewis was at pains to point this out in *The Tatler*, when rounding on a critic who had described a film as 'almost callow enough for the *Boy's Own Paper*'. Wrote Wyndham-Lewis:

Callow (unfledged, innocent, inexperienced, downy) is the last epithet we should have applied to that paper, which we remember from our golden infancy to be full of tough, hairy, conquering Nordics plunging through trackless forests and lethal swamps, wrestling with huge apes and enormous cobras, foiling villains of Latin origin, crammed with experience and philosophy and knowing practically everything. If the story was by Gordon Stables, R. N., moreover, they turned out to be Scotsmen, and therefore twice as conquering, hairy, noble and scornful of civilized Southern fal-lals.

If, on the other hand, the critic boy meant by 'callow' that vintage B.O.P. heroes never used beastly language, like a modern school-girl, he was correct. In the tightest corners they merely 'uttered a hasty exclamation'. More often than not, faced with fearful odds, they simply gnawed their lips, thus:

'I fear,' said Black MacTavish quietly, 'we are surrounded. Meanwhile do you, MacIntosh, hand me MacNab's knife. I fear his leg is no longer of service.'

It was the work of a moment to amputate MacNab's leg. A substitute was briskly carved from the nearest *njama*-tree by Sandy. MacNab at once leapt up and expressed himself ready to march all day. As he spoke a shower of poisoned spears rattled through the bush and laid three of the little party prostrate.

MacTavish gnawed his lip.
Callow, huh? . . .

An early volume selected at random (1887–88) and opened at random contains a passage no less tough than Wyndham-Lewis's imaginary one. Morgana, a dark and *décolletée* matron, is being trodden to the floor of a collapsing tumulus by a blind man, whose leg she is attempting to hack off with a golden sickle. With her other hand she is trying to pour out a goblet of poison. Before she can make much progress either way the tumulus crashes on both of them. An appropriate comment comes from one of her adherents: 'It is time for us to become Christians.'

The same volume of the *Boy's Own Paper* contains a drawing of a newly decapitated man with blood pouring from his trunk, and another of a man hanging from a tree. But more gruesome than any fictional item in this volume is a series of practical hints on taxidermy for boys, by Lieut.-Colonel Cuthell, late 13th Hussars. Here is one of the lighter passages on stuffing birds:

The Head. – If the head is very much larger than the neck, cut the throat lengthways to remove the head. It is immaterial whether the eyes are taken out before the head is skinned down or after. The gouge should go well to the back of the eye and separate the ligament which holds it to the socket. Should the gouge go into the eye, it will let out the moisture, which often damages the skin. Some people crush the skull slightly to make it come out of the skin easily, but this I do not advise. Remove the brains by taking out a piece of the skull at the back as you cut off the neck. Pull the eyes out of their cavity and fill up their place with wool soaked in arsenical soap. Anoint the skin of the head and the neck well with asenical soap, and place in the neck a piece of stick covered with wool, the end of which put into the hole made in the skull for extracting the brains.

Lieut.-Colonel Cuthell has another memorable paragraph which begins: 'And now for the treatment of the head of a horned animal ...'

When the *Boy's Own Paper* held its jubilee luncheon in 1929 the then Home Secretary, Sir William Joynson-Hicks, recalled how, in youth, the *Boy's Own Paper* had incited him to build rabbit hutches and chicken pens, but he said nothing about ventures in taxidermy. Nor did anyone else.

Like many boys' magazines the *Boy's Own Paper* mellowed with the years. It became a monthly in 1914 and stayed faithful to its standards until the end came in 1967.

The *Boy's Own Paper* could boast many famous names among its contributors, but it fell to James Henderson, publisher of *Young Folks* and *Nuggets*, to serialize the most famous adventure story of all: 'Treasure Island'. The cold fact remains that this was the least successful of the three stories by Robert Louis Stevenson to be published by Henderson in the eighties, the other two being 'The Black Arrow' and 'Kidnapped'. 'Treasure Island' appeared as the work of Captain George North and was a 'flop'. Very little happened for the first half-dozen chapters, and if the editor had retained Stevenson's original, unimaginative title of 'The Sea Cook' the readers of *Young Folks* might have abandoned it completely. As it was, they were very critical. To Henderson, the story was worth no more than the ten shillings per thousand words that Stevenson was paid for it. 'The Black Arrow', though admitted by its author to be 'tushery', was a success, because it was written as a serial should be written.

Chums, a paper which enjoyed almost the same degree of parental approval as *Boy's Own Paper*, did not appear until 1892. It was published by Cassell and the first editor was Sir Max Pemberton, who resigned after a year. Though *Chums* can hardly be said to have prospered under his direction, his serial 'The Iron Pirate' did much to rally it when its health was causing anxiety. Pemberton's editorial in the first issue, which had an unattractive lay-out like that of a weekly review, struck an urbane, unaggressive note:

Have you, most excellent readers, too many boys' papers? And without suggesting unkindness towards my rivals, have you such good boys' papers that another may not enter into friendly rivalry with them? I think you will say that you have not.

Although 'Treasure Island' had already been serialized in *Young Folks*, *Chums* published the now-famous story again in 1894. The news of Stevenson's death in Samoa was received just as the last instalment was going to press.

Chums entered on a new, vigorous career just before the turn of the century and became as full-blooded as any of its contemporaries. Today it is chiefly remembered, perhaps, for the pirate stories of S. Walkey, illustrated by Paul Hardy – 'Rogues of the Fiery Cross', 'Under The Black Flag', 'Yo! Ho! For The Spanish Main' and many others. For more than thirty years S. Walkey contributed his fast-moving tales of villainy on the deep, varying them with stories of Red Indians, highwaymen and the French Revolution. Other well-remembered contributors were D. H. Parry, Captain Frank H. Shaw ('The Secret of the Sargasso Sea') and Captain Charles Gilson.

A third 'respectable' boys' magazine was George Newnes's *The Captain* (1899), edited by R. S. Warren Bell, and famous for its school stories by the young P. G. Wodehouse. It was perhaps more light-hearted in its tone than the *Boy's Own Paper*, but lacked the rumbustious appeal of the later *Chums*. Many other famous authors, in their younger days, contributed to it, among them John Buchan and Alec Waugh. According to Captain C. B. Fry, who was the Athletics Editor, *The Captain* 'never persuaded advertisers that it was read by parents. Advertisers did not believe that boys are likely to buy such articles as soap and whisky. I have always thought that the disbelief of advertisers in the capacity of boys to absorb soap was the snag which eventually tripped up the career of ,*The Captain*.'

The class of reader at which the *Boy's Own Paper*, *Chums*, and *The Captain* were aimed may be gauged, in the first-mentioned, by the qualification to the take-a-cold-bath advice given by the editor – 'Do not make more splash than you can help so as to give the servant trouble'; in *Chums*, by the use of such phrases as *O quantum mutatus!* in the editorial: and in *The Captain* by the preoccupation with public school sport.

A feature of almost all the boys' magazines of the pre-Harmsworth era, irrespective of the class of reader at which they were directed, was the very firm handling of

THE BOY'S OWN PAPER

No. 482.—Vol. X.

SATURDAY, APRIL 7, 1888

Price One Penny.
(ALL RIGHTS RESERVED.)

A TALE OF THE NAVY
NINETY YEARS AGO

By GORDON STABLES, C.M.,
M.D., R.N.,

*Author of "The Cruise of the Snowbird,"
"Wild Adventures Round the Pole," etc., etc*

CHAPTER I.—INTRODUCING SEVERAL
OF OUR PRINCIPAL CHARACTERS.

WOULD it snow?

That was the question uppermost in everyone's mind at Agincourt Hall on that still December morning of seventeen hundred and ninety-three.

Would it snow?

"God save the King!"

'God save the King!' A characteristic B.O.P. cover (1888)

correspondents and the parading of a strong editorial authority. Supposed pictures of the editor usually showed him to be a bearded gentleman in the sixties, with a let-me-mould-your-future look in his eyes. A reader of the *Boy's Own Paper* was very smartly slapped down for his mistaken assumption that certain articles were written by boys – 'they are written by *men*'. Corespondents were kept firmly in their place and told what was good for them. A youth who wrote to the *Boy's Own Paper* expressing an interest in party politics was lectured as severely as those youths who confessed to 'sinful habits'; the editor did not say so in so many words, but the impression gained was that a cold bath was the cure for both types of aberration.

At all times the editor was cautious not to set his readers against the established order, even when the established order was at its most trying. To one reader he said:

Fifteen hours a day is, we consider, much too long for a boy of fourteen to have to work; but we do not see what you can do except complete your apprenticeship. You should not have chosen a trade in which such long hours are customary.

Nor could anyone say that he went out of his way to encourage 'Cavalryman':

If you get a commission you *might* rise to be a field-marshal! But we do not think you would. Suppose you limit your notions to your becoming a sergeant?

The editor of the *Boy's Own Paper* may have been pardoned a certain asperity towards his readers, as so much of his mail seems to have consisted of carelessly packed beetles and broken eggs, hopefully submitted for identification. One feels that he got a certain amount of malicious satisfaction out of such answers as:

'BERTIE CLERK will know by this time whether the squirrel is dead or alive.'

Edwin Brett also took a stern line towards his readers and trusted them no farther than he could see them. In announcing a new competition in *Jack Harkaway's Journal for Boys* he warned that anyone submitting the work of another person would be not merely disqualified but PUBLICLY EXPOSED; and just to be on the safe side he ruled that no prizes would be sent off to winners until a month after the results of the competition were published. Brett by that time had few illusions left about readers, authors or fellow-publishers.

If editors did not trust their readers, the reverse appears to have been true. The editor of the innocent *Nuggets* had to counter allegations that his competitions were swindles, that nearly all the prizes went to London, and so on. One reader challenged him to a duel.

The competitions run by Brett and Henderson were mostly on a higher intellectual plane than those privately-run contests which were advertised in small type in *The Young Briton's Journal* (1888). (This magazine was edited by Guy Rayner, contained a serial entitled 'Guy Rayner Among the Brigands', and an editorial assurance that Guy Rayner did really exist – he was 'an Englishman staunch and true'.)

Here is a selection of the catchpenny contests which were to be found in every issue:

Genuine Competition. R . . E B R I T . . N A. Fill in five letters and form two words. A postal order for 10s. sent to every reader who correctly solves above puzzle. Fee 3d. only. Answer advertised. Mr John Lewis, 2 Wait's Buildings, Staple Hill, Bristol.

Prof. Robzart offers three prizes for the most words from R O B Z A R T. Entrance fee 6d. First prize 6s. worth of conjuring tricks; second, three shillings worth; third 1s. 6d. worth. List must be sent in by July 14. – 29 Fleet Street, Southsea.

Grand competition! Journ . . . Add two letters to form a common word. 1st prize, Viaduct watch (splendid condition); 2nd, Handsome Harry, Cheerful, Daring, Wonderful and Young Ching-Ching; 3rd, Broad-Arrow Jack, Bravos of Alsatia, Dick Turpin and first number of Cassell's British Battles. Entrance 6d. to W.R., 16, Trafalgar Square, Peckham.

Genuine Competition. – Nearest to the number of times

letter 'A' occurs in the Book of Titus. First £1 1s.; second 10s. –
Cummings, 53, Hurworth Terrace, Darlington.

Boys, this is genuine. Whoever guesses right or nearest
number of my watch will be owner of it. 92 ... It is a centre-
second stop-watch, full jewelled and real silver. Guesses 6d.
for one, 10d. for two. Insufficient entries, 4d. and 8d. returned.
Addresses C.A.H., Reading Rooms, Brixton, London S.W.

Sheer impecuniosity must have been the reason why
Rayner accepted advertisements like these – impecuniosity
which made him invite his readers to submit stories of
'not more than six columns and not less than three' and
offer *half-a-crown* for all printed, with 20s. for the best.

In fairness to Rayner it must be pointed out that similar
– and much bigger – advertisements were to appear a
couple of years later in a much more prosperous rival,
Comic Cuts. This had an advertisement by a firm in
Boston, Lincolnshire, offering £200 for counting the H's
in the Book of Daniel (entry fee 2s.), £100 for counting
the T's in the first eight chapters of Romans (entry 1s. 6d.),
and £50 for counting the R's in the first six chapters of
Genesis (entry 1s.).

Meanwhile, the 'penny dreadful' was by no means extinct. Indeed, the state of popular juvenile literature was
reducing the *Edinburgh Review* and *Quarterly Review*
to a state of near-apoplexy. 'If Fagin the Jew, Baron Mun-
chausen and Jack Sheppard had set up work as joint
editors of a Thieves' Library they could well have been
proud of the whole series now before us,' wrote the *Edinburgh Review's* critic in 1887.

Even Bill Sykes, if driven to pen and ink, can sign his name;
and any one of his numerous offspring can read with fluency
the weekly Police News or the last edition of the Newgate
Calendar, and criticize the details of the latest burglary, outrage or murder with the flippant ease of a connoisseur of
crime. Murder as one of the fine arts is not too much for him;
his library is both extensive and varied, and to be had at the
rate of a penny a volume. It is to be found anywhere and
everywhere throughout the whole domain of poverty, dirt,

hunger and crime. It tempts him under a hundred different seductive titles alike in country and in town. Every alley and foul court in Babylon reeks with it, and the remotest hamlet can no more escape from some sign of it than from the ubiquitous placard of the last new transparent patent soap.

One of the stories dissected by the *Edinburgh Review* was entitled *Joanna Polenipper, Female Horse Stealer, Foot-Pad, Smuggler, Prison Breaker and Murderer*. The critic's indignation was divided between the style of writing – 'bombastic rant, high-flown rhodomontade and the flattest fustian flow from the lips of all speakers alike' – and the inadequate retribution visited upon Joanna for the havoc she made of the Decalogue, as indicated at the end of the story:

Joanna was transported for her crimes, retrieved her character in Australia, married a rich settler and lived for many years respected and beloved by all who knew her.

The *Quarterly Review's* assault was made three years later. This journal, which had savaged Keats and called Dickens vulgar, had already wrinkled a fastidious nose over the domestic romances and tales of high life published in mid-century, exclaiming incredulously, as it said every normal person must be tempted to exclaim on first dipping into one of these works, *Quis leget haec?*

Despite the advance of education, complained the *Quarterly*, such works as *Joskin the Body Snatcher* and *Three-Fingered Jack, the Terror of the Antilles,* were still there 'to dispute the favour of the poorer class of readers with translations of the improving romances of MM. Zola and Paul de Kock ... In a lane not far from Fleet Street is a complete factory of the literature of rascaldom – a literature which has done much to people our prisons, our reformatories and our Colonies with scapegraces and n'er-do-wells.'

The *Quarterly's* critic claimed to have private knowledge of the authors of many of these penny publications – 'not as a rule very distinguished members of the Repub-

lic of Letters, though in some few instances their antecedents are better than might be expected'. One, it
appears, was a beneficed clergyman who had cast off his
cloth. Another, who translated 'dubious French novels'
on weekdays, actually officiated on Sundays at 'some sort
of Dissenting Chapel'. The critic knew of a maidservant
whose father wrote novels from ten to four for a cheap
publisher; also of a cook who, taxed with dilatoriness in
the preparation of meals, explained that she was busy in
the kitchen writing novels.

Other cooks, of course, were busy in the kitchen reading
novels. And they, in company with the footmen, the pot
boys and pit boys, the errand boys and apprentices, were
not going to be cheated out of their blood and thunder.

In the late eighties emerged a new source of fierce and
bizarre enjoyment – the Aldine Publishing Company, under Charles Perry Brown. Over the next forty years or so
it was to put out a profusion of 'libraries' on every subject
from highwaymen to horse racing. In its early years,
which were its most successful, it specialized in reprints
of American stories, notably those featuring Frank Reade
(Chapter X) and Buffalo Bill and Deadwood Dick (Chapter XV). For home-bred heroes it remained faithful to the
tried and tested figures of folklore – Robin Hood, Dick
Turpin, Claude Duval, Jack Sheppard and Spring-Heeled
Jack. The Aldine titles were as richly fantastical as any of
an earlier generation, witness 'The Silver Skeleton, or
Dick Turpin and the Queen of the Pirates', and 'The
Fiends of the Forest, or the House of Eternal Midnight'.
Equally promising were some of the Robin Hood titles:
'The Demon of the Forests', 'The Lord of the Wolves'
and 'Through Foam to Freedom'. Chalton Lea was one
of Aldine's most fertile romancers; another was Stephen
H. Agnew.

It was the Aldine Company that published, in the nine-
ties, two school stories of more than ordinary popularity.
These were *The Lambs of Littlecote* and *The Island
School,* both by E. Harcourt Burrage (Frank Swinnerton

is one who admits having read the penny instalments with avidity). The principal of Littlecote Abbey was Fontenoy Snicker, an H-dropper with 'a face which Nature must originally have intended for a racecourse welsher'. He drank. His assistant was P. Y. Bunn, or Penny Bunn, who in off-duty hours allowed the boys to tie him up with ropes. From the fact that his nose was 'the colour of a faded cabbage rose' it is not difficult to guess that he shared his principal's hobby. The pupil teacher was the cruelly tormented Awful Rooker, and he too, with perhaps more justification, found solace in public-houses. Mrs Snicker, when not correcting her husband's failings ('*Taters!*' repeated Mrs Snicker, 'will you never remember the *per*?'), was supposed to spend her time beating out a pound of butter to cover two acres of bread. When the author tired of barrings-out and treasure hunts in the vaults of the abbey, he set his Lambs adventuring round the world under the tutelage of a sinuous Oriental, Chunder Loo, who had joined the Littlecote staff in odd circumstances.

The Island School had a Mediterranean setting and the characters included: 'Napoleon Farrell, the too-ambitious Founder of the School; Jim Gordon, the Youth of Action, abounding in health and courage; Morse, the Chemist, the Young Designer, the youthful "Moltke" of the island; Lucia di Valo, the proud, revengeful Spanish beauty; Espardo Reonardo, the Invader of the Island; the Smuggler Band; "Charley", the Tame Bear; and Macbeth, Hamlet and Romeo, a trio of Darkies who more or less fill in the whole duty and characteristics of the nigger.'

Take away Lucia di Valo, and *The Island School* might well have held its own among the outrageous schools featured in the *Hotspur*, of more recent memory.

CHAPTER VII

CUCKOO IN THE NEST

While the scramble went on for the pennies, and even the halfpennies, of the new Board School generation, one publisher, James Henderson, was lending encouragement to a young freelance journalist who was fated one day to buy up Henderson's firm, after crowding many of his other rivals from the map. This cuckoo in the nest was Alfred Harmsworth,[1] founder of the Amalgamated Press.

Harmsworth's first publishing enterprise was not aimed at the juvenile market; this was *Answers to Correspondents*, quickly shortened to *Answers* (1888). It was modelled on George Newnes's *Tit-Bits*. The new paper had a shaky start, but thanks to the famous competition in which readers were invited to earn £1 a week for life by estimating the total amount of gold and silver in the Bank of England on December 4, 1889, it was soon on the road to riches. Each entry in this competition had to have five supporting signatures – and there were more than 700,000 entries. Thus some three million potential readers were introduced to *Answers*. The winner of the contest, Sapper Austin, of the Ordnance Survey Department at Southampton, guessed within £2 of the correct amount.

In 1890 Harmsworth, in conjunction with his brother Harold, published *Comic Cuts*, as a halfpenny challenge to *Ally Sloper's Half-Holiday*, the leading penny comic of the day. It was an intoxicating success almost from the start, though the brothers had to fight a brisk battle with 'reactionary' newsagents who objected to handling halfpenny papers. To readers who expressed surprise that it was possible to offer 50 pictures and 18,000 words for a halfpenny, the Editor explained, 'Well, it is possible, but that is all.' But the Harmsworths were quick to see that

1. He became Lord Northcliffe in 1905.

they had hit on a highly successful formula, and they hustled forward plans for *Chips*, which appeared (as *Illustrated Chips*) only two months after *Comic Cuts*. Still the battle with the newsagents went on. Indignantly, Alfred Harmsworth denied that his intention was to whip up big circulations for his halfpenny papers and then raise the price to one penny. He printed numerous testimonials from readers, one of whom thought that *Comic Cuts* was 'a jolly sight better than *Punch* at three-pence'. Among those who had succumbed to the lure of 'One Hundred Laughs for One Halfpenny', it appeared, was Mr Gladstone, who 'could often be seen marching about the garden at Hawarden, a smile upon his lips and a *Comic Cuts* in his hands'. The Marquis of Salisbury was claimed as another addict and Sir Lyon Playfair was said to have been seen reading the paper surreptitiously in the House of Commons.

At the outset *Comic Cuts* and *Chips* were aimed at adolescents and young people, not at the very young. The comic strip technique had still to be popularized. *Chips* held on to its comic characters more successfully than *Comic Cuts*. That famous pair of workshys, Weary Willie and Tired Tim, first appeared in 1896, under the names of Weary Waddles and Tired Timmy. These 'merry mirth merchants', or 'frisky fun furnishers', ambled, cooed, crooned, tootled, wuffed and burbled without intermission on the front page of *Chips* until 1953, when the paper ceased publication. Although these papers were classed as comics, much of their appeal was in their serial stories, notably about convicts and ticket-of-leave men. *Chips*, for example, published the famous 'Convict 99' by Robert and Clare Leighton (it was run in *Answers* in 1892). Stories about convicts, wrongly convicted for preference, did much to strengthen the foundations of the early Harms-worth empire.

A couple of years after *Comic Cuts* was launched Harms-worth was claiming a readership of two and a half million a week (presumably on a basis of several readers to each copy). The seam cried out for further exploitation. In quick succession appeared the *Halfpenny Wonder* (1892) and the *Halfpenny Marvel* (1893).

Harmsworth appears to have convinced himself that it was his moral duty to conduct a crusade against 'penny dreadfuls'. In *Comic Cuts* he contented himself with producing a 'fighting editor' whose job it was to throw downstairs, in addition to poets, all authors of 'penny dreadfuls' who sought to sully his pages with their unsolicited contributions. Soon afterwards the campaign became bitter; Harmsworth hurled into it all the reckless fervour which he was to bring to his later and more famous crusades. Number One of the *Halfpenny Marvel*, which was to carry the first stories of Sexton Blake and Nelson Lee, bore a slogan: 'No more penny dreadfuls! These healthy stories of mystery adventure, etc., will kill them.' An editorial deplored the number of boys who, inflamed by reading 'penny dreadfuls', were robbing their employers, buying revolvers with the proceeds and setting themselves up in the back streets as highwaymen. 'This and many other evils the "penny dreadful" is responsible for. It makes thieves of the coming generation and so helps to fill our jails. If we can rid the world of even one of these vile publications our efforts will not have been in vain.'

A later issue of the *Marvel* quoted a 'penny dreadful' with 'three spelling and six grammatical errors to every page', and mentioned that one publisher of such works cleared £7,000 a year. 'Of course, he does not give one-fiftieth of the value we do.' There followed letters supporting Harmsworth's campaign from a police sergeant and a magistrate, quotations from court reports and a story of how a 'walking library man' had been making 24,000 per cent profit from office boys and printers' devils in Fleet Street by repeatedly re-issuing copies of 'penny dreadfuls' at half-price. Happily, he had now seen the error of his way and had undertaken in future to sell only the *Marvel*: and to sell it outright.

In a later number of the *Marvel* was quoted a letter

from a reader revealing another insidious aspect of the
'penny dreadful':

> In front of shop windows you may see at any time through
> the day a crowd of children eagerly, breathlessly following as
> far as they can through the glass the fortunes of some idiotic
> abortion of a lunatic writer's brain. Physically and morally,
> could there be anything more harmful to our children? No
> wonder they are taking as a matter of course to spectacles.
> Years ago we used to make fun of the Germans in this respect.
> In another decade or so we too shall sail our ships and fire our
> guns and go about our daily work spectacled.
> Investing in 'Rats, the Boy Ferret' and 'Humboldt Harry,
> the Hurricane',[1] I read them and have had horrid dreams ever
> since. There is not one good, honest paragraph in the lot; not
> one sentence worth a moment's lingering over ... Were Board
> Schools established for the purpose of teaching children to
> amuse themselves with such stuff as this?

This reader who so oddly confessed to suffering from
nightmares inspired by paragraphs which were not worth
reading went on to say that eight out of ten boys in the
streets of London had 'penny dreadfuls' in their pockets.
It was, he thought, almost a case for State intervention.

Shortly afterwards the *Marvel* published prominently on
its back page a tribute from the Rev. C. N. Barham, of
Nottingham, expressing his pleasure that the contents of
the magazine should be so 'pure and wholesome in tone'.
It is conceivable that the Rev. Mr Barham regretted writing this testimonial when he saw the front cover of the
issue in which his letter appeared. The picture shows a
man being tortured by Greek brigands, with the caption:
'The gaoler screwed up the horrible machine until the
brigand's bones were nearly broken and he shrieked aloud
for mercy, though none was shown.'

That was Harmsworth's problem: to discredit 'penny
dreadfuls' and their publishers, and yet to provide his
readers with strong enough meat to replace the fare to

1. Both of these were Aldine titles.

which they were accustomed. It called for a nice balancing of values.

Another congratulatory letter quoted in the *Marvel* was 'from a personal friend who has a son at Harrow. He informs me that at all the public schools there is a great rush for the *Halfpenny Marvel* and boys read it with evident enjoyment.'

Next came *Union Jack* and *Pluck* (1894). The former bore slogans like these across the bottom and top of almost every page: 'The *Union Jack Library* will consist of pure, healthy tales only'; 'The *Union Jack* is a market for only the very best literary and artistic wares.'

'There will be nothing of the "dreadful" type in our stories,' pledged the *Union Jack*. 'No tales of boys rifling their employers' cash boxes and making off to foreign lands, or such-like highly immoral fiction products.'

The *Boys' Friend*, launched in 1895, contained a still fiercer onslaught against 'penny dreadfuls'. Oddly enough, this broadside contained ammunition which had already been fired in the *Quarterly Review* in 1890; and the editor of the *Quarterly Review* had been smartly reproved at the time for his intolerance and snobbishness in the pages of Harmsworth's *Chips*.

Innocent boys who got hold of 'penny dreadfuls', said the *Boys' Friend*, little dreamed of the trickery and deceit which went into their manufacture. What could they know about 'the miserable beer-swilling wretches who write them ... if such a word as write could be applied to their work?'

As a rule they are drunken, sodden creatures whose lives have been one long unbroken story of failure. Sometimes they are University men who in the flower of their youth gave promise of becoming noble men but giving way to the temptations of drink they have gradually sunk lower and lower in the scale of life until at last they reach the depths of degradation and their natures have become so debased that they are fit only to write evil stories which fill the pocket of the man who prints and sells the 'penny dreadful'.

'Editor', it seems, was a misnomer when it came to describing the person who commissioned 'penny dreadfuls' – 'his capability for editing is not to be measured with his capability for drinking intoxicants'. His practice was to get hold of old and worn type which printed in 'a blurred, sight-destroying way', and then cast around to find a set of second-hand blocks to serve as illustrations. Then he ordered a story to be written around the blocks, no matter what the pictures showed.

It is a daunting thought. Who will withhold sympathy from a hack presented with, say, six pictures showing a redskin dancing round a captive, two Frenchmen fencing, a highwayman holding up a coach, a smuggler's boat landing in a cove, a detective looking at a footprint through a magnifying glass and a bound and gagged woman, with instructions to 'keep it down to 20,000 words' and call it 'Guy Gaspereau, the Brigand Chief?

Next the *Boys' Friend* asked: Where do they write? And supplied the answer: communal kitchens of cheap lodging-houses, the bar parlours of dirty, back-alley public-houses. The head of a beer cask was sufficient for table, and the man who used ink was a man of means 'compared with the usual run of this pitiful class'. Notepaper consisted of 'backs of old bills' and any dirty wrappers which happened to be handy.

Finally the *Boys' Friend* got around to asking: *What* do they write?

If you buy a copy of 'Guy Gaspereau' you will find it consists of some 16 pages vilely printed and with woodcuts which look as though they had been carved with a chopper. No paragraph is longer than four or at the most five lines.

'Guy paused.
'The villain clenched his teeth.
'The situation was terrible. No help within a league.'

There is generally a hero, bold, dashing, handsome and gifted with every possible accomplishment. There is a villain, often a hunch-back and always pitted with small-pox. There is the hero's great friend, a simple country youth who follows his chum through thick and thin and saves his life every other week.

It is curious to find Harmsworth magazines holding up the short paragraph to ridicule when it is remembered that not so many years later the *Daily Mail* offices were to contain enormous notices exhorting 'Paragraph! Paragraph! Paragraph!' and any sub-editor who allowed long-winded contributors to get away with unbroken slabs of prose was quickly on the carpet.

Alfred Harmsworth in the nineties was very concerned to give his readers value for money. He reminded them constantly that in his 'long complete' stories they were getting a shillings-worth for a halfpenny. He even apologized for leaving the inside covers of the *Union Jack* bare of text. The paper was so thin that to print on the reverse side would have ruined the picture on the cover. Harmsworth believed in taking his readers into his confidence and telling them all about the problems of printing and block-making.

Instead of spending money on first-class glossy paper, thick cardboard covers and large type we shall give the very best value possible ... It would be easy to sell for 1s., but where one man will spend a shilling 5,000 will risk a halfpenny.

There was the Harmsworth theory of business in a nutshell.

One can believe that much of the wrath Harmsworth bore against the publishers of 'penny dreadfuls' was inspired, not by the supposed peril to the younger generation's morals or eyesight, but by such underhand and 'unprofessional' devices as using second-hand blocks. Not that such a practice was unknown in the twentieth century.

Publication of halfpenny magazines forced some of the other boys' publishers to follow suit. Brett, for instance, put out an orange-covered *Halfpenny Surprise*, containing a 'long complete' and a short serial. After a few years

Harmsworth raised the prices of his boys' papers to one penny, and thereby achieved a higher standard of production. There is no doubt that the type in some of his half-penny papers was even more trying to the eyes than that of some of the maligned 'penny dreadfuls'.

A claim to be the most successful of the Harmsworth boys' thrillers launched in the nineties – judged by length of life – has been lodged on behalf of the *Union Jack*, which ran for almost forty years; but a strong case can be made out for the *Wonder* ('Funny But Not Vulgar') which, under the titles of the *Wonder*, the *Funny Wonder*, the *Wonder and Jester*, the *Jester and Wonder*, the *Jester* and the *Jolly Jester*, ran from 1892 to 1940. True, it was primarily a 'comic', but like all the Harmsworth 'comics', it had a powerful stiffening of adventure stories. In the *Jester*, as it was best known, these ranged from tales of sleuths, iron tortoises and human bats (one performer in this category is pictured sleeping upside down with his feet in a slot) to sporting curates, convict earls and girls without a home. At one period no issue of the *Jester* was complete without a buxom heroine trapped on a target ship or pinioned in a lion's den. Serials would run on for year after year; in this department Herbert Allingham was a star performer.

The pink-covered *Union Jack* (which bore the same title as a short-lived publication with which W. H. G. Kingston and G. A. Henty were associated some years previously) ran from 1894 to 1933, when it was merged in the new *Detective Weekly*. Number Two contained 'Sexton Blake, Detective' (of whom a great deal more in the next chapter). A certain modesty was noticeable in the announcement of future stories; 'The Phantom Dwarf', for instance, would be 'in the approved Rider Haggard style and written by the celebrated author Maxwell Scott. Do not imagine, however, that we would compare our series with the work of that great writer whose every new book causes its readers to go into raptures.'

The early stories were mostly open-air tales of redskins, explorers, prospectors and sailors, with a few detectives thrown in. Titles like 'Fighting for the Flag' were common, heroes being drawn from the Zulu, Matabele and Ashanti wars. One story at least was written by a woman. Readers were invited to send in copies of the *Union Jack* with their comments inscribed in the margin, a prize going to the critic who wrote most neatly.

Gradually Sexton Blake stories began to grow more frequent and after the magazine reached penny status it was devoted to the detective exclusively.

The green-jacketed *Marvel*, which ran for almost thirty years until merged with *Sport and Adventure*, published much the same kind of story in its initial stages. It had been planned as the *Miracle*, but the name was changed at the eleventh hour to avoid offending religious susceptibilities. Though it carried early adventures of such celebrated characters as Sexton Blake and Nelson Lee it did not hold on to them, and it is probably chiefly remembered for the unending tales of Jack, Sam and Pete by S. Clarke Hook, a descendant of Theodore Hook, the novelist and lampoonist.

These three jovial adventurers flourished in the pages of the *Marvel* from 1904 to the last number in 1922 – a fair indication of their perennial popularity. Jack was a roving English lad, Sam was a skilled American hunter and Pete was an iron-fisted Negro of frightening physique and no less frightening *bonhomie*. It was not long before Pete, who added ventriloquism to his attainments, was the dominant figure of the three. They spent much of their time roaming the less civilized corners of the globe, one week frustrating a revolution in Peru and the next cleaning up the elections in Mexico. Often they were in a state of most gratifying affluence, thanks to the frequency with which they unearthed one golconda after another, but affluence never corrupted them. It was nothing for Pete to charter a special train to reach the scene of the next adventure, but the three had a marked preference for travel by balloon. Scrupulously in the first paragraph of

each story the author would name the country in which
the trio were adventuring that week, then throw in a per-
functory mention of mangrove or cactus as required; after
that it was substantially the same story, with the trio
swinging into their familiar routine of flattening bullies
and discomfiting snobs (notably, hotel managers who
looked askance at 'niggers', even rich ones, and head
waiters who refused to shake hands). Pete's approach
to a stranger, however dignified, was to slap him on
the back and address him as 'old hoss'. He was as
easily amused as his victims were insulted, and the line

                'Yah! Yah! Yah!' roared Pete

peppered the saga as freely as 'Ha! Ha! Ha!s' in the
saga of Greyfriars.

There was a strong slapstick element about these stories
which set them a little apart from the purely blood-and-
thunder class, but once at least Pete was solemnly brought
to the edge of 'death's dark portal'. After long spells
abroad the three would be called home to undertake provincial tours. They did not confine themselves to big cities
like Glasgow and Manchester, but even found lively adventures in modest towns like Northwich. In Northwich
or in the foothills of the Andes Pete never failed to prosper, no matter how improbable the enterprise to which he
turned his attention. The titles tell their own tale –
'Pete's Pierrot Troupe', 'Pete's Pantomime', 'Pete's Boarding House', 'Pete's Chinese Laundry', 'Pete's School',
'Pete's Dairy', and so on.

A comic Negro, or Chinese, or Eskimo figured in many
boys' stories of the day, and no doubt a thesis could be
written showing how the Englishman's amused contempt
for the 'lesser breeds' is traceable to such fiction. The
authors of these tales no doubt considered that in introducing funny foreigners they were doing their bit to break
down racial prejudice

It might be thought that a weekly stint of Jack, Sam
and Pete for nearly twenty years was enough for one man,

but S. Clarke Hook wrote in many other boys' papers, even launching an occasional rival trio, like Dan, Bob and Darkey in the *Boys' Friend*.

The *Boys' Friend*, which ran for thirty-two years, was a vigorously conducted weekly under one of the 'livest' of boys' editors, Hamilton Edwards. Not only did he publicize himself freely in its columns, but he played up his authors, which was something of a departure for those days. The *Boys' Friend* ran school tales ('Bob Redding's Schooldays'), romances of the Boer War, of exploration, even historical tales, and also featured from time to time all the leading performers of the Amalgamated Press – Sexton Blake, Nelson Lee and Jack, Sam and Pete. Many remember it for those 'invasion of Britain' extravaganzas (Chapter XI). Others recall the Ferrers Lord stories, which ran under one title or another for years. 'Wolves of the Deep' (1900) was styled 'the story of a grim battle of life and death between two of the wealthiest men the world has ever known'. With this was linked an editorial pronouncement which, once again, sounded like a confident expression of the publisher's philosophy: 'There is no limit to the power of colossal wealth when wealth is linked with brain.'

The nature of the stories of Ferrers Lord (not to be confused with Ferrers Locke) may easily be judged from the *dramatis personae*, which included the inevitable comedy characters:

Ferrers Lord.	A British inventor. Two immense submarine boats he has constructed. A staunch patriot.
Michael Scaroff.	A Russian prince and Lord's bitterest enemy. He stole the plans of Lord's submarine ship and built a similar boat – the Tsaritza.
Rupert Thurston.	Lord's companion.
Ching Lung	A Chinese prince. He is an expert conjurer and always up to some fun.
Prout and Maddock.	Two seamen of the Lord of the Deep.

Kennedy.   An Irishman in Yang's army.
Pierre Bovrille.   A funny Frenchman.

Lord and his rival were made to symbolize the rivalry
between Britain and Russia. 'Lion Against Bear' was the
title of the second series. Everything that could and could
not happen under water happened to the rival millionaires. The fertile author was Sidney Drew.

The *Boys' Friend* had companion papers in the *Boys'
Realm* (1902) and *Boys' Herald* (1903). All were under the
editorship of Hamilton Edwards. Hardly was the *Boys'
Herald* launched before Pearsons, who already published
the *Big Budget* (1897), announced the *Boys' Leader*; what
was more, they bought space in Hamilton Edwards's papers to advertise it. In his editorial notes Edwards complained about 'so many confusing advertisements' for boys'
papers and urged his readers to remember the names of the
Big Three: *Boys' Friend* (on green paper); *Boys' Realm*
(pink) and *Boys' Herald* (white). It seems likely that
Edwards had words with his advertising department about
the *Boys' Leader* announcements; but in boys' papers
advertisements are notoriously hard to come by, and, if he
protested, he was overruled. 'It isn't quite playing the
game to be issuing a paper and allowing boys to think I
am editor of it when I have nothing to do with it,' he
wrote. His most mortifying moment came when a facsimile of page one of the new rival was inserted in copies
of his *Boys' Herald*. Assuredly, business was business in
those days. Hamilton Edwards had the last laugh; the
Boys' Leader collapsed after a fairly short run. The *Big
Budget*, which had a strong comic element, continued as
a challenger until 1909.

All three of Hamilton Edwards's papers were served
by the same writers, whose names or pen-names included
Sidney Drew, Maxwell Scott, Herbert Maxwell, S. Clarke
Hook, T. C. Bridges, Reginald Wray, Henry Johnson,
Alec G. Pearson, Henry St John, John Tregellis, John
Hunter, Murray Graydon, Robert Leighton and Arthur
S. Hardy.

The two famous school story magazines were next in the field – *Gem* (1907) and *Magnet* (1908) (Chapter XIII). In 1912 came that curious trio, the *Dreadnought*, the *Penny Popular* and the *Penny Wonder*. The *Penny Popular* offered a multiple bargain. A typical issue would contain a Charles Hamilton school story, a Sexton Blake story and an adventure of Jack, Sam and Pete, all much shorter than usual. In the writer's possession is a copy of the *Popular* containing a St Jim's story by Martin Clifford, an instalment of 'The Rio Kid', by Ralph Redway, a Rookwood story by Owen Conquest and a Greyfriars story by Frank Richards, all those authors being Charles Hamilton, who was probably also the author of the anonymous story in the same issue about Ferrers Locke.

The *Penny Wonder* was a curious blend of fiction for boys, girls and even housewives. It had John Flood, the River Detective, for the delectation of male readers; for women readers there were Galloping Gloria the Lady Turpin, Grace Daring the Girl Chauffeur, and a third heroine whose proficiency with bow and arrow made her invaluable at firing lifelines, sending messages to prisoners in towers, and shooting down hanged men. For hearthside reading there was 'What Will Become of Her?' It was the story of 'A wife without a husband, a mother without a child, who faced the world alone.' The *Wonder* was curiously old-fashioned in that its heroines were still being lashed to windmill sails or left dangling on the clappers of church bells while more progressive journals were binding them to aeroplane propellers or suspending them from airships. Nevertheless the *Wonder* contrived to work out some novel predicaments with the aid of the old-fashioned windmill, clock tower and water-wheel. Notable was the plight of a man who, pushing his head through a grille in a clock face, had his head gripped between the hands at the lethal hour of twenty minutes to nine; a situation which was considered sufficiently dramatic to repeat in the *Boys' Friend* fifteen years later. But the most curious throwback in the *Penny Wonder* was a Gothic story entitled 'The Secret Dread, or The Mystery of Castle Hume'. Edward Lloyd would have been happy to print it in his day. Said the editorial prologue:

This story is founded upon a real-life mystery and its central character had in fact his counterpart in actual existence. There are skeletons in the cupboards of our ancient noble families – skeleton secrets so awesome and so forbidding that knowledge of them needs to be kept a profound secret from every human soul but the head of the house in question. There are strange uncanny things in secret chambers, to which no light can come, that breathe and die unknown and unnamed; things that cause a shadow in the eyes of those that know them. And of such a Secret Dread this tale relates.

According to a later synopsis, the secret dread turned out to be a very old friend:

It is midnight at Castle Hume and a dread tempest of thunder and lightning rages without. Guests and retainers are assembled to celebrate the coming of age of the heir of Hume, who tonight must hear from the old Earl's lips the dread secret of his race. On the stroke of twelve, after the lightning has struck a goblet known as the Luck of Hume from the hand of Lord Douglas, the heir, the old Earl leads his son to the Blue Chamber to unfold the secret to him. And as the Earl makes known to his son the hidden secret, the solitary portrait of the wicked Earl Malpas is split in twain and there appears through the rent – the face of a Horned Man. Immediately flames burst into the Blue Chamber, the castle now being on fire. Scrymgeour Hume reaches the battlements in quest of the Lady Elaine, the destined bride of the heir of Hume, only to see the Horned Man with the girl in his arms leap from the battlements.

Though Alfred Harmsworth had vowed to have no rogues as heroes in his boys' papers, highwaymen and high-waywomen began to creep in, perhaps as a challenge to the Aldine stories. Claude Duval performed in *Pluck* at an early stage. The *Boys' Friend* published a serial in 1905 called 'The Idle Apprentice', which revelled in the 'strange yet wonderful, mis-spent career' of Jack Sheppard. In the last chapter Jack was borne to Tyburn but his execution was not described. It was made clear, too, that before his death Jack had undergone a spiritual reformation.

In many of the stories in the early Harmsworth boys' papers there was a heroine. The *Marvel* usually gave her a head-and-shoulders illustration to herself. In the actual story she played a negligible part; her duty was to rebuff the advances of the villain and to marry the hero in the last chapter at the village church. She was a sop for older readers.

There was a vogue, too, for Rider Haggard queens of the 'She' type – mysterious pale-skinned princesses ruling lost kingdoms of Negroes, or reigning over albinos in the craters of volcanoes.

Heroines were as nearly as possible sexless, even the 'She'-like queens, who wore long thick white nightdresses, sometimes with pigtails. The 'penny dreadfuls' had occasionally offered a heroine whose bosom, in stress of motion or emotion, had escaped from captivity, or on whose bare back a playful pirate was proposing to brand his mark. In the early magazines of the Brett type, matrons with generously proportioned and lightly clad torsos were no rarity, either as symbolic figures like Britannia or Marianne, or as Boadicean-style heroines. Even James Henderson's *Young Folks* regaled its readers with a front-page picture showing Queen Mab appearing before the dazzled hero clad only in a wisp of gossamer. But the Harmsworth heroines were careful not to flaunt their sex appeal, in which resolve they were aided in those pre-1914 days by the prevailing fashions. About 1912 it became a deliberate policy to play up a 'girl chum' – possibly as a concession to the large female readership, possibly as a concession to reality. Cousin Ethel of the *Gem* was a good example (Chapter XIII). Considering the strenuous adventures which befell them, such girl chums as Eileen Dare, Nelson Lee's assistant, contrived miraculously to keep their calves concealed – even when descending fire escapes or hanging on to aerial cables. What was just as important, the crooks who tied them to railway lines were always

commendably careful not to disarrange their clothing.[1]
Daisy Dare, the Girl Reporter of the *Dreadnought*, would
blush innocently and retract her feet under the desk
whenever a baronet paid her a formal compliment as a
prelude to consulting her in some case which had baffled
Scotland Yard. There is a drawing of Daisy perched at
the top of a telephone pole tapping the wires, clothed
entirely as Mrs Grundy would have wished. All these girl
chums as featured in the illustrations had a tendency towards flat chests and low heels. Their faces were pretty
in a chocolate box style, but their figures were strictly
non-voluptuous – even those over whom schoolboys were
occasionally allowed to go 'soppy', until ragged out of it
by their comrades.

Now and again readers would seek personal advice on
the subject of feminine friendships. Wrote the editor of
the *Magnet*:

A most interesting query comes from Roy Walker, of South
Shields, who asks my view about boys having girl chums.

My older members know exactly the opinions I hold about
boy and girl friendships. I feel they can serve a healthy and
useful purpose if they are carried on with the full approval of
the parents on both sides, provided no foolish thought of
courtship is indulged in. A lad feels there is something in the
friendship of a girl chum that uplifts him, and fills him with
the desire to live well, keep steady, and do great deeds. And so
long as both parties to the friendship remain true to themselves, I am sure no fair-minded man or woman would wish to
deny them the happiness they enjoy.

In all these papers the editorial chat was a prominent
feature. Hamilton Edwards sought to strike a less formal
note than the Beetons and Hutchinsons. 'In most cases,'

1. James Cameron in his autobiographical *Point of Departure* tells
of an incident during his apprenticeship on *Red Star Weekly*, the
D. C. Thomson paper for factory girls. He commissioned from an
artist a cover picture to illustrate a story about a 'man with glaring
eyes' who went about slaying young women. The artist showed a
girl lying in a dark alley with her throat slit horribly from ear to
ear. The editor exploded: 'You must be mad . . . look at the lassie's
skirt, it's awa above her knees.'

he wrote, 'boys regard the editor of their paper as an austere, domineering old gentleman, to whom they should write, if occasion should compel them, in terms of utmost humility and deference. This is wrong.' Yet Hamilton Edwards had his stern moments. He warned his readers repeatedly against those habits which could lead only to 'an early and miserable death', and in a special note to parents urged them to introduce into their sons' lives some such daily discipline as 'an hour's woodchopping'. Otherwise the lads would assuredly behave in such a way as 'to bow down their grey-haired parents in sorrow'.

He and his fellow-editors between them advised their readers on every affliction, physical and psychological, which could beset the adolescent – blushing, pimples, short stature, pigeon-chestedness, freckles, bandy legs, protruding teeth, nervousness with girls; told them how to stop smoking, and how to remove not only blackheads but tattoo marks.

The founder of these papers did not lose interest in them, even when he had *The Times* in his possession. According to Tom Clarke, 'to the end of his day *Comic Cuts* in expensively bound volumes had proud place in the bookcases in his magnificent sanctum at Carmelite House.' Sir John Hammerton, who looked after the 'fortnightly parts' publications of the Amalgamated Press, tells in one of his books how angry the 'Chief' was when he heard that a member of the staff had jokingly referred to the 'hooligan department'. At an early stage Harmsworth was so keen that no vulgar slang should creep into his boys' stories that he instituted an office censor for the purpose. Sir John Hammerton was offered the job but declined it. Hammerton's book suggests that he was not especially interested in the boys' fiction department. Could it have been in retaliation for this that one of Sexton Blake's adversaries was christened Hammerton Palmer?

In souvenir volumes published by the Amalgamated Press to celebrate important milestones in the firm's history are brief – rather too brief – references to the boys' magazines on which the Northcliffe fortunes were built. In 1912 the claim was made that 'these [boys'] journals aimed from the first at the encouragement of physical strength, of patriotism, of interest in travel and exploration, and of pride in our empire. It has been said that the boys' papers of the Amalgamated Press have done more to provide recruits for our Navy and Army and to keep up the esteem of the sister services than anything else.' The author of *The Romance of the Amalgamated Press* (1925) asserted: 'There is no paper with which the firm has ever been associated that, whatever its other defects, could not at any time have been placed in the hands of the most puritanical man, woman or child without raising a blush or causing the faintest thrill of distaste.' That sentence contains enough negatives to be ambiguous, but the intention is clear and most readers will endorse the truth of it. The late A. A. Milne was hardly fair when he wrote: 'It was Lord Northcliffe who killed the "penny dreadful" by the simple process of producing a ha'penny dreadfuller.'

The man who had sounded the death knell of 'penny dreadfuls' nevertheless lived to see his own publications called by the same name, though some people styled them 'bloods', which was a shade more flattering. Long after his death the publications which he founded were still carrying paragraphs like this from the *Nelson Lee Library*:

Glad to hear, Frank Nicholls, that since your father has read some copies of the Old Paper he no longer regards them as 'penny dreadfuls'. I wish a few thousand other fathers would follow his good example.

Northcliffe today is remembered as the founder of the *Daily Mail*, the purchaser of *The Times*, the arch-foe of Germany, the propagandist for aviation, the eccentric tyrant of Fleet Street. In his obituaries and biographies only the most summary mention is made of his boys' papers. Just as the obituaries of Edward Lloyd had omitted to state that he was the sponsor of Sweeney Todd, so the obituaries of Northcliffe omitted to state that he was the sponsor of Sexton Blake.

CHAPTER VIII

THE ODYSSEY OF SEXTON BLAKE

THERE was once a radio quiz in which a girl was asked to name a famous detective who lived in Baker Street. Her reply 'Sexton Blake' did not satisfy the BBC quizmaster, though in thousands of homes it was doubtless accepted as the correct answer. Even when the quizmaster resorted to transparent prompting – 'No, I mean some detective or detectives who had *homes* in Baker Street,' the girl obstinately clung to her original reply.

To offset this, there was a radio occasion in 1945 when several writers of detective stories were asked to name the most famous detective of fiction. This time Sexton Blake was not mentioned.

Sexton Blake has been called, patronizingly, the office-boy's Sherlock Holmes. Those who take detective fiction seriously claim that his successes are due less to pure deduction than to calculated coincidence, an ability to recover almost instantly from concussion, and such specialized attainments as the power to out-stare cobras. Show Blake a sheet of writing in which the fist is alternately regular and irregular, and he will be unable to tell you, from the incidence of the palsied patches, that it was written in a train travelling between Norwood and London Bridge. But nail him down in a crate and throw him off the bridge at Westminster and while you are still dusting your hands and saying 'That's that' he will be right there behind you. Only an adult will accept a *tour de force* like the first. Only an adult will sneer at a *tour de force* like the second.

Miss Dorothy Sayers cited Sexton Blake when she wrote that detective blood-and-thunders were 'the nearest approach to a national folk-lore, conceived as the centre for a cycle of loosely connected romances in the Arthurian manner'. If Sexton Blake is not a legendary hero of England ranking with King Arthur and Robin Hood it is not the fault of his chroniclers, who have spun thousands of millions of words about him; or of the film makers, whose efforts are not to be decried because they have rarely been seen in the West End of London.[1] To refer to Blake as a 'legendary hero of England' is, in any case, parochial; his exploits have appeared in Swedish, Norwegian, Finnish, Dutch, Spanish, German, Portuguese, Italian, French, Arabic, Hindi and Afrikaans. In the unlikeliest corners of the globe tattered copies of Sexton Blakes are treasured. Behind the Japanese lines in the Second World War, Lieutenant-Colonel F. Spencer Chapman alleviated his boredom with a chance-found copy of 'The Murdered Mahout' (see *The Jungle is Neutral*).

Ever since the 1890s the interminable casebook of Sexton Blake has been profitably rummaged by syndicates of authors. It is still yielding its secrets today, though not quite in such profusion. There is no closed shop in the Sexton Blake industry; more than one hundred authors have done their bit to build up the legend. It is the peculiar, though unavoidable, fate of most of them to be remembered not for their Blake but for the adversaries they pitted against him, or for the *femmes fatales* they introduced. Some of the names are known pseudonyms; others have that pseudonymous look about them.

In latter years – since it became policy to play up authors' names – those who have created outstanding opponents for Blake, or who have done much to fortify his reputation, include Robert Murray, George Hamilton Teed, Gwyn Evans, Anthony Skene, Edwy Searles Brooks, Lewis Jackson, John Hunter, John G. Brandon, Mark Osborne, Coutts Brisbane, Andrew Murray, Cecil Hayter,

---

1. Sexton Blake appeared in films as early as 1914. It is claimed that the first films to be made under the British Films Quota Act were based on Sexton Blake adventures; Langhorne Burton played the detective and Micky Brantford the part of Tinker. More recent films featured David Farrar.

Walter Tyrer, Anthony Parsons, Donald Stuart, Rex Hardinge and Gilbert Chester. The first-mentioned, Robert Murray, was the son of William Murray Graydon, an early, and fertile, writer of Blake stories. One who must not be omitted from the Blake roll of honour is the indefatigable artist Eric R. Parker, who was also the designer of the Sexton Blake bust, now something of a rarity. The bust went to reward readers who pulled in other readers and to console competitors who failed to win Austin Sevens. It was also widely distributed at cinemas which showed Sexton Blake Films.

Sexton Blake can be traced back, without much difficulty, to the year 1893, but only a rash researcher would claim that this was positively his first appearance. Sherlock Holmes, on whom Blake is commonly supposed to have been based, made his début in 1887 in *A Study in Scarlet*, attaining much wider popularity four years later in *The Adventures of Sherlock Holmes*. But it is noteworthy that the Sexton Blake who appeared in the sixth number of Alfred Harmsworth's *Marvel*, published in 1893, in a story called 'The Missing Millionaire', had almost none of the characteristics of Holmes. The illustrations showed a well-built, not particularly distinguished Victorian gentleman with a high-crowned bowler, carrying a heavy walking-stick. Nor did he work in Baker Street but in New Inn Chambers (the next story put him in offices in Wych Street, off the Strand). He was operating at that time in partnership with a French investigator, Jules Gervaise. In those days it was a privilege to be linked with a French detective, so well had Messrs Gaboriau and Leroux done their work.

The author's name was given as Hal Meredeth – which looks like a pen name. Whether this writer himself invented the name Sexton Blake is open to doubt; a survivor of those days states that the original intention was to call the detective Frank Blake, but the demand went up for a more unusual first name, with a dash of the sinister. Somebody hit on Sexton – and the name stuck.

Blake was of the 'new order of detectives', which could have been a reference to the Conan Doyle stories, the French school or the American school. In the nineties detectives were spawning in both hemispheres, as the next chapter will show.

Number Seven of the *Marvel* also contained a Sexton Blake story. He and Gervaise seemed to be doing fairly well, for they had a clerks' office 'with three doors'.

Even at this stage there was a woman in Blake's life. Not for the last time the detective was to feel tenderly towards a young woman who was destined to be kidnapped and not restored till the last chapter:

'I never believed until now,' reflected Sexton Blake, 'that I should ever seriously fall in love and especially at first sight: but I must confess that if I could succeed in winning the affections of Lillie Ray I should account myself the luckiest of earthly mortals. Bah! I'll not trouble the office any more to-day . . .'

It was not long before Blake and the arch-crook of this particular episode were fighting hand-to-hand in the basket of a balloon drifting over the Channel. Neither man could break his adversary's grip.

He [Blake] then determined on taking a desperate course, for the present position of matters had become maddening. He pulled the trigger of his revolver and sent a bullet crashing through the silk of the balloon! The gas came hissing from the rents and the two men descended with a rapidity which robbed both of them of their senses!

What exactly happened after this Blake could never tell. When he had at last opened his eyes it was to find himself in the comfortably furnished cabin of a steamer . . .

The heroine, once rescued, came into a good deal of money. Blake was distressed at this development:

For a little it seemed to Blake that her accession to such vast wealth placed another barrier between them; but she has given him more than half a promise that she will some day reward his devotion to her in the way he most desires.

Sexton Blake in mid-career. – The Union Jack, 1915.

In spite of which Blake was destined to remain a bachelor. Or was he? Reginald Cox, writing in *The Saturday Book* (sixth year), mentions a crony who claims to have heard of a companion paper of *Union Jack* in which there are disconcerting references to a Mrs Blake. Whatever the truth of this, it must have been borne in upon Blake's sponsors at an early stage that while it was not unreasonable for him to cheat death at least once a week, it would invite accusations of profligacy if he fell in love with a different woman every week.

To return to the *Marvel*. Blake made only spasmodic appearances in this journal, which like all Harmsworth's new publications was exceeding the Editor's 'most sanguine expectations'. Some of the stories were attributed to Harry Blyth – probably Hal Meredeth's real name. Blake took turns with stories about gold prospecting and the Matabele wars. Then in Number 25 came the announcement that 'Sexton Blake has been secured by the *Union Jack*', due to make its début in April 1894. It was this pink-jacketed newcomer, then also a halfpenny paper, which was to make Sexton Blake famous. Not that it held any exclusive title to him, for he has appeared in *Boys' Friend, Boys' Herald, Penny Popular, The Jester*, and of course the *Sexton Blake Library*, which started as a separate institution during the First World War.

A redskin story – 'The Silver Arrow' – was selected to open *Union Jack*. Then in Number Two came a Sexton Blake story with a cover picture showing an exhumation in a churchyard. The editorial preamble said:

Some time ago we arranged with Mr Sexton Blake, the celebrated detective, to furnish us with particulars of the most remarkable and sensational cases he has been concerned in. From some of the materials he has placed at our disposal we have framed the following exciting and authentic narrative, feeling sure that its strange details will excite world-wide interest.

Heroes and villains in these early stories were not hard to identify. No detective (or reader) would be likely to waste time checking up on the credentials of Ernest True-love, or Harry Armitage; or of Ninian Joyce, 'the sweetest maiden that Heaven ever blessed with a dainty form and a beauteous grace'.

It was early made clear that Blake was not interested in money. To a naval officer who consulted him, he said:

'I would rather work for nothing for a naval man like your-self, one of the best protectors of our precious flag, the pride of England, than I would take bank-notes from those who are careless of the honour of old Britain.'

The naval officer was relieved to hear that, and even more relieved to hear:

'With Heaven's help, my word shall be kept. The promises of Sexton Blake are written in adamant.'

To the villain, when finally unmasked, Blake said:

'Your cunningly erected edifice of fraud has now collapsed and you stand a good chance of being involved fatally in its ruins.'

In *Union Jack* Blake's adventures still alternated with stories of the Matabele and Ashanti wars, and in a readers' poll he took third place to 'Fighting For the Flag' and 'The Silver Arrow'. His popularity easily survived a brief spell during which the editor of *Union Jack* printed abridged versions of works by Dickens, Scott and Fenimore Cooper.

In the *Marvel*, Blake explained his working principles in near-Johnsonian prose:

'We do not interfere in disputes between man and wife, nor do we pursue defaulting clerks, but if there is wrong to be righted, an evil to be redressed, or a rescue of the weak and suffering from the powerful, our hearty assistance can be readily obtained. We do nothing for hire here; we would cheerfully undertake to perform without fee or reward. But when our clients are wealthy we are not so unjust to ourselves as to make a gratuitous offer of our services.'

Hereabouts the Editor of the *Marvel*, claiming that 'thousands of correspondents' had written demanding more Blake stories, invited criticisms of the stories published to date. Puzzlingly soon afterwards appeared a Hal Meredeth story of Jules Gervaise in which Blake received only a passing mention.

What Blake needed, obviously, was a build-up. At some early stage he became hawk-like, incisive, and acquired the habit of putting on his dressing-gown in order to think. He ceased to talk like one of the more virtuous characters in the Red Barn. He no longer said 'Hist!' Probably it was sheer pressure of public opinion which forced him into Baker Street. Clearly he needed someone to look after him, someone old enough and respectable enough to be called a housekeeper and not a 'housekeeper'. Hence Mrs Martha Bardell, with her 'Hevvings!' her 'Lawks-a-mussy!' and her genius for malapropism. It was a happy stroke to furnish Blake with a bright boy assistant instead of a dull fellow modelled on the lines of Watson. Blake badly needed someone to prevent him being pompous. At the same time it was probably considered that an errand-boy reader could more easily project himself into the narrative by imagining himself to be Blake's assistant. So arrived Tinker, that young man of doubtful years (old enough to pilot an aeroplane) and doubtful antecedents, irrepressible, resourceful, susceptible to female charm, addicted to suits 'which would have made Solomon want to retire from the glory business', and possessing a fathomless admiration for the 'Guv'nor'. On one of the occasions when Tinker was 'wanted for murder' (a misunderstanding, of course) the police posters with which Britain was placarded showed him to be an intelligent, eupeptic-looking youth, with curly hair.

Reginald Cox claims in the *Saturday Book* that Tinker had three predecessors. The first, a Chinese boy called We-wee, was dropped for reasons which may readily be conjectured; the second was a waif called Griff; and the third was one Wallace Lorrimer. Tinker did not arrive until 1904. He is supposed to have been living on the fringe of the underworld, though later evidence has it that he was also a regular soldier. Blake educated his assistant rather sketchily. He himself had been brought up at two distinct public schools and had subsequently studied at both Oxford and Cambridge, so that he may well have decided that a man can have too much education.

Tinker survived the great purge of 1904 when Blake – heavily overworked – dismissed all the other members of his staff and retired to the country under the name of Henry Park. 'Tinker always would remain. They were part and parcel of each other's lives.' Tinker at this time was refusing bribes of £5 to disclose the detective's private address to importunate clients. Then came the day when Henry Park was falsely accused of theft, and Blake had the stimulating experience of being engaged to track himself down. (He relished that kind of operation. Once he wagered £500 with the police that he would disappear in London and that they would not find him. He joined the police who were hunting him.) The unusual case of Henry Park convinced Blake that he would never be able to give up the game of detection. 'I shall remain in harness till the end,' he said.

There was another addition to the household – the bloodhound Pedro. He was sent to Blake with £100 by a well-wisher called Mr Nemo. And then came the Grey Panther, which sometimes turned out to be a motor-car and sometimes a monoplane (designed by Blake himself). This was confusing, but latterly the name Grey Panther was reserved exclusively for Blake's bullet-proof Rolls.

Thus equipped and befriended, Blake was able to settle down to his ordained task of combating the Brotherhood of Silence; the Brotherhood of the Yellow Beetle; the Criminals' Confederation (featuring Mr Reece); George Marsden Plummer, the Scotland Yard renegade, and his beautiful accomplice Vali Mata Vali; Huxton Rymer and his equally beautiful female accomplices Mary Trent and

Yvonne; Leon Kestrel, the Master Mummer, whose real features no one knew; Waldo the Wonder Man; Mr Mist, the Invisible Man; Dr Ferraro, who demanded £1,000,000 for not blowing up London; Dr Satira; Carlac; Professor Kew; Paul Cynos; Krock Kelk; the Baron von Kravitch, 'luxury-loving aristocrat by night and picker-up of cigarette ends by day'; the reincarnated Prince Menes; his criminal majesty King Karl II of Serbovia, director of the Double Four gang (which included a female impersonator, a circus strong man and a baby-faced midget); Zenith the Albino, afflicted with a colourless skin but far from colourless personality, whose possession of infra-red binoculars put all London's wealth at his peril; a variety of numerical groups like the Black Trinity and the Council of Eleven; an endless succession of megalomaniac banditti calling themselves the Slasher, the Phantom, the Vulture or the Spider; and a lesser but equally interminable rout made up of German spies, Soviet trade spies, anarchists, apaches, mad scientists, hooded terrors, fraudulent Atlantic flyers, crooked lawyers, rascally rajahs, American racketeers and human bats.

Not all Blake's adversaries sought to destroy him, or he to destroy them. Mr Mist, who caused some dislocation in the nation's business by stealing the Mace from the House of Commons and spot-lighting a Budget scandal in which the Chancellor's wife was being blackmailed, sent the detective the friendliest of notes (beginning *Morituri te salutant*) when he decided to go out of business. Waldo the Wonder Man cherished no hard feelings. Blake could show magnanimity too – even towards Leon Kestrel who went round impersonating the detective, thus fogging the issue to a bewildering degree. And it was hard to be cross with Miss Death, the lady with six months to live, who broke the law in order to speed up her measures for the underdog.

Other adversaries were definitely out to 'get' Blake. One of the more ruthless arranged to have him fired to the Moon by rocket, but Blake, with nine hours to go, cut himself free with his pocket hacksaw. King Karl locked him in an Iron Maiden which happened to be lying about the palace; but because the Maiden had received inadequate care and maintenance the iron spikes which should have pierced Blake's flesh and eyeballs had rusted away at the tips sufficiently to cause him only minor discomfort. Then there was a scientist who sought to rob Blake of some of his surplus energy. This 'man who stole life' sat the detective in a glass chair and threw over the master switch. Blake seemed well worth robbing, in contrast to the previous occupant of the chair ('That girl was tired. I was only able to take a little life from her'). But Blake was able to escape with his life force unimpaired.

To every famous detective, if he stays long enough in the business, comes the day when he pits his wits against his double, arrests the chief of Scotland Yard, finds himself in jail (Blake was lashed to the triangle and all but flogged at Bleakmoor), sees his lodgings blown up (dynamitards visited Baker Street in 1912), reads about his death and attends his own funeral. When Blake was reported dead in 1927 an illustration showed page-boys and top-hatted City gentlemen all with stunned expressions gathered round a newsboy, united in their common loss. And the detective's Fleet Street collaborator, Splash Page, was so overcome he could hardly bring himself to turn out the required two columns on 'Sexton Blake As I Knew Him'. (The placards 'SEXTON BLAKE DEAD' which advertised that issue of *Union Jack* had the effect of greatly inflating the circulation, for hundreds of ex-readers bought copies to see what had happened to their youthful idol. Blake was revived with the aid of the then new drug adrenalin; and as soon as his circulation returned to normal so did that of *Union Jack*.)

The call for Blake's services came from every corner of the globe, from rajahs and Red Indian chiefs, from the Lord Chancellor, the Bank of England (repeatedly) and even from a local authority worried at the number of men who were disappearing and leaving their wives chargeable

to the rates. One of Blake's major assignments was that in
which he was granted plenary powers over everyone in the
country for twenty-four hours; one of his minor assignments was when he intervened to save a Highland laird
from an addiction to the bottle. (This story, entitled
'Drink!' bore one of the few monosyllabic titles in the
long list.) Once at least Blake had a taste of the fate which
was to overcome his professional rival, Nelson Lee. A
serial in the *Boys' Friend* described how, in order to break
up some fell conspiracy, he joined the staff of a public
school; Tinker, of course, became a schoolboy. It is worth
noting that Sexton Blake and Nelson Lee, though rivals,
were perfectly good friends. A story by Maxwell Scott,
'The Winged Terror', in the *Boys' Herald* of 1910, had
Blake stepping in to warn Lee of an impending attempt
on his life by an ex-convict. Together the two detectives,
aided by Tinker and Nipper, tracked down their man in
a highly mechanized campaign which cost the nation the
Tower Bridge and London Bridge. When, at one stage,
Lee drove the car in which he and Blake were travelling
into the hedge, to avert a calamity, Blake said, 'It was a
smart idea of yours, old boy . . . an inspiration of genius.'
To which Lee modestly said, 'It was a choice of evils.'
This was by no means the only occasion on which Blake
and Lee joined forces.

The era of short skirts and the shingle produced a succession of beautiful and unscrupulous heiresses who sought
to compromise Blake's reputation as a bachelor *sans
reproche*. One night, returning to Baker Street, he found
in his bedroom a young woman dressed in a kimono and
not much else who coolly asked him to go outside while
she slipped a dress on. Mrs Bardell denied having admitted the hussy. It turned out that she had entered disguised as Tinker, carrying nothing but a change of
clothes and £100,000 in jewels. The girl was Olga Nas-
myth, alias the Girl of Destiny, who was taking time off
from her implacable pursuit of her family's foes to vamp
the detective. When the scent of her hair was in his nos-

trils and her lips were very close Blake pulled himself together and 'put her from him gently'. Piqued, the girl blew smoke in his eyes and under cover of this ground a glass phial under her shapely heel. When the detective came to, Olga had vanished. It was good riddance.

Then there was the affair with Roxane. For a man of Blake's well-tamed instincts it was quite a sultry little episode. He found himself on some pretext or other aboard the lady's luxury yacht (she was his client at the time). Roxane was a reigning beauty and her picture was constantly in the shiny weeklies. On this occasion she made it clear that her patience was exhausted:

'I'm not going into details again,' she said slowly, 'but I am forced to ask you once more if you will join me ... It is true that I have reached the limit of endurance. I want some – happiness in life. Am I ugly? Am I repulsive? Am I lacking in intelligence? Other men have not found me so.'

'Nor have I,' said Blake in strained tones. 'You are none of those things. It is necessary for me to tell you that you are very lovely and very, very desirable.'

'Then why won't you ...?'

He shook his head.

'No. If I admit any of the softness of what you suggest into my life it means my career would suffer. I have always put it first and must continue to do so. I am sorry, but I can't.'

Roxane had no glass phial, but she had something just as good – a gas pistol. She fired it, not at Blake, but at herself; a white cloud suffused her lovely head. Blake caught her as she slumped, 'the warmth of her body intimately close through the wisp of silk that covered her'.

Blake was in bad shape. He implored her to tell him with which gas the pistol had been loaded, so that he could search in the yacht's laboratory for an antidote (it was that kind of yacht). Nor did he stop there, but promised recklessly that he would do anything she wished. 'It was a bursting of the forces of control such as Sexton Blake had never experienced ...'

In due course Roxane came to and before he realized

what was happening 'she was drawing his head lower and lower until his mouth was upon her half-open lips. How long they stood thus neither could have said.' But at least they kept standing.

Suddenly Roxane smiled and announced that the whole thing was a hoax. She had filled the gas pistol with harmless scent. 'I tested you,' she said.

Blake had no time for bitter reflection on the treachery of women, for at this moment the infamous Felix Dupont, entering without knocking, announced that he had witnessed the whole episode, that he had photographed it and proposed having the picture of the detective 'embracing with such fervour ... this clouded bit of nudity' published in a disreputable journal.

This was Blake's bad day. He whose name was a 'synonym for austerity' would be disgraced and forced out of his profession. London, Paris and New York would ring with the news of his downfall ...

Happily this fate did not come to pass. But it was a narrow escape, and perhaps a salutary warning. Already Blake had been lucky in the case of June Severance, a charmer whom he had gone out of his way to assist. His enemies might have made a good deal out of the fact that he had set her up in the antique business.

During the ten years preceding World War One Blake had a long and curious association with Kaiser Wilhelm. His adventure entitled 'The Conscript, A Tale of the German Army' (1908) ended with Blake thrown into a Prussian prison. He had failed in his object of extracting a British recruit who had been forced into the German Army. To his surprise Wilhelm came to visit him in his cell. The Emperor was displeased:

'On former occasions you have come to my country to do me service. This time your hand has been against me, and you have broken my laws.'

However, in recognition of the esteem in which he held the detective, the Emperor magnanimously decided to grant him a free pardon and a passage home; this dispensation also covered Tinker and Pedro, each languishing in their separate cells, and even the young Briton whom Blake had sought to rescue.

'Again I thank Your Majesty,' exclaimed the detective. 'Never will I forget your great kindness.'

His voice 'choked with emotion', and in his gratitude he kissed the hand of the Kaiser. The last sentence described the party of four leaving for England, 'thanks to the mercy and generosity of the Emperor'.

Blake did not allow his gratitude to the Kaiser to outweigh his patriotism. When, shortly afterwards, the British Prime Minister asked him to investigate some ugly reports connected with the German Naval manœuvres, Blake warned:

'I have had the pleasure of meeting the Kaiser – having worked both for him and against him – and I can assure you that even his wildest speeches have truth in them – a good foundation of truth.'

'The only man in Britain for the task,' was the Prime Minister's comment when Blake left the room, and mentally made a note to put him down for a peerage. Blake refused this almost on the same day that he declined the Kaiser's offer to appoint him head of the German Secret Service. At that time it really looked as if he had succeeded in persuading the Kaiser that his doctrine of 'might is right' was folly. But it was hard to reconcile the Kaiser's 'reform' with an intercepted document in which Wilhelm rashly committed to paper a plan whereby Bulgaria was to receive her 'independence', the Emperor Franz Josef was to annex Bosnia, the Kaiser was to march on Paris and Britain was to come cap in hand to the peace table.

Five years later – in 1913 – Blake again undertook a mission for the Kaiser. A telegram delivered at Baker Street read: 'Come here at once. Wilhelm.' He wired back to Potsdam: 'Regret too busy to accept honour.

*An Eric Parker portait of Sexton Blake to celebrate the
detective's return from the dead: 1927*

Sexton Blake.' But eventually he went to Berlin. He had
already been followed by German Secret Police in London, somewhat to his surprise. ('I wonder what the deuce
the man wanted to follow me for. If the man had been a
Russian I could have understood it, but –.') The Kaiser
ordered him to recover a document stolen from the German War Office. It was to be returned with seals unbroken and the contents could not be divulged even to
Blake. To assist him, the Kaiser gave the detective a ring
which he had only to show to receive every official co-

operation. Blake and Tinker recovered the document, which was 'a most complete and detailed plan for the invasion of England', and returned it to the Kaiser, after sending a photographic copy to Whitehall, with the detective's compliments. The Kaiser did not seem put out at this. He recognized in Blake not only a clever sleuth but a great patriot, and realized that a patriot could have done nothing else. Indeed he presented Blake with a ring in recognition of his services, in exchange for the original *laissez passer* ring. Everyone parted on good terms. It was a puzzling episode.

One by one Blake cleaned up the big cities of Britain – 'Sexton Blake in Nottingham', 'A Manchester Mystery, Sexton Blake in Cottonopolis', and so on. It is impossible to escape the conclusion that his provincial tours were prompted by the circulation department. (One Sexton Blake editor was given the task of impersonating the detective in various towns, a prize being awarded to the first person who recognized and challenged him.) Then came a series of crimes which involved the assumption of the most improbable disguises – 'Sexton Blake, Bath-Chairman', 'Sexton Blake, Ice Cream Man', 'Sexton Blake, French Gardener', 'Sexton Blake, Tax Collector', 'Sexton Blake, Trainer', 'Sexton Blake, Santa Claus', and so on.

Next, one by one, Blake tackled the rackets which were disfiguring Britain – slum landlordism, the sale of children, the worn-out-horse traffic, food profiteering and hire purchase abuses. This perhaps was Blake's finest hour (if one excepts his war service).

There were the occasional political cases too. Once, to Tinker's pained surprise, Blake insisted on going out of his way to record his vote at an election. It is not disclosed how he voted, but from his admission that he happened to own property in the constituency it is possible to make a guess. His attitude on the question of votes for women was clear-cut. At one stage Mrs Bardell joined the Women's League of Freedom and said, in reply to a query about some insignia she was wearing:

'That lurid thing, sir, as you 'ave called it, is a mark of honourable extinction and in no wise deserving of the finger of scorn. I would not part with it for orders or jewelled garters or for the Company of the Bath nor for any other boasted insignitaries of 'igh degree. It is a toking of the fact that I have joined the Women's League of Freedom. Sir, I am proud to state that I 'ave become an 'umble decipher of the great Mrs Spankhard ...'

Exasperated, Blake spoke sharply to Mrs Bardell and threatened to pack her off bag and baggage at a week's notice. This was probably the only time he really lost his temper with his loquacious housekeeper. But he was no snob where Mrs Bardell was concerned. Did he not, on one memorable occasion, invite her to the Hotel Magnificent's Regency dining-room – 'the smaller private one' – to join with the Yard and Home Office chiefs in celebrating the downfall of the Criminals' Confederation?

Another time Blake was called in to tackle the case of the Labour M.P., Honest Tom Mills, who 'was respected by everyone throughout the land'. Unfortunately, Honest Tom's son was suspected of selling the plans of the new Australasian defence scheme. Blake recovered these just in time to avert the collapse of the Government. Thanks to George Orwell, one is left harbouring a possibly base suspicion that Blake would not have exerted himself quite so hard if it had been a Labour Government in jeopardy.

About 1910 it was revealed in 'Sexton Blake, Territorial' that the detective, like Tinker, had once been a regular soldier, which might account for his political orthodoxy. For the purpose of this story Tinker also had to join the Territorials. Those who expected him to chafe at Army discipline were disappointed. He was sorry he had ever laughed at 'Saturday soldiers', and found that the service did him a power of good. It was noticeable that Blake and Tinker never missed an opportunity to put in a good word for the 'Terriers'.

Despite his regular training, when World War One came along Blake was in a reserved occupation. True, he

did a certain amount of snooping about the Low Countries in disguise, with pot-shots at the odd Uhlan, but
mostly he was too busy at home recovering kidnapped
Ministers or preventing the gassing of Greater London.
Usually he was briefed by Sir John —, but sometimes it
was Sir James —. Once Sir James — offered him a C.B.
even before he had begun his investigations, but the
detective brushed this aside pretty snappily.

Blake was relieved, it may be supposed, when the
nightly dumping of spies on these islands ceased, and he
was able once more to choose his own cases. But all too
often extravagant crime persisted in occurring around
him when he was trying to avoid it, or in circumstances
which made it impossible to disregard it. There was the
'Case of the Silent Jury', for instance. The detective was a
spectator at the Old Bailey. Ordinarily he did not care to
watch his man being sentenced, but it was important to
take precautions; the judge might turn out to be Leon
Kestrel in disguise, or the court attendant might have
omitted to test the witnesses' drinking water for arsenic.
On this occasion Blake had stayed to hear the judge's
summing up – a masterpiece of lucidity. Then the jury
retired. Their verdict was a foregone conclusion. But the
jury failed to emerge after a reasonable time. They refused to answer a knock at the door. When the door was
broken down there they were – all mysteriously dead. The
judge, a fellow club-member of Blake, was worried by a
remark of the detective, and said:

'Good heavens, Mr Blake, you surely are not insinuating
that this is the result of foul play?'

The judge put Blake on the case at once. It was a very
sticky one. The next shock was when the murderer whose
fate the jury had been discussing was delivered to Blake
dead in a crate. It was not long before Blake found himself being prepared for a crate, too. If he had not filled the
villain's hypodermic with water the annals of Sexton
Blake would have closed there and then.

The murderer? It was one of those cases in which the least-likely person is the guilty one. Yes, the judge. 'We do not credit Old Bailey Judges with the passions and emotions of ordinary men,' explained Blake. They found in the diary of this unhinged justice the entry:

'Presiding at the Royal Courts of Justice, and listening to the incredibly fatuous cases of criminal stupidity has become a weariness unto the flesh. Now that my retirement is due I shall put into execution a crime unique in the annals of the Old Bailey or indeed of criminology . . .'

To this end the judge had inserted a capsule containing a deadly, volatile, odourless gas in the keyhole of the jury-room door. Turning of the key had crushed it and the dust cover on the keyhole had prevented the gas blowing back into the court room.

In the later issues of *Union Jack* leading Blake authors were persuaded to pit their wits against each other. The first test of strength was a series in which six authors had to write separate stories all building up to a common climax: the discovery of Sexton Blake unconscious from a blow on the head on a tram top at Wood End depot. There was a good deal more to it than that, however. Slumped on a seat beside Blake was to be a stoutish, clean-shaven, elderly man, dead of heart failure. Other stipulations were:

At his (the dead man's) feet lying on the floor is a rolled-up banner, such as is used for processions. The wording on the banner is: 'We Demand Justice For Our Fellow Sufferers.'

On the seat beside him, tied up roughly in brown paper, is a brass fireman's helmet with a dent in it. The helmet is tarnished. The window of the tram on the man's left is broken. Only a few fragments of glass – not enough to fill the hole – are inside the tram.

The man's name proves to be Albert Mowbray Pound, and his age is about 45. He is wearing an ordinary grey lounge suit, but there is no sign of hat or cap. The contents of his pockets are:

COAT

One pawnticket for a mandoline.
One pawnticket for a carpet.
A pipe and pouch of tobacco (shag).
A packet of postcards of London views, banded with a paper band, and obviously just bought at a shop. There are only eleven cards in the packet, one presumably having been extracted.
A map of the London underground system.
A map of the London tram system.
A break-back mousetrap, wrapped in paper.

WAISTCOAT

An old silver watch.
Two pencils; one H.B., one blue.
A packet of book matches.
An electric torch in the shape of a fountain pen.
A wallet containing a 10s. note.

TROUSERS

4s. 9d. in coins.
A knuckle-duster.
These articles may or may not be relevant to the events which lead up to his presence on the tram. The conductor of the tram says he looked on the upper deck when he arrived in the depot before signing off for the night, but did not see either the man or Blake.

Readers were invited to vote on the respective merits of the six tales which ensued, with a prize of a pedigree bloodhound to the one who correctly put the tales in their order of popularity. The nervous were informed that this prize could be commuted to £10 in cash. It had been rashly assumed that the winner would take the cash; when he demanded his bloodhound the country had to be scoured for one.

In the final issues of *Union Jack*, just before it became *Detective Weekly*, appeared a Blake serial – 'The Next Move' – instalments of which were written by four authors in turn – Robert Murray, Anthony Skene, G. H. Teed and Gwyn Evans; the editor was the 'referee'. Thus

Robert Murray would end an instalment with Roxane
locked in an air-tight safe of which only she knew the
combination, and leave it to Anthony Skene to extract
her. Skene would leave Blake drowning in an underground catacomb (and Roxane still in the safe), and hand
over to G. H. Teed. Finally Robert Murray brought the
whole thing to a plausible end. Readers were invited to
give their opinions of this experiment. Some may have
found literary exercises of the kind disillusioning; for
there have always been a minority who believe Blake to be
a real person and who from time to time pluck up the
courage to write to him, congratulating him or seeking
his aid. Women have even applied for the job of housekeeper on Mrs Bardell's retirement.

The *Detective Weekly* (1933) proved to be modelled
on the more spacious lines of the *Thriller*, which had
emerged from the same stable with loud trumpetings in
1929, and which had published in its first number a full-
length story of J. G. Reeder by Edgar Wallace. Some of
the Sexton Blake 'regulars' had also been writing for the
Thriller: it had carried, too, 'Saint' stories by Leslie
Charteris and tales by Sydney Horler. It was time to give
Blake a fresh boost, to sustain him against the strenuous
competition of the thirties.

The nature of the Blake build-up in the first number of
Detective Weekly was not calculated to disillusion the
credulous who believed in a real-life Sexton Blake.
Readers would discover, it was stated, that 'Sexton Blake
is not merely a name or a puppet figure of fiction. From
our stories, phase by phase, will emerge the real and
rounded portrait of a living man – and one who has already won and held the attention of a world-wide audience. Sexton Blake it not a detective; he is *the* detective.'

The build-up contained a wealth of imaginative detail.
Blake, it was claimed, had 'added much to the foundations
of criminology laid down by such pioneers as Lombroso
and Charles Goring, M.D.' The reader was blithely referred to a list of his monographs in Appendix B of that

great German crime classic *Der Verbrecherkreig*, by Ludwig Schroeder. Blake's titles were said to include:

Some information on the use of methylene blue as an antitoxin.
Single-print classification.
Finger-print forgery by the chromicized gelatine method.
Speculations on ballistic stigmata in fire-arms.

It may be noted in passing that Blake was up against gelatinous forgery, not merely of finger-prints, at a very early stage. In one of his first cases he accidentally put his hand on an unconscious man's face, and the 'face' came away in his hand.

The *Detective Weekly* went on to remind readers that Blake was an honoured figure at international police congresses at Vienna, Paris and London, and referred to his early training in the world of medicine (his father Berkeley Blake, of Harley Street). It seemed a little hard, after this, that the first issue of *Detective Weekly* should have sought to drag a skeleton from the Blake cupboard – the only one there, as far as is known. However, the author, Lewis Jackson, had Blake's 'full permission'.

It appeared that the detective had a brother Nigel, a waster, whose conduct had brought 'the grey hairs of his old father in sorrow to the grave'. Blake had met Nigel in the Cameroons, where he was drinking himself to death in a fever swamp, with occasional time off to beat his wife; and Nigel had ordered him away at the revolver point, calling him a 'snivelling parson'. Blake left, and tried to think no more about the distressing episode.

Twenty years later in his study in Baker Street the detective was looking through his earliest collection of finger-prints. In his youthful enthusiasm he had finger-printed his family and even himself, heading the list with 'Sexton Blake, His Mark'. The adjacent print was Nigel's. Gazing horror-stricken at this, Blake recognized it as the same print left by a mysterious forger currently enjoying an unusually prosperous season in London. Blake, in fact, already had all his resources marshalled on the case, and aiding him was Nigel's son, whom the waster had deserted along with his wife. Once again Blake was faced with a diabolical problem. It was the Roxane dilemma afresh:

He could picture the stories, the publicity and scandal of it. 'A brother of the world-famous private detective.' How one or two at the Yard would relish it; and what a titbit for some of his 'friends' in the criminal fraternity!

Luckily it proved possible to hush up the criminal's capture, and Nigel was shut away in a fortress-like house in Buckinghamshire; but not before brother Sexton had had a show-down with him, exclaiming in a voice 'acid with bitterness': 'Nigel Blake – forger and crook! What would our mother have said to that!'

That may well be the only reference to Sexton Blake's mother.

No sooner was Nigel locked away than Leon Kestrel, who never knew when to let well alone, began to go about made up as the wastrel brother. His object was the theft of Blake's Magnetic Picklock, which in conjunction with Blake's Manual of Crime was calculated to make him a considerable menace to society.

The *Detective Weekly* inaugurated a 'round table' at which readers were invited to criticize the fare provided. There were some readers who wanted to see Blake married off; there were even some who wanted him killed off. Both proposals provoked an angry reaction from the faithful. When the Second World War came along there was an agitation for Blake to tackle the Hun, but there was an even stronger agitation to keep him out of uniform. When he did tackle the occasional Gestapo plot 'it was only after all the skill and resources of Scotland Yard, aided by the British Secret Service, had failed'.

In the closing days of *Detective Weekly* there was a serial by Edward Holmes – 'A Case For Sexton Blake' – which ran in conjunction with a Tuesday night serial on the radio – a piece of pre-Dunkirk escapism featuring a man in an iron mask. Then, in the issue of 25 May 1940, came the half-expected announcement that *Detective Weekly* was closing down on account of paper shortage – but that the *Sexton Blake Library* would go on.

After Hitler's war Blake took on many of the characteristics of those tough, disillusioned American detectives, and in a rough-and-tumble he was not always so punctilious about where he hit; which was perhaps understandable in a man who, for sixty years and more, had been beaten up by every enemy of society from Nihilist to Teddy Boy. Much, perhaps too much, of his activity was confined to Soho. Rarely did his latter-day adversaries rival the endearing megalomaniacs of old. To be sure, Hitler's war spawned such an improbable company of megalomaniacs that a writer of fiction might well admit himself defeated. What a splendid ready-made villain for a Blake story was Walter Schellenberg, head of Hitler's Foreign Intelligence, sitting in his microphone-riddled room behind a desk like a fortress with is rotatable machine-guns, with his two false teeth containing, respectively, cyanide and microfilm, devising invisible inks which became visible when mixed with blood, and plotting to kidnap the Duke of Windsor!

Yet, from time to time, Blake was called upon to unravel a plot as bizarre as anything he tackled in the old days. Take, for instance, 'The Mystery of the Three Demobbed Men', one of the early post-war stories. In this remarkable adventure Tinker, accustomed to peculiar behaviour by his master, is astonished to see him not only accepting a bribe from a lawyer but demanding that the original offer of £1,000 be doubled. Blake observes his assistant's misgivings;

'I owe you an explanation, Tinker. You've been very helpful to me. You see, before I went to see Mr Gradstone I took a small dose of a certain Eastern drug. We didn't know the effect of it and we wanted to find out. It appears that a measured dose of this drug lulls the moral sense. In other words, it makes the victim blind to common honesty and capable of any theft or unscrupulous piece of work.'

He sat up, his nostrils quivering impatiently.

'Tinker,' he said, 'on the shelf in the bathroom you will find a small box containing a white powder. Bring it to me and bring me half a glass of water as well. Quickly!'

There's a nasty situation for you. One false step, and Blake will become a criminal, with Tinker as his hunter. But Tinker is equal to the occasion. He darts to the bathroom and destroys the remainder of the drug. Blake is exceedingly angry, but after a tremendous struggle with himself he shakes off the effects of the powder. He then gets down to the task of exposing the activities of a demobbed soldier from the Middle East who is incorporating the drug in the old-fashioned headache-powders manufactured by a respectable firm in the North. The result is a wave of minor crime in Lancashire. Women of unimpeachable integrity, after taking a headache-powder, start to steal each other's clothes pegs off the line, or to lift packets of sugar at the grocer's without paying. The drug happily causes only minor peccadilloes, but the statistics of petty crime have the police chiefs worried. No more insidious threat to the nation's well-being has ever been removed by Sexton Blake.

In 'The Case of the Night Lorry Driver' Blake found himself drawn into the sort of case which, but for his strong sense of public duty, he would doubtless have preferred to decline, if only out of respect for Tinker's youth. The crime he is invited to investigate begins to look ominously like something out of the *News of the World*. This conversation occurs between two characters:

'Tell me, Dr Gribley, what inclines you to the idea that the woman had been criminally assaulted?'

'She was young and rather attractive and in my opinion slightly hyper-thyroidal.'

'What does that mean in Basic English?'

'I would say,' said the pathologist, smiling, 'that she was not under-sexed.'

'Theories, eh?' said Harker with a grin. 'Anything else?'

Blake, who did not grin, had his own theory. Tinker held no very firm views; he was a little out of his depth, one hopes. And Blake was using words like 'empirically' and 'militating', which put a strain on Tinker's vocabulary; possibly more than one long-standing reader read with raised eyebrows:

Blake had investigated a large number of what the police called 'sex crimes' in his time and had studied the reactions of a large number of sadists.

But while Blake was wiser in the ways of human wickedness, some readers began to wonder whether he was quite his old resourceful self. In 'A Date With Danger' he was driving in his Grey Panther on the heels of a car-load of crooks. Unluckily he was cut off by the closing of level-crossing gates. He waited two minutes – two minutes! – and then hailed the signal-box.

'Can't you open up for us, signalman?' he called. 'I'm a detective in pursuit of crooks. They're getting away.'

'Sorry, sir, but there's no openin' of gates once they're closed. The train's due, and orders is orders.'

Blake went back to his assistant.

'We've had it, old chap,' he announced.

That flat acceptance of defeat was un-Blake-like. Was this the man who, forty years earlier, had allowed Tinker to drive a Packard through police barricades on a wild dash to London? Why didn't he say, 'I'm Sexton Blake' instead of 'I'm a detective'? In the old days, of course, every signalman would have recognized not only Sexton Blake but the Grey Panther, and cheerfully risked dismissal or the wreck of the Irish Mail to speed his passage.

If any readers thought that Blake was growing old, or losing his grip, they were disabused when, in the summer of 1956, they started to read 'Frightened Lady', by W.

Howard Baker. In this historic story they learned that pressure of work had obliged Blake to open offices in the West End – in Berkeley Square, no less. His door ('Sexton Blake: Investigations') was reached by way of heavily chromed swing doors and an expensively carpeted staircase. In his outer office sat a silken-eyelashed young brunette whose full black skirt made a whispering noise as she rose. It appeared that Blake had entered into 'reciprocal co-operative arrangements' with investigators in Los Angeles, New York and Paris, and intended to widen greatly the scope of his activities; he had also 'discarded a lot of his old equipment and methods in favour of new'. Hardly had the startled readers adjusted themselves to the idea of a pretty girl in a whispering skirt on Blake's payroll when they found him signing on as secretary the frightened lady of the story, Paula Dane. *What was going on?* Would this Paula Dane turn up in the next story?

She did. For better or worse, Paula Dane became part of the legend. She was a tall, slim honey-blonde with high cheek bones and – when first encountered – a 'near-mink' coat. Before Blake rescued her from her oppressors, she had been trying to write advertising copy, but had not really relished persuading people to buy what they did not need with money they had not yet earned. Paula dared not admit to herself her real feelings about her employer. She accompanied him on a holiday to Positano where they dallied innocently on the beach until a corpse was washed up at their feet. In the ensuing investigations she knocked out an armed adventuress with a blow to the jaw.

Marion Lang, the receptionist, 'breathless and forever helpful', took time to adjust to the atmosphere of sudden death. She had stimulating notions of what to wear in the office. According to Paula, she spent most of her time thinking of two subjects, both of them men. Paula doubtless noticed that when her employer made a telephone call from the outer office his eyes were liable to 'slide carelessly' over the 'softly rounded young body' of his recep-

tionist. Neither Paula nor Marion addressed Blake as
'Sexton'. That forbidding first name, so obviously defying
contraction, is at once a stumbling-block and a protection.

It was a relief to older readers to find that Tinker was
still there and pulling his weight, though he was increasingly referred to by his real name, which most of us
had forgotten, if we ever knew it:

'My assistant, Edward Carter,' Blake said. 'Everyone calls
him Tinker. Don't ask me why.'

Tinker was 'no longer the boy assistant, but a sturdy,
hard-key man in the Blake menage'. His slang, which used
to be a blend of 1900 *Comic Cuts*, 1920 Wodehouse and
1930 Hollywood, was now as up-to-date as the last head-
line. He showed no jealousy of Paula. If, on one occasion,
he noticed her put her hand on Blake's behind the desk,
he made no comment. (Blake 'gave Paula back her hand'
fairly quickly.) In the old days Tinker saw 'the old war
horse' work up a mild 'pash' on many a nubile young
woman, but he could be fairly sure that nothing serious
would come of it. He and his master enjoyed that perfect
understanding which comes only of being clubbed and
chloroformed together, down the generations. They
differed slightly in their attitude to Marion. Whereas
Blake ran his eyes over her, Tinker ran a friendly hand
over her.

It was all a big jolt for the older fans of Sexton Blake.
Only gradually did they learn that the detective was still
enough of a traditionalist to maintain a home in Baker
Street, and that Mrs Martha Bardell, far from having been
pensioned off or having walked out in a huff, had come
back from nursing a sick relative to look after her employer and stuff him with hot buttered crumpets. It also
turned out that she was looking after the 'faithful and
salacious' bloodhound Pedro, truly a marvel for his age,
and a newcomer in the shape of a Siamese cat.

The shocks were not yet over. In 1963 the *Sexton Blake*

Library ceased its run of nearly fifty years and the great 'Arthurian cycle' seemed to have come to an end. There was something of a wake in Fleet Street. A personal message from Blake, a somewhat teasing one in the circumstances, was published in the last issue. The detective said: 'It's over now. We can get on with the job of fighting crime without having to stop and think: "Now, how's this going to look in print?"' The message was signed 'Sexton T. Blake', with a postscript: 'Hah! That middle initial was something I always managed to keep to myself.' Well-known Blake authors also sent messages. Jack Trevor Story, a popular novelist in his own right, said: 'The *Sexton Blake Library*, in common with other dead publications, lacks everything it takes to appeal to the mass audience now emerging from the new eleven-plus machine: it lacks dullness, it lacks puerility, it lacks sterility, it lacks pictures that could obviate reading altogether ...'

The tears and jeers were premature. Thanks to the industry and resource of W. Howard Baker, Blake re-emerged in a run of forty Mayflower paperbacks. He also appeared in a series of hard-back books, some of them 'omnibus' two-in-one volumes, bearing the imprint of the Howard Baker Press. The prolific author-publisher who had given the detective Paula Dane and Marion Lang was determined not to let him escape again. In 1972 Jack Trevor Story, who said those hard things about the eleven-plus generation, wrote a notable Blake story called 'Company of Bandits'. It was a tale about a £2 million train robbery in which the loot found its way to starving peoples. Most of its readers will have formed the conclusion that Blake, with a little more determination, could have frustrated this escape of funds, but he seemed very happy about the outcome. It was clear that he had developed a strong distaste for some of the ways of capitalism.

Perhaps the shocks are only just beginning.

CHAPTER IX

MORE DETECTIVES

SEXTON BLAKE lived to lead the field of popular detectives, but he was only one of a huge and struggling bunch of runners when he made his first appearance.

The setting up of private detectives was a major literary industry in the nineties. When 1900 dawned the Aldine Company alone could boast more than 250 detective titles. Earnest attempts were made to spin a web of romance round the private investigator, however squalid his role might be in real life. Said an Aldine advertisement in the nineties:

These thrilling SHADOW REVELATIONS of the deep and cunning meshes of concealment woven by astute and criminal men and women often in high positions and spotless before the world and the deadly dangers besetting the daring professional MAN HUNTER are vividly depicted in these absorbing narratives.

Most of the Aldine man-hunters were imported from America, where Old Sleuth and Old Cap Collier had long been dazzling readers of Munro's Dime Novels. Some of the more peculiar titles, in the Aldine publications and elsewhere, were *The Demon Detective*; *The Jew Detective*; *New York Nell, the Girl-Boy Detective*; *Fritz, the Bound Boy Detective*; *Old Stonewall, the Shadower*; *Lynx-Eye, the Pacific Detective*; and *Old Electricity, the Lightning Detective*. Female sleuths included Daisy Bell, Sarah Brown and Kate Scott, the Decoy Detective. Then there was a whole range of specialist detectives, such as The Post Office Detective, The Revenue Detective, The Naval Detective, The Hansom Cab Detective, The Science Detective, The Actress Detective and The Mountaineer Detective. There were also brother detectives, brother-

and-sister detectives, father-and-son detectives, father-and-daughter detectives, uncle-and-nephew detectives, husband-and-wife detectives – there may well have been man-and-mother-in-law detectives; and there was no scarcity of dog detectives.

Allan Pinkerton of the famous Pinkerton Agency had put out a series of supposed selections from his firm's casebook, with the Pinkerton eye – 'We Never Sleep' – on the cover. These had encouraged other publishers to issue 'casebooks' linked to reality only by a couple of hairs. Many of these were reprinted in Britain and enjoyed ephemeral life.

Since the competition was acute, it followed that the mortality rate was high. A sleuth would be hailed as 'none other than the celebrated' so-and-so (though he might never have achieved print before), would flourish for an instalment or two and then vanish into limbo. Others, more modestly introduced, would crop up at long and irregular intervals in unexpected places. A good detective might outlast a poor magazine, but equally a poor magazine could ruin a promising detective. It was not necessarily a tribute to a detective's brilliance that he survived; it was just as likely to be due to the publisher's financial staying power or to the size and brilliance of the coloured plates he could afford to give away. No one will ever know how many stories written around a given detective were rejected and then successfully re-submitted to another publisher with another detective's name substituted; nor how many stories, once accepted by an editor, had the hero's name changed to that of another detective to meet some emergency of publishing.

A challenge to Sexton Blake for fully a generation was Nelson Lee, the detective who turned schoolmaster. There was a real-life Nelson Lee who figured in the 1850s as some sort of theatrical impresario, but there is no evidence to show that he mingled detection with his other accomplishments. The fictional Nelson Lee, again, was a Harmsworth detective, and his earliest appearances were in the

Marvel and *Pluck*. His creator was Maxwell Scott (Dr John Staniforth), who planned his stories so meticulously that he knew exactly what would happen in chapter 30 before he had written a word of chapter 1.

Lee's first exploit in the *Marvel* – 'A Dead Man's Secret' (1894) – was the solving of a blow-pipe murder mystery on the West of England Mail. Nipper, his future assistant, figured in this story, arriving at Gray's Inn Road to claim half a sovereign for information.

Readers of *Pluck* who missed this story in the *Marvel* must have been puzzled by their first introduction to Nelson Lee. This mettlesome weekly, started in 1894, was described as 'Stories of Pluck – being the daring deeds of plucky sailors, plucky soldiers, plucky firemen, plucky explorers, plucky detectives, plucky railwaymen, plucky boys and plucky girls and all sorts and conditions of British heroes.' An editorial in the first number said that *Pluck* would contain true stories, but no one was to imagine that truth would be dull. The first number carried stories of General Gordon and of Nelson's powder-monkey; succeeding numbers featured Lobengula, Livingstone and Lord Roberts. In the fifth issue was a story of 'Roland Dare, the greatest fireman America ever had'. As a name like Roland Dare plainly invited suspicion the editor disarmingly admitted that it was a false name but said that the hero's identity was 'so thinly veiled that it will be readily recognized by most readers'. In Number Eight came another announcement which may or may not have caused misgivings:

Long ago and with irresistible acclaim the world gave Gideon Barr, the famous detective, one of the highest places among the men who have immortalized themselves by strenuous deeds of courage. It was he who accomplished one of the most brilliant achievements in recent social history by so coolly dealing with an already lighted bomb that he saved the best part of a large city from destruction.

His noble bearing in the fearful mining disaster in Wales will hold the memory for ever; and who can forget that Gideon

Barr single-handed was the valiant one who subdued and banished that infamous confederacy of highly trained and murderous criminals known as 'The Black Vultures'?

This time the editor did not state that Gideon Barr was a disguised name. It is doubtful whether any of his readers were sufficiently interested in establishing Barr's *bona fides* to search for Baylard's Inn off Holborn and there hunt out a lithe, blue-eyed detective whose flaxen hair had a 'golden glow'.

Succeeding issues of *Pluck* were still sprinkled with the adventures of such incontestable characters as the Duke of Wellington. An examination of these early numbers suggests that while fact may have been stranger than fiction, fiction may have sold better than fact. Was it proved that 'real life' was as dubious a recommendation for an adventure story as 'home made' for a windowful of cakes?

But what of Nelson Lee? In Number 23 came this announcement in bold type on the back page:

Some of our readers may remember reading the newspaper account of the wreck of the steamship Sandown, which took place on the 19th of last December. It was rendered more than usually interesting by the fact that the ill-fated steamer was bringing an enormous amount of bullion (or bars of gold) from Capetown to England, and that after the wreck no less than twenty of these bars (valued at as many thousand pounds) have been stolen. The Steamship Insurance Company, with whom the vessel was insured, place the matter in the hands of Mr Nelson Lee, of Gray's Inn Road; and the celebrated detective after nearly three months' sojourn in foreign climes has now returned to England, flushed with success. Newspapers and magazines have vied with each other in publishing more or less fanciful accounts of his latest and most brilliant triumph; but thanks to our arrangements with Mr Maxwell Scott the true and complete account will appear in the pages of *Pluck*. It will be published in the next issue under the title of 'A False Scent, or the Adventures of Nelson Lee in Search of Sunken Gold.'

So out of this half-world of fact and fiction, emerged

Nelson Lee, hero of Lhasa and Limehouse, confidant of
Lloyd George and Kitchener, the man who in later life (in
the hands of a successor to Maxwell Scott) saved from
nameless and numberless disgraces the venerable public
school of St Frank's.

Lee was introduced in his headquarters in Gray's Inn
Road 'pacing his room with the rapid stride and mut-
tered growls of a caged and hungry lion'. He was offered
10 per cent of the value of the Sandown's missing bullion,
if he recovered it.

'That is £2,000,' said Nelson Lee, musingly. 'You will pay
me £2,000 if I succeed, but what will you pay me if I fail?'

A foolish speech, as he realized at once when his client
reminded him with a smile:

'There is no such word as "fail" in the dictionary of Nelson
Lee.'

It was easy money, as it turned out, involving nothing
more arduous than an underwater fight with long-handled
axes.

Later evidence showed Lee to be aquiline, with sunken
yet clear eyes – 'he could even be called good-looking'. He
was a dressing-gown detective, liked comfort and Turkey
carpets. His chief vice was a continuous knitting of the
brows. It appears from the *Boys' Realm* of 1902 that Lee
was working in uneasy alliance with another of those
French detectives, Jean Moreau. But Moreau, though
brilliant, was treacherous, and Lee did well to shake him
off.

Lee's adventures appeared in many of the Amalgamated Press journals. In 1903, readers of the newly-
founded *Boys' Herald* learned how Lee met his boy assistant Nipper, a street urchin of unnatural distinction who
preferred to live by supplying information of comings and
goings at half a crown a time. Under the dirt and rags 'his
features, like his hands, were perfectly modelled'. When
Nelson Lee demanded, 'Who are you?' he replied, ' "My

name is Norval. On the Grampian hills –"' then began to
walk round Lee's room on his hands, 'whilst at the same
time he gravely intoned those well-known lines of the
Roman poet, *Facilis descensus Averni*' – faultlessly, for
four lines. A few moments later Nipper was on his hands
again, singing a German drinking song. The mystery
which Nelson Lee was then attempting to solve was a
trumpery indeed compared with the mystery of Nipper.

It was not until 1915 that Nelson Lee achieved the distinction of being chronicled in a library all his own. There
was as yet no serious paper shortage, and readers were invited to compete for a 3½ h.p. Rudge-Multi by getting the
names of as many boys as possible to read the *Nelson Lee
Library*. Five thousand lads at once rose to the bait. The
motor cycle eventually went to Master Willie Jones, of
102, Wellsby Street, Grimsby, who submitted 8,634 names
and addresses. It was probably the hardest earned motor
cycle in history.

Gray's Inn Road was the scene of thinly disguised
criminal activity in those days. One afternoon the detective, still served by Nipper ('pert as a magpie, keen as a
weasel, and clever as a cartload of monkeys'), was looking
idly out of the window. To Nipper he said:

'Do you see that man there? European clothes, but with the
slant eyes of a Chinaman. Probably his pigtail is coiled up in
his bowler hat.'
'You mean the lame one, sir – the one with the club foot?'
Nipper, the young assistant, answered brightly.
'The man who appears to have a club foot,' Nelson Lee
corrected. 'If you watch him closely you will see that the bend
of the knee is not natural, that his leg would be the same
length as the other if he cared to stretch it out and –'
'But what's the idea of that?' Nipper demanded.
Nelson Lee shrugged his shoulders and the expression on his
face suggested that he was bored to death.
'Opium smuggling,' he answered briefly. 'I have often
thought that there was a depot of that kind round King's
Cross and now I am sure of it.'

Nipper wanted his master to take action, but the detective said it was an affair for the police. He was bored with routine small-time stuff. With an ill grace he consented to rescue an American millionaire's kidnapped son, receiving for his pains a cheque for £10,000. Nipper suggested that this was 'almost enough to take us away for the weekend', but he received curt instructions to distribute it among the detective's ten favourite charities. Lee did not care for the way the millionaire had made his money and declined to be corrupted by it.

When the Great War came the State had first call on Lee's services; he was kept busy stamping out the 'serpent of secret service that writhed its insidious coils through every town, city and hamlet in the British Isles'. With the 'fervent thanks of his grateful country ringing in his ears' he could afford to take a very off-hand attitude towards the War Office. When a Staff major rang him up late at night and asked him to come at once, he exclaimed,

'Bally Government offices! Deuced cheek I call it. Think everybody's got to dance attendance on them. Jolly well wish I hadn't said I'd come.'

And it was only a trumpery little matter of preventing the Goswell Road district being asphyxiated by barge loads of German 'fertilizer'.

It seems probable that Nelson Lee was overworking at the time. As Nipper pointed out when the phone rang:

'My word, sir, Mr Lloyd George hasn't given you much rest since he appointed you Inspector of Government Factories.'

When Lee, in response to the phone call, went across to see the Premier he was received instead by Sir Reevely Chart, Lloyd George having been suddenly called away. This was a disappointment for Lee, to whom Kitchener was always at home, but then Lloyd George was a busy man too. Sir Reevely Chart got down to business:

'Look at this Table of Output. Over 2,000 hands are employed yet the number of rifles, shells and small ammunition is a bare half of what it should be.'

'This is grave indeed,' said Lee. 'I am at a loss to account for it.'

'They were running at full speed when you were down there?'

'Day and night, double shifts. No lathe or machine idle.'

Here an unworthy thought occurred to Sir Reevely Chart. He asked:

'Do the men drink?'

'No. There may be a slacker here and there, but the bulk of them are splendid fellows – good, honest, hard-working Yorkshiremen.'

The villain in the piece turned out to be General (*'und tousand teufels'*) von Schoffen, who was out to weaken output before giving the signal for a mass insurrection of Germans from prisoner of war camps.

Much timely and versatile assistance was given to Nelson Lee by Eileen Dare, the girl detective. She was of special use when he wanted to plant a parlourmaid in some house of mystery. Nipper, knowing that there were limitations even to his powers of disguise, seems to have borne no ill-feelings – rather the reverse. When Eileen Dare was around he paid more attention to his appearance, and slicked back his hair. He always called her 'Miss Dare', as did Nelson Lee. It is improbable that the girl detective shared the bachelor quarters in Gray's Inn Road, but she was always readily available. The partnership lasted many fruitful years.

Nelson Lee's first visit to St Frank's was with the object of hiding from a gang who were pursuing him too hotly. But if he hoped to find calm in the groves of Academe he was mistaken. His professional rival Ferrers Locke was continually being called to Greyfriars or St Jim's to investigate a stabbing or kidnapping, planting his juvenile assistant in the Remove or the Shell as required. It must have been to the mutual advantage of Nelson Lee and

Dr Stafford, the Head of St Frank's, when the detective agreed to join the staff; doubtless the Head was astounded to see what new, unsuspected and perverse machinations the detective was to uncover. Nipper enjoyed the move to St Frank's. He had never had any formal education, but held his own among the Sir Monties and Hon. Douglases. Only occasionally was he 'framed'; then he speedily cleared himself.

Now and then Nelson Lee and Nipper slipped back to Gray's Inn Road to keep the old practice going, but these reversions were not popular with the imperious readers of the *Nelson Lee Library*. The editor had to admit that separate stories of Lee and Nipper, divorced from St Frank's, were 'about as popular as fog at a football match'. 'You want the detective element, but you want it intermixed with a school yarn. All right, you shall have it.' And have it they did, right to the end, when the *Nelson Lee Library* was merged with the *Gem* (1933).

The Aldine detective, Dixon Brett, was a highly organized performer when Blake and Lee were still comparative tyros; the archives show that he had routed many an anarchist by the middle nineties. This scientific sleuth owned one of the first Mercedes race cars. He was usually to be found cigar-smoking at the wheel, wearing 'immaculate evening dress' under a fur-lined overcoat. The 'Night Hawk', his car, was a redoubtable performer too, and did not seem to suffer from the heartless way in which the detective set her in motion. ('The sleuth put in the clutch, slipped it in gear and let the clutch back again with a jerk. A second later the great car leaped forward ...') Beside Brett in the 'Night Hawk' was usually to be found his Number One assistant, Pat Malone; his Number Two assistant, Bill Slook, was more often left to look after the chambers in Lincoln's Inn. Slook was a curiosity – 'a freak even', in that he was 32 years old but looked like sixteen. His youthful appearance was the more remarkable when it is remembered that Brett plucked him from a life of degradation in an opium den. There were obvious ad-

" I am serious, Lee, and your flippancy is not in keeping with the present circumstances ! " snapped the Night Owl. " I have come here for the Don Santos Treasure, and I shall take it away with me ! "

vantages in 'combining the face and form of a boy with the age and ripe experience of a fully-grown man'. But for all his ripe and specialist experience Slook seems to have caused the detective a good deal of worry. In case after case he was rescued only at the eleventh hour from sudden death, or would turn up at Gray's Inn Road 'foaming and chattering like an ape' from a musk-maddened tarantula's bite. Malone was often a liability, too; he narrowly escaped torture by liquid air one day and by heat ray the next.

When not tearing about the country in his Mercedes, Dixon Brett sat in his loose dressing-gown in a deep chair, smoking an 'evil-smelling briar' or 'igniting a choice weed'. For a man with so many enemies it seemed odd that he should have had a speaking-tube extending down from his sitting-room to the front entrance; and for a man of his acumen it seemed even more odd that he should have been unsuspicious of a sweet scent in the room, and, having detected it, that he should have dismissed his giddiness with 'Shall have to put in a bit more exercise. Nerves getting a bit slack.' For Dixon Brett knew as well as the reader that Fan Chu Fang, the Wizard Mandarin, was abroad in London.

Fan Chu Fang, 'a veritable archangel of evil', was one of the few fictional villains to raid Buckingham Palace successfully. The Chinese Government used regularly to deny that the Mandarin was an agent of theirs, but Dixon Brett knew better.

Fan Chu Fang, like the more famous Fu Manchu, seemed to have unpleasant optical trouble.

'At last he unveiled his green and evil orbs, and with something very like a shudder of disgust Dixon Brett observed that with the uplifting of the heavily folded eyelids a filmy grey substance was likewise drawn upward over the pupils, something like the moving membrane – the *membrana nictitans* – seen in the eyes of a bird.'

Soon after the Mandarin left a young man called, 'an

obvious neurotic, slender, fragile, eager'. He had wide-open blue eyes with broad pupils 'in which could be seen plainly the characteristic "hippus" – the incessant change of size which marks the unstable nervous equilibrium'.

The eyes of Brett himself 'glowed a cat-like green' when he was excited. A hand-to-hand struggle between him and an albino would have been good value.

As a scientific sleuth Brett had an up-to-date laboratory. Some of his triumphs today would seem like the pottering of a small boy with a chemistry set, but he performed one feat at least which would still take some rivalling. It was necessary to identify some small seeds which looked like being an important clue. Brett laid them on soil which he steeped with a secret fertilizer, and then turned on the Röntgen rays (maintained by him for detecting forged banknotes).

In about ten minutes the shoots had reached the height of nearly an inch, and were then observed to grow much slower. Brett tipped the remains of the fertilizer from the phial into the jar.

The effect was almost magical; slowly but surely the shoots stretched upwards until the tops were at least eight inches from the earth. They then began to swell until they formed a dry-looking bud which a moment later burst, bringing forth a magnificent flower of a deep red colour.

'Great Scott! A poppy!' gasped Malone.

He was right. There was no mistaking the nature of the beautiful flower.

'Quick, Pat!' rasped Brett. 'Switch off the current of the rays and pull back the curtains.'

Why Brett got so excited at the end, or why he was operating behind drawn curtains, is not clear, unless it was that he did not want to be caught monkeying with the forces of Nature.

Although no mean scientist, Brett had not neglected his modern studies. When Dr Yoshimaro, to whom he took the poppy for identification, greeted him with 'Welcome, O Friend of ten thousand virtues!' Brett took a deep breath and countered with 'Greeting, O faithful son of ten million illustrious ancestors! The sight of thy radiant countenance, beside which the sun at noon is even as a dishonourable farthing candle, has healed me of all things. O Yoshimaro, the wise, beside whom the Sacred Owl of Wisdom is a babbling and absurd idiot!'

Nobody could complain that the characters in a Dixon Brett story died by natural causes. Leon Markheim collapsed suddenly, not from that overworked arrow poison but from sipping what he thought was a bottle of cognac and which turned out to be a flask of liquid air. 'His throat had been frozen solid the second the terrible liquid touched it, every blood-vessel in his neck being instantly congested.' Another victim was literally scared stiff by seeing an evil figure beckoning to him from what he had supposed was a mirror; another fell to the whispering death, a sibilant, all-pervading voice which urged him to get up and hang himself (one of many anti-social uses to which the innocent microphone has been put).

It was about 1900 that a powerful American rival strode on to the scene: Nick Carter. Perhaps it would be better to say that he was dumped on the scene. 'Remainders' of the Nick Carter Publishing House in New York were put on the British market at a low price, and enjoyed a considerable success. The house of Harmsworth, who had done their best to undercut their rivals a few years before, tried to enlist the wholesalers against this threat, but failed. Nick Carter established a beachhead, and began to fan out. But his weakness was in his supply lines. When the remainders were exhausted Nick Carter had to withdraw and await his next chance, hoping that his legend would survive.

Not that his reputation depended only on remainders. He made many appearances under the aegis of one publisher or another. And he was a much-translated detective. The Germans, for instance, saw in him a challenge to the dubious sensational fiction from which their market suffered. He had a keen following in France and Belgium.

So many incarnations had Nick Carter, in so many places, that it is uncommonly difficult to chart his career. He appears to have been created by John Russell Coryell, in the *New York Weekly* in the 1880s. Most of the Nick Carter stories, however were the work of Frederick van Rensselaer Dey, who turned them out endlessly at the rate of 30,000 words a week. He died by his own hand in New York.

When the *New Nick Carter Weekly* was published in Britain in 1911 – with a New York address – the Amalgamated Press promptly took the opportunity of pointing out that Sexton Blake was a BRITISH detective, and issues of *Union Jack* bore the notice 'This is NOT an American reprint.' Number One of the *New Nick Carter Weekly* showed the detective examining a safe on which a robber had been considerate enough to leave, not just a fingerprint, but an entire handprint, or as entire a handprint as he could leave with only three fingers. It seemed as adequate a clue (or clew) as any detective had a right to expect.

There was a powerful piece of promotion for the benefit of those, if any, who had never heard of Nick Carter:

The name of Nick Carter has spread to every land where the English tongue is spoken, and his exploits have won tremendous popularity in the picture palaces everywhere. He is undoubtedly the cleverest detective and criminal investigator the world has ever known. Nick Carter, with the aid of his two assistants, Chickering Carter, generally termed Chick, and Patsy, has unravelled more astounding mysteries and been the central character of more thrilling adventures and hairbreadth escapes than any other man. He ranges his wonderful powers on the side of law, order and justice against the criminals of five continents.

Notice that Nick Carter is credited with two assistants. (Chick, just to make things difficult, sometimes made up as Nick.) There were many others, though not all stayed the exacting course. When it was suggested to the Grand Duke Ivan that Carter was just the man to mop up the nihilists ('The nihilists! The nihilists! That cry which is the most awful that can be heard in Russia!') the Grand Duke asked:

'Does he know anything about Russia? Does he speak the language?'
'My dear Cousin, Nick Carter knows every country and speaks all languages like a native.'
'Then let us send for him.'
'By the way, there is more than one of him.'
'What do you mean by that?'
'He has two or three assistants, I really don't know how many, and they usually work together in big cases. We'd better have them all, hadn't we?'

Really only a Grand Duke or a Maharajah could afford to take all Nick Carter's assistants on the payroll. Moreover, the assistants had wives who sometimes joined, or were called into, the chase. On the rare occasions when they were home in New York they all lived together *en famille*. Patsy Garvan and his wife had a private sitting-room, but they dined with the detective, who sat at the head of the table. It was by no means unusual to find Nick smoking a cigar in the library with Adelina (Patsy's wife) curled up opposite him with her embroidery. This was a striking break with the masculine traditions of Baker Street. Adelina, 'beloved by every member of the household', would sometimes 'take liberties with the detective that others would not think of doing'. All this meant was that she would sometimes rally him when he was unduly silent or secretive.

There was a girl called Ida Jones who would cross oceans at the detective's request; there was the 'youngest assistant', whose name was Jack Wise; and there was an Indian called Jack Rabbit. The household also included a 'faithful servitor' called Joseph and a housekeeper, Mrs Peters.

On the top floor of the house was the strong room, a high windowless room which came in useful from time to time. Nick thought nothing of locking up a couple of women crooks inside the strong room and holding them, without fear of *habeas corpus*, until he had decided what to do with them.

Nick Carter went to great pains when disguising himself. He would cheerfully run the clippers over his hair, stain his teeth and torture his ears with gold wire. And when he became a hunchback – his strong line – he was not content with a hump which came away when he removed his coat (as some operators apparently were): the hump lay 'deeper than the coat or the flowered waistcoat that covered it. It was deeper than the shirt beneath the heavy, coarse woollen undershirt he wore, in fact, so that if occasion should arise to remove his coat, as was likely to happen, the hump was still there.' Even when he took the last garment from his back you had difficulty in spotting that the hump was a dummy. When not in use the hump was kept in a cupboard and must have baffled Mrs Peters when she came round tidying up.

Yet when Nick Carter joined the nihilists in order to bore from within, his skill at disguise and facility at languages proved inadequate to convince the evil Vlasda that he was the peasant Beppo who lived 'about ten versts from Tver'. She ordered him suddenly in French to sit down, but Nick did not fall for that one. Nor did he bat an eyelid – this illiterate peasant – when told to report to the arch-crook with an open document which said that he was Nick Carter, a traitor. Soon he was in a rough-house, punching his assailants 'in American fashion' under the back of the skull, and at the same time exclaiming, 'That's English, if you understand it, you villains.' Had he fought a less clean fight he would not have landed in Siberia, chained to a murderer and a thief.

Carter was at his best when pitted against beautiful, unscrupulous women. Deliberately he courted a battle of wits with a female Svengali in Paris. He wanted her to believe that she had him in a state of hypnosis, whereas he would still (he hoped) be in possession of his wits. It was tough going. Under the lady's gaze he felt a tightening of his throat, 'a feeling like that of a rubber band around his brows'. He allowed himself to be lured to an easy chair where the lady stroked his forehead, covered though it was with beads of sweat.

'Nicholas Carter,' she said, with odd formality. Then sharply, 'Answer me.'

Nick did not answer, but continued to play 'possum'.

'I am about to waken you now. You will believe that you have slept. You will believe that you held me tightly in your arms; that your head has been pillowed upon my breast; that you have told me of your love for me; and that I have confessed my love for you. You will implicitly believe all this when you awaken.'

Nick declined to 'awaken' fully, and his adversary put him to sleep again. Just then the master villain came in and suggested that it would save a lot of trouble if the detective in his hypnotized state were sent out onto the boulevards with instructions to jump in the Seine. For private reasons the lady was unwilling to do this. The plot hereabouts became very complicated, but at no time did Nick yield the initiative.

After enduring many a trying experience like this, Nick Carter was entitled to hold strong views on his pet subject:

'Throughout my experience I have been repeatedly annoyed by the escape of criminals whom I have arrested only after great and continuous effort. With the aid of my two assistants I track down a criminal and get him or her in durance vile and then some official turns his back and permits that criminal to escape. No man likes to do his work over a second time, no matter how much he may be paid for doing it. But this present case out-Herods Herod . . .'

It is disconcerting, after studying 'this wonderful American' against his cosmopolitan background, to find that in 1915 he apparently took up permanent headquarters in, of all places, Manchester. (*Further Exploits of Nick Carter, Detective*: C. A. Pearson, Ltd.) He was down to one assistant, Chick Wilson, who was familiarly, if un-originally, known as the Nipper, but still enjoyed the power to arrest or to say to police officers, 'You will arrest –'

Another English publisher – George Newnes – put out stories of Nick Carter against a sometimes ambiguous background, which could have been either Britain or America. Perhaps that was all part of the secret of the popularity of the Nick Carter stories.

In 1933, Nick Carter made a notable come-back in the *Nick Carter Magazine*, published in New York. The stories were stated to be 'by Nick Carter', although the narrative was in the third person. Nick Carter the author did not hesitate to praise the initiative and acumen of Nick Carter the detective.

Carter was by now very busy and very rich; too busy to observe the normal courtesies, and perhaps too rich to care. He lived in a house on Fifth Avenue with a Filipino valet 'whose name was changed every time Nick Carter felt like it'. Adelina was no longer there to practise her gentle raillery. She would have found the new Nick Carter very hard and self-sufficient, and would almost certainly have been snubbed if she had tried to jolly him along. Chickering Carter was still alive and serving the sleuth faithfully.

Nick was now tackling big gangster organizations and kidnappers. Experience had taught him to practise an even higher degree of personal preparedness. Here he is at breakfast:

Holding his glass of orange juice in one hand, Nick started deftly shucking the envelopes off his mail with the other. It was an unwritten law with the master detective never to use two hands for anything if he could possibly manage with one. This was because there were so many times in Nick Carter's life when he couldn't use one hand because it had a gun in it.

One out-of-the-way case involved the recovery of a stolen yacht loaded with a drug which had been hailed as the new anaesthetic, but which, belatedly, had been found to drive patients crazy and to give them the characteristics of apes. Carter searched for the yacht from his own aeroplane, which was fitted with a large magnifying glass in the floor. Being Nick Carter, he was allowed to mount offensive weapons on his aircraft and to carry bombs, even while flying over New York.

He also routed a master crook who had hit on the happy idea of priming his unwilling helpers with the details of cracking a chosen crib and then clamping on their heads an electric helmet which paralysed cerebrum and cerebellum, leaving the *medulla oblongata* still functioning. The victim would then proceed to execute uncritically the last instructions registered by the *medulla*.

With the *Nick Carter Magazine* was launched a Nick Carter Club, members of which were given a badge resembling a police shield. This accorded the wearer no special powers, but he was expected to help uphold the law on all occasions, to give evidence in the face of intimidation and to resist all demands for protection money. The hope expressed by the sponsors was that there were 'hundreds of thousands of citizens who will no longer remain passively standing by while crooks drench our streets with their bloody killings and flaunt their crimes before us'.

Certainly Nick Carter set an example of incorruptibility. To a father who offered him two million dollars to save his son from the consequences of his folly, he merely said, 'Your son is going to burn.'

He had become a very hard man indeed. But not so hard as he was to become forty years later in Tandem paperback. By then he was known among agents everywhere as Killmaster.

Among English detectives who dared to be different was Falcon Swift, who flourished in the pages of the pink-jacketed *Boys' Magazine*[1] (1922). He was a sporting detective; not the first of that genre, for Aldine had run a *Dr*

1. Later absorbed in the *Champion*.

Grip, the Sport Detective, nearly a generation before. But Swift was the only detective to play in international soccer wearing a monocle.

This sleuth with the 'keen aristocratic face' was a Cambridge triple blue who was equally proficient at boxing, soccer, sculling and fencing. He had his headquarters in what was described as a 'cosy' sanctum hung with boxing gloves, rapiers and many trophies of the chase. Here sat his assistant Chick Conway – 'the London street urchin whom he had literally taken out of the gutter'. Chick spent all his time reading the *Sporting Chronicle* and trying to match up his master for a prize fight. The *châtelaine* of this establishment was Biddy Malone, who cooked the meals when she was not lying clubbed or drugged in the kitchen.

One of Falcon Swift's early adversaries in the ring was a bruiser, who was also a member of an international gang of crooks. Swift found himself facing this rugged character in the ring on one of those days when everything had gone wrong. Chick Conway had vanished in suspicious circumstances, and just before the contest was due to begin it was revealed that the box office had been robbed of the £10,000 takings. A lesser man than Falcon Swift might have been put off his form. But he prepared to do battle.

The men shook hands. What a contrast! Swift with a skin of satin whiteness looked a picture of the English fighting man, with long arms and slightly sloping shoulders. And the Smasher. A man who might have been carved out of old mahogany, his body tanned to a red-brown hue, his mighty neck and shoulders suggesting some great forest oak.

A dirty blow in the stomach nearly knocked out Swift in the first round. He played for time, trying to recover his wind. Then during one of the intervals, while he was breathing heavily, a note was pushed through the ropes.

'I am sending this to the house by pigeon post. Biddy will bring it to you. Come at once, Boss, Mellish has trapped me. I am locked in an undergrond cell with the tide coming in through the grating. By eleven o'clock I shall be flooded and drowned. The Owls are robbing the box-office. Come as soon as possible to the Blue Lamp Laundry. Wharfside Alley, Rotherhithe. It's sos, Boss.'

It was ten o'clock when Swift received this note. Chick Conway was due to die in an hour's time. If he left the ring now, on whatever pretext, Swift would be mobbed by 'a thousand angry men'. What could he do? What could anyone do, lacking the vegetable resources of a Popeye? Hastily he scribbled a note to Scotland Yard. Then the gong went.

Swift boxed listlessly. But just as the Smasher was moving in for the kill the detective suddenly became 'a thing of fire and tempest', and in no time at all the Smasher was dead meat. Exactly five minutes later Swift was climbing into his Hispano-Suiza – in full evening dress – for another spell of slogging, this time in the alleys of Rotherhithe.

With remorseless regularity Falcon Swift's adversaries in sport turned out to be master crooks. Playing football one day he charged the crack opposing player – a man with bright red hair – and dexterously pulled out two of his hairs in the process. The hairs were not red right down to the roots: they were dyed. The player was an escaped convict.

Soon afterwards Swift was given a temporary commission in the Black Dragoons (Conway being taken on as batman) with instructions to locate a traitor in the regiment. It was all too easy. When the toast of 'The King' was given in mess only one man – the major – did not drink. As glasses were dashed to the floor the major's glass left a red puddle, and Swift was the only one to spot it. It fell to Swift to fight the major with foils, though why he had to fight on a roof top with a sheer drop behind him is not clear. Swift was for ever being drawn into these unequal combats.

It was an adversary called Claude Montana – who sounds like a dance band leader but was the arch-crook of five continents – who gave Swift his most worrying weekend. Montana was fond of a 'dare', and he sent Swift the following document:

'As perhaps you and I are the greatest rivals for fame – each in his own method of interpreting the British Laws – I am challenging you to a little combat of wits before putting up the shutters on what I can proudly boast to be the most successful career in the history of crime. I have decided to take possession of the English Cup at Stamford Bridge Ground to-morrow, Saturday, April 9th, at 3 p.m. precisely. There promises to be a record crowd present, and after all have paid admission I will call round and collect the gate money. I am retiring from active life and I feel that I cannot write success on the last page and close the book until I cross swords with you in this last adventure. One word of warning – be careful that this little affair of mine is not your last as well. I am hoping to bring off a big coup.'

In the succeeding operations Chick Conway was kidnapped again. It is doubtful whether that mirror ring he wore in order to see behind him was really much use. But bruised as he was, he was able to unscrew the perforated sphere, twice the size of a cricket ball, which he habitually kept underneath his jacket (and which his captors unaccountably overlooked) and release a miniature pigeon with another message to his master.

Montana kept his promise. He did succeed in seizing the English Cup and the 'gate' at the time appointed. It was all done from the air, with smoke bombs and lassos, and a confederate here and there on the ground. But Swift's plane was hard on his heels and after a brief chase Montana was shot down.

Swift's adversaries frequently turned out to be exhibitionists. There was one who caused a warning charade to be projected on to the vacant wall of a building. It showed the master crook about to drop the glove which was the signal for shooting a row of gagged and bound victims. But the criminal who best combined a sense of the dramatic with a sense of humour was the one who had Chick

Conway suspended upside down in such a way that when Falcon Swift came to his rescue the opening of the door would lower his assistant into a cauldron of acid. There was an attractive simplicity about his scheme; it required less technical preparation than an alternative device in which the opening of a door closed the circuit which fired a gun aimed at the victim's head.

All the detectives noted so far were content with modest premises in which to live and consult their clients. Not so Martin Track, the detective of the *Dreadnought* (1912). Here was an operator who attached high importance alike to his personal comfort, his personal dignity and his personal safety. He lived in a barbaric palace which looked like a lamasery, built on a high pinnacle over the North Sea. Round the base of the hill ran a high wall a mile in circumference, guarded by armed men, and without visible entrance. Baffled visitors seeking an audience would find themselves suddenly and disconcertingly confronted by a Chinese dwarf dressed in a monk's robe, who would blindfold them and lead them in by an underground passage. Others would be netted from the wall and whisked over the parapet. Still others would be picked up eagle fashion, by padded claws operated from underneath Track's box-kite aeroplane homing to its eyrie, and dropped down a chute on to something soft, there to await the master's pleasure.

Once inside, the clients were usually so overawed by the owner's bizarre taste in furnishing that they would forget to be indignant about the manner of their delivery. The main reception room was resplendent with ottomans, rich silks, tapestries, wild beasts' skins and stained glass windows. Priceless objects of art lay all around; any rash visitor who, fancying himself unobserved, picked up one of these to examine it was liable to find himself surrounded by a device resembling a giant glass cake-cover dropped from the ceiling. Through this the gipsy features of Martin Track would be seen registering disapproval. The chamber was frequented by Grip the Chinese dwarf, two

Japanese servants, a parrot, a raven and a white dove – sometimes all together. There was another audience chamber where Track occasionally chose to receive his clients. It was a cavern cut in the living rock, and patrolled by lions and tigers, which ambled up to sniff the suppliant. Track sat on a stone throne, with a black eagle perched above his head. He wore neither the beard nor the leopard skin which such a situation seemed to call for, merely a lounge suit of undistinguished cut.

In spite of the elaborate defences with which he surrounded himself, Track spent a good deal of time repelling attempts to assassinate him by syndicates of criminals. Once his castle was bombarded with six-inch shells by a pirate cruiser; another time there was an attempt to dynamite his castle rock. Spies who succeeded in crossing the wall were liable to fall into the 'pit of treachery', already littered with the bones of the too-inquisitive. Others were set to work night and day in an underground chamber, in an 'enforced repentance'. Even though they fully repented they were never allowed to emerge; they were lost to the world as irrevocably as Mrs Lovett's pieman in Bell Yard.

Martin Track was a real literary curiosity – a Gothic detective who employed the latest inventions of science. There is no record of him ever playing in a Cup Final.

CHAPTER X

PURE INVENTION

In the late Victorian years was born a fashion for tales of invention – pure invention, invention for invention's sake.

All too soon was Science to become the bride of Mars. But in those closing years of the nineteenth century warfare and invention were still two separate conceptions. Warfare meant donning a frogged uniform and riding down Zulus or Fuzzy-wuzzies; invention meant nothing more sinister than labouring with two chums in a secret workshop to devise a more gratifying means of locomotion in the air, on land or under the sea – in other words building an aeronef,[1] a steam man or a submarine.

Electricity was still a miraculous and exciting novelty, all the more fascinating because it was imperfectly understood. The writers of early science fiction did not go to any great pains to brush up their subject, or to make their inventions plausible. Their machines, whether aerial, terrestrial or submarine, were frequently driven by a baffling mixture of pure electricity, hydraulics, steam or liquid air. The more cautious authors kept to ballooning. It was hard to make any technical *gaffes* in a story of lighter-than-air craft; and if it was essential to cover vast distances rapidly it could always be done by harpooning a whale and hanging on.

The heavier-than-air machine which did service for the best part of a decade, in scores of aerial romances, was shaped like a short, fat airship, with a railed observation platform on top. Above the platform an array of propellers revolved horizontally. These served to raise or lower

1. Jules Vernese for power-operated flying machines. Verne's output of scientific romances began in the eighteen-sixties and continued into the twentieth century; those of H. G. Wells were published between 1895 and 1905.

the vessel, and to scare off pterodactyls. At the front and rear of the craft were vertical airscrews, often two or three to a shaft, and any protuberance in the design was also fitted with an airscrew for good measure. Occasionally the craft had rudimentary wings, usually shaped like those of a bat.

Now and again, however, an inventor turned out something really original. In an early *Marvel* story – 'The Witches' Clutch', by Owen Meredith – was described a flying contraption (if any thing 700 feet long can be called a contraption) based on a principle which seems to have been overlooked by the de Havillands and the Messerschmitts. The artist who illustrated the story baulked at drawing the machine. Let the inventor explain:

I have simply adopted the old theory of Professor Lanis, which was based on the fact that if a vessel is exhausted of its air it becomes lighter than the air and will float in it. He suggested that a metalline vessel might be made so large that when emptied of its air it would not only be able to raise itself but to carry passengers along with it. This is a fact admitted on all sides, but hitherto no metal has been found which could be beaten out sufficiently thin to float in the atmosphere and at the same time be able to resist the external pressure.

The secret of making such a metal is mine. I can manufacture steel which when rolled out into sheets as thick as tissue paper will defy the assaults of any bullet you can fire at it. With this wonderful steel I have constructed an immense tube some 700 feet long and nearly 150 feet in diameter. This, exhausted of its air, will raise a prodigious weight any height. Internally it is divided into chambers which, by a contrivance of my own, can be filled or deprived of air at will. Thus I can regulate the speed of ascent or descent, or if I wish we can remain motionless suspended in space . . .

Along each side of the tube large collapsible wings are attached. They are reversible in action, and guide as well as propel. So closely do they fold up that when in this position they are not easily discernible. Rigidly suspended beneath by hollow columns through which my machinery works is a commodious car built in the shape of a ship. Here is luxurious

NEW BOYS PAPER—GRAND NEW STORIES.

The Boys' Herald 1d.

A Healthy Paper for Manly Boys

EVERY FRIDAY

No. 7 Vol. I. EVERY FRIDAY—ONE PENNY WEEK ENDING SEPTEMBER 19TH, 1903

An Exciting Scene from This Week's Instalment of our Great Airship Serial.

WINGS OF GOLD.

AN AIR-SHIP STORY

The Story of the Most Terrible
and Amazing Journey Ever
Made by Man.

Edited from the Notes of Robert Fordham, Esq.

By the Author of
"BEYOND THE ETERNAL ICE"

[For early chapters see next page.]

A SHRIEK AWOKE THE ECHOES OF THE CLIFFS CROOKS SPRANG ROUND SILHOUETTED AGAINST THE SKY HE SAW A BLACK MONSTER DROPPING TOWARDS HIM ON OUTSTRETCHED WINGS, IT SWAYED AND DROPPED LIKE A STONE. CROOKS FIRED BOTH BARRELS, AND YELLED.

Perils of aviation – 1903

accommodation for hundreds of passengers and here are placed my electrical engines which control the great wings and the air-exhausting pumps. I have invented storage batteries which will re-charge themselves automatically. The nature of the fluid I use is again my secret.

That this invention was packed with menace towards others besides the passengers was admitted by the designer:

Consider how soon I could make the greatest city on earth a seething mass of ruins if I assailed it from my airship with a sufficient quantity of the proper explosive, and I be out of harm's way all the time! In less than half an hour I could sweep the combined armies of the old world off the face of the earth. Therefore I say my discovery will make war impossible.

He was, alas, only one of a long line of fictional vision-aries who were confident they had found the secret of making war impossible. So obsessed was this designer, nevertheless, with the danger of his invention falling into the wrong hands (thus making war possible) that he had it built by Red Indian slave labour in a remote town-ship, suitably called Eureka, of the American West.

Another bizarre flying machine was that which figured in a story, 'King of the Air', by 'Professor Gray', also in the early *Marvel*. Its body was shaped like a launch. Rising from its decks were two pairs of bats' wings, and extending horizontally fore and aft from the body were shafts bear-ing multiple propellers. The test flight was conducted rather optimistically from the top of a tower, instead of from the ground. Here is the inventor's explanation:

'The reason why the outside appears so much greater than the inside is that all round are air-tight chambers in sections. These are filled with gas, and the gas can never escape. Not-withstanding this, I say the tendency of the machine is to gradually approach the earth, though very slowly. Were no one in it, but only the dynamo and batteries which work the wings, it would keep almost level in the air. Get in, and I will show you that theory put into practice.'

Somewhat dubiously, the hero consented, and with difficulty found room among the rifles, pistols, ammunition, provisions, condensers, chemicals and electric stoves which the 'Bat' contained. In no time at all they were shooting buffalo from the air and rescuing a young woman from mutilation by a tribe of gorillas.

The most successful and industrious of the inventors for invention's sake was Frank Reade, whose adventures were retailed under the Aldine banner, in the *Invention, Travel and Adventure Library* ('Jules Verne outdone!'). There were, in point of fact, two Frank Reades – father and son – but nothing is gained by distinguishing between their exploits. A great number of the stories were the work of Luis P. Senarens, an American dime novelist of prodigious output.

According to the first tale in the Aldine series:

Frank Reade was noted the world over as a wonderful and distinguished inventor of marvellous machines in the line of steam and electricity. But he had grown old and unable to knock about the world as he had once been wont to do. So it happened that his son Frank Reade, junior, a handsome and talented young man, succeeded his father as a great inventor, even excelling him in the variety and complexity of invention. The son speedily outstripped his sire.

The great machine shops in Readestown were enlarged by young Frank, and new flying machines, electric wonders and so forth were brought into being. But the elder Frank would maintain that inasmuch as electricity at the time was an undeveloped factor, his inventions of the Steam Man was really the most wonderful of all.

For all his fecundity of imagination Frank Reade, junior, persisted in designing machines in the form of men and horses. His justification was that his Steam Man was a magnificent sight, far more impressive than any puffing billy of the age. The coloured cover showed what looked like an outsize suit of armour, surmounted not by a casque but by a top hat, from which flames were issuing. In his hands the Steam Man held the shafts of a small chariot, which was walled with bullet-proof mesh, and contained apertures for rifles. The young inventor, looking just a shade anxious, held the reins and appeared to be calling on his robot rickshawman for a spurt. In the wake rode a band of hostile cowboys.

For the benefit of new readers, every story contained a summary of how the Steam Man operated:

Steam was the motive power. The hollow legs and arms of the man made the reservoir or boiler. In the broad chest was the furnace. Fully 200 pounds of coal could be here placed, keeping up the fire sufficient to generate steam for a long time.

The reins operated the throttle and whistle respectively. In the chariot at the rear was a store of ammunition and a box of surprises.[1]

Hardly had the Steam Man emerged from the shops than the call for his services came from the West. Reade, junior, with his faithful retinue, Barney O'Shea and Pomp the Negro, jumped aboard, and 'the Steam Man plunged at once into the unexplored wilds of the mighty West . . . for hours he kept on with long strides'.

His normal speed seems to have been between 30 and 40 miles an hour. He could negotiate rivers, always supposing that the water did not come up to his furnace-chest.

The Comanches had thought themselves proof against the shocks of the White Man. But the Steam Man panicked them. It bore down on their encampment, trampling the tardy under its metal feet and scything the horses' legs with the Boadicean knives attached to the chariot's hubs.

1. *The Aldine Garfield Boys' Journal* (named after America's canal-boy-to-White-House President) contained, *c.* 1894, a description of a steam man made by a Mr George Moore in Canada. The designer had been obliged to clothe his invention in medieval armour instead of the contemporary frock coat. Inside the chest was a boiler filled with water, and steam was expelled from a cigar between the model's teeth. The steam man was five feet six inches in height, developed half a horsepower and was credited with a speed of between five and eight miles an hour.

When beating up an Indian camp or a Western township it was important to keep the Steam Man going all the time. If he was faced with a physical barrier he was finished. Running out of fuel was not the problem it might have appeared. Usually 'a coal mine chanced to be near and the bunkers were refilled'. Eventually, after a running fight with desperadoes on a railway train, and the rout of cowboys who sought to halt its progress with lassos, not to mention the rescue of its inventor from the stake, the Steam Man plunged over a cliff and was destroyed.

Frank Reade, junior, did not mind. He now had the opportunity to build a Steam Horse. It was a fine-looking beast, with steam gushing from its nostrils and powerful pistons in its flanks. The chariot was rather better armed and armoured, and could tackle anything up to cannon. There was no need to feel nervous at night, out in the Comanches country, with the Steam Horse for company:

The eyes of the horse lit up by the fierce glow of the magnesium coils threw a brilliant light far out upon the level plain. Frank pulled the whistle cord, and the Steam Horse sent forth his shrill note of defiance.

After surviving peril from quicksands and theft by the Red Indians, the Steam Horse blew up, inexplicably, in a fire. But another was ready in time for the next instalment, an improved model with rubber joints and capable of running on sea-coal, wood or even turf; which did not mean that it could be turned out to graze. Then came the great day when the Steam Horse and a new Steam Man set off across the prairie together. The Man, as was only to be expected, lagged a little, so the Horse had to be throttled down. The two were capable of very effective combination against the Indians; at one point they bore down upon a bunch of braves with a trip wire extended between man and horse. When it was desired to frighten the Indians by night, chemical fire in a variety of colours was discharged from the hollow uprights of the chariot.

The box of surprises now included an electric stockade which could be laid out at night. Redskins who touched the wire could not let go and were plucked off when a suitable opportunity arose.

The next development was obviously a Steam Team. This equipage, which could easily exceed fifty miles an hour, needed a certain amount of skill to handle. When cornering it was necessary to slow down one horse and speed up the other (it was never explained, incidentally, how the other steam monsters were steered). The Steam Team could also be reversed. Each horse possessed, besides fire in its belly, a searchlight in its head. Barney was right when he described the Steam Team as 'illegant'. Yet Frank Reade never succeeded in wholly taming his steam horses. One of them mysteriously began to kick and plunge, then bolted, snorting fiercely, and committed suicide by smashing itself against the walls of a building.

In time Frank Reade, junior, grew really ambitious and invented such hybrids as the Electric Air Canoe, which could hover under its 'suspensory rotascopes' and train a dynamite gun on any object desired; and the Electric Submarine Boat in which the three adventurers travelled under the ice to the North Pole. But it is by the adventures of the more modest steam men and horses that Frank Reade is best remembered.

There is something of a mystery about Frank Reade's rival inventor, Jack Wright, who also had a town named after him on the eastern seaboard of America. It is entirely possible that Wright, who figured in the Aldine *Cheerful Library* (1894), was Frank Reade under another name, though why Aldine should have wished to change his name is not apparent.

Almost parenthetically, the reader was told in the first story of a project on which Wright was working in his spare time – a project which made Edison and Faraday look like amateurs of Science:

Behind Wrightstown there was a vast mass of iron in the ground, a mile long, a mile wide and several miles thick, around the top of which miles of wire had been wound by the young inventor. He had formed an induction circuit in which he was going to have the most powerful of electric currents, and as telephones are made by running wire round the top of a magnetic bar, when this one was charged with electricity the boy expected to hear the explosions which are supposed to be going on continually upon the sun by this big telephone.

Although he was able to squander vast quantities of raw materials merely in order to listen in to the rumblings of solar indigestion, Wright was conscious of his duty towards the town of Wrightstown:

In the central building the boy constructed various kinds of submarine and other kinds of boats; in the right wing he devised the most singular-looking vessels for navigating the air, while the left wing was utilized for building overland contrivances, run, as most of his inventions were, by electricity, steam, compressed air, gas, vacuum and wing force.

It was Jack's concern to provide his township with bigger stores and better factories. Perhaps that is why his inclination was towards building under-water craft rather than flying machines; for it was a bad day if one of his submarine catamarans or electric turtles (with jaws which could snap off a ship's rudder) did not come back with the gold of a sunken galleon.

Jack Wright also penetrated the West from time to time in extravagantly conceived vehicles. One of these was the 'Magnetic Motor', which had a cowcatcher, a pneumatic gun, a searchlight and a steel-meshed cabin for the protection of the occupants. Carried externally was an imposing array of spare 'horse-shoe' magnets, arrayed in neat patterns. These were to be operated, in some unexplained way, 'to increase the speed of the locomotive if it became necessary'.

In this vehicle the intrepid inventor made a Thermopylae stand against hordes of Apaches. When he pulled a lever the vehicle imparted electric shocks to any Indians who were rash enough to touch it. But the Indians seized him nevertheless, tied him to a golden stake and set fire to the faggots. He was rescued just as the warriors were commenting on how bravely he burned, and they probably did not grudge him the load of gold he shipped away, to defray expenses. After that Wright went back to submarine navigation, where the worst that could happen was being sucked halfway into the sac of a giant octopus.

It is fortunate that neither Reade nor Wright entertained dreams of world conquest. They were restless experimenters, and never seemed satisfied with one invention for long. Mere accumulation of wealth was no object. Otherwise they might have been tempted to equip Readestown or Wrightstown on Willow Run lines in order to mass-produce steam men or herds of iron horses, with results which defy contemplation.

Over-soon, this halcyon age of pure invention was to end. The Harmsworth boys' magazines began to see in the fertility of inventors all manner of threats to the security of Britain.

CHAPTER XI

BRITAIN INVADED

At the start of this century Lord Northcliffe did his noisy best to convince the adult citizens of Britain that they were in danger of invasion. He also did his utmost to alert and alarm their schoolboy sons. The boys' papers he founded published a remorseless spate of serials which described the descent of foreign hordes upon these shores and their subsequent bloody repulse at the cost of a sacked St Paul's and a shattered Clock Tower at Westminster.

So fierce became the propaganda against Germany, chiefly in the *Daily Mail*, that in 1910 an American newspaper was prompted to exclaim:

> It will be a marvel if relations with Germany are not strained until war becomes inevitable as a direct result of the war-scare campaign inaugurated and carried on with the most reckless and maddening ingenuity by the Northcliffe syndicate of newspapers.

The 'maddening ingenuity' might well have been a reference to the campaign as conducted in the *Boys' Friend, Boys' Herald*, the *Marvel* and other Northcliffe boys' papers.

The enemy was not always Germany. In 1897 Hamilton Edwards wrote in his *Boys' Friend* a serial, 'Britain In Arms', described as: 'The story of how Great Britain fought the world in 1899, showing what Britons can do for their Queen and Country in the hour of need. A tale of loyalty and devotion to the Old Flag.' Its chief claim to notice is that it envisaged a form of Mulberry Harbour, nearly half a century before that well-publicized device was put into service.

The story opened with joint French and Russian invasion fleets steaming on Britain, Germany being privy to

the plan. After the repulse of the invaders, by the Royal
Navy and the 17th Lancers, Lord Roberts was ordered to
lead an expeditionary force against the 'confounded
French' (Lord Roberts' phrase) to teach them a lesson.
There was a surprise in store for the avenging troops
when they neared France:

As they steamed in towards shore the soldiers were astonished
to find that a landing stage had been erected for them, and
everything was ready for the ships to run alongside and the
British troops to land.

The move of Lord Roberts had been well calculated. A de-
tachment of Royal Engineers had constructed a floating wharf
made to fit this particular point in the shore. This wharf had
been towed across the Channel and fixed while the British
Fleet was bombarding Havre.

In a few hours everything was complete and 60,000 British
troops, 50,000 cavalry and 300 guns were landed on the French
shore.

It was not long before Lord Roberts and General Sir
Redvers Buller had occupied Paris. The French agreed
to pay an indemnity of £100,000,000 and to limit their
army to not more than a million men. 'This,' said the
author, 'indirectly worked for the benefit of the French
people who were relieved from the horrible conscription
which every year sucks the lifeblood of the best of the
younger generation of Frenchmen.'

What Lord Roberts thought of this story, if his attention was ever drawn to it, we can only guess. At one
point he was made to say, *à propos* a traitor on his Staff:
'The low scoundrel! He deserves to be strung up to the
nearest tree; and by Jove! I have a good mind to do it if he
ever returns to the camp.' Certainly Lord Roberts would
have deplored the reference to 'horrible conscription'.

In 1900 the *Boys' Friend*, already heavily weighted with
drawings showing Boers riding down fleeing natives, shooting up flags of truce and bombarding the Red Cross,
carried a series of pictures of warships at death grips. One
which was headed 'What Will Happen in the Next Great

Naval War' bore the caption: 'Here is seen the sinking of a French man o' war battered by the guns of the British Navy. There can be no question that our Navy is more than equal to any two of the great European powers. Long may it be so!' Another in the same issue was captioned: 'This sketch shows a French warship trying to enter the Thames being blown up by a submarine mine.' A third bore the legend: 'The Russian Fleet being driven back into the Baltic by a flying squadron of British warships. This is what would happen if war between Russia and Britain broke out.' To bring the peril right home there was also a drawing, supposedly based on an incident in the news, showing a Frenchman beating an Armenian beggar for daring to address him in English. It bore the title: 'How The French Love Us.'

This policy appears not to have received wholehearted acclamation, for shortly afterwards an editorial note revealed that a reader had pleaded for fewer war pictures to be printed:

He [the protesting reader] will already see that the *Boys' Friend* has once more returned to its old serene style of being purely a boys' paper.

It was all very well making a burst of patriotism when the war first commenced, but to maintain it would be to my mind unnecessary and calculated to annoy my readers. So my friend will find that war will not occupy a very prominent position in the only boys' paper in the future.

Hence those of my readers who have objected to war pictures will now find their objection no longer exists.

The note was a little premature, for in the issue in which it appeared there were more than a dozen pictures of warlike incidents. Soon afterwards the editor, who seems to have repented of his decision, returned to the urgent theme:

Will my readers believe that there are at the present time but a few hundred trained soldiers in this country to resist any attack an antagonistic foreign nation might choose to make on our little island home?

An issue or two later the *Boys' Friend* carried a full-page drawing on its cover showing a shell exploding smack in the middle of Big Ben, with stampeding horse omnibuses in the foreground. The heading and caption ran: 'Bombardment of London – The French at Our Doors: Indeed then would come our great hour of woe when French shot and shell fell in horrible rain along the fair streets of the Empire's City. One shell, for instance, would strike the Clock Tower of the Houses of Parliament, flinging it down in a hail of destruction.'

On an inside page Hamilton Edwards described how easily Britain could be invaded from the Continent. He wrote:

'The Invasion of England' – it is no wild dream of the imaginative novelist, this threat of an invasion of our beloved shore. It is stolidly discussed in French and Russian – ay, and in German – newspapers.

The Frenchman and the educated Russian talk of such a thing as coolly as we talk of sending out a punitive expedition to the Soudan or up to the hills of North-West India.

The *Boys' Friend* returned to the theme week after week, month after month, year after year. So did the companion papers. The *Marvel* gave up one of its issues in 1900 to a 'grand patriotic story' describing an invasion of England by Chinese war balloons. It ended with the Dowager Empress of China being placed in lifelong confinement in a Chinese island, 'vigilantly guarded by British cruisers'. In 1903 the *Boys' Herald* had a series describing how a Captain Strange fought a one-man war against the French in the English Channel. (In the *Boys' Realm* a Captain Handyman performed a similar office.) Strange's vessel was equipped with a giant grab, and he would steam triumphantly into harbour trailing a bantam-weight submarine which he had discovered exploring the British minefields. From it would be decanted a handful of 'shaken Froggies'. Captain Strange also frustrated various treacherous attacks on Gibraltar by the French.

He was quick to realize the deadly peril contained in the announcement that 'M. Santon Dumas', the aerial inventor, had put his knowledge and his wonderful flying machine at the disposal of the French Government. In no time at all M. Dumas's craft was sinking the British Fleet at the rate of one bomb, one battleship.

In 1905 a *Boys' Friend* serial, 'Rule Britannia' (containing a Lion and a Bear in the heading design), described a British punitive expedition to St Petersburg rendered necessary by the outrageous act of the Russian Fleet in firing at defenceless fishing vessels on the Dogger Bank. This story was stated to be on the lines of 'your editor's story "Britain in Arms" '.

Meanwhile, with almost monotonous frequency Sexton Blake in *Union Jack* was uncovering plans by the German High Command to invade Britain. These documents he would send with his compliments to the Cabinet or the War Office. His work did not go unappreciated (indeed he was offered a peerage), but nobody thought of getting down to the job of reorganizing Britain's defences.

The warning was sounded even in the stories of Greyfriars and St Jim's, of Rookwood and St Frank's. Some Territorials taking cover near St Jim's were mistaken for Germans. One of the schoolboys said: 'It can't be the Germans. We all know they are coming some day, but they have not finished their fleet yet.'

In 1908 the *Boys' Herald*, introducing a new serial of aerial warfare, printed a symposium of views by famous military leaders and statesmen on 'Will there one day be a world at war?' Wrote the editor:

It is no secret that the Britisher is hated abroad. In many countries a Britisher is not safe from insult or assault. In parts of Germany, to give one example, our countrymen are openly reviled and sneered at. Why? Because of our huge possessions and colonies, because of our prosperity as a nation, because of our enterprise and grit. Foreign nations are jealous of our progress. They fear that one day we will make a bid to be the conquerors of the world, that one day Britishers will rise up from their homes in every part of the world and make a concerted blow at every other nation.

Foreign spies in Great Britain and our possessions abroad have for years been gathering information with regard to our fortifications and defences, the weak points on our coast line and a thousand other items invaluable to a Power intending one day to strike a blow at us.

As 1914 neared the invasion stories came thick and fast. John Tregellis was the name under which many of them appeared. In 1912 this author had 'The Flying Armada' running in the *Boys' Friend*, and 'Britain Invaded', followed by 'Britain at Bay', in the *Marvel*. In the *Dreadnought* was 'The War in the Clouds', not to mention a serial called 'Doom', which told of a great cataclysm overtaking the earth.

'Britain Invaded' started with the sudden cutting of the North Sea cables and the simultaneous dawn landing of five Army Corps – totalling 200,000 men – at Hull, Boston, Cromer, Lowestoft and Frinton. In the battle from the word 'go' were the cadets of Greyfriars (not *the* Greyfriars) who rapidly became an *élite* corps. The Kaiser, whose yacht was on the scene at an early stage, was not to be killed. That instruction came from 'higher up'. He was to be taken alive.

Britain's gallant armies, under General Sir Sholto Nugent and Lord Ripley, could not hold back the invaders from the northern half of London. Uhlans and Prussian Grenadiers marched through the city. Von Krantz ran up the German flag over the Mansion House, which he made his headquarters, and accepted the keys of the Bank of England. The Lord Mayor elected to remain in office rather than leave his beloved capital, or what was left of it. St Paul's, once again, had become a casualty. The dome was crushed in at one side, like an egg assaulted by a spoon. Big Ben was cleft down to the clock face, and London Bridge was broken down. On the occupied side of the river the Londoners were bearing up 'wonderfully well on the whole … as patient as heroes'. In parts of the

West End life went on much as usual, though there were no cabs as the War Office had commandeered all horses. Food was not plentiful, but the rich were able to buy commodities which they were decent enough to share with the poor. Rioting by the still far-from-docile population was frequent, and was bloodily put down, men, women and children being shot in batches. Barricades were thrown up in Covent Garden and defended to the last woman and boy. Von Krantz began to get desperate. Perhaps he had heard that the Colonies were sending shiploads of arms to the defenders. His worries were not lessened by the destruction of a second wave of German troops in the North Sea. Two cadets of Greyfriars had accomplished this feat by spilling petrol over the ocean, sailing powder hulls into it and then tossing in a match when the German vessels came near enough. Setting the sea on fire had been thought of long before World War Two.

Helping to maintain the morale of Londoners in the southern half of the city was the *Daily Mail*. In the northern sector it came out under German censorship, but in the south it was free to report, with suitable comments, each German ultimatum. Typical headlines were:

THE KAISER'S DEMANDS
BRITAIN TO PAY INDEMNITY OF £100,000,000
CESSION OF NATAL, TRANSVAAL AND RHODESIA
EGYPT AND CAPE COLONY TO BE GERMAN
   PROTECTORATES
HALF THE NAVY TO BE SURRENDERED TO GERMANY
A GUARANTEE NOT TO BUILD MORE THAN TWO
   SHIPS PER YEAR IN FUTURE WITHOUT THE
   GERMANS' CONSENT
DISARMAMENT AND SUBMISSION TO GERMAN RULE

This was greeted by the loyal populace with cries of 'No surrender!' 'God Save the King!' and the hoisting of every Union Jack in town.

'The 'smartest of the afternoon journals' – oddly enough, the Northcliffe *Evening News* – commented:

The great fact remains and the blame with it lies not with our military or naval leaders but with those above them.

WE ARE NOT READY!

We have been taken unprepared; the greatest military nation of the age has caught us napping. Thanks to this belief in our security we have been sleeping, dreaming of universal peace. This is our awakening.

The Northcliffe boys' papers were not alone in their forecasting of war with Germany. In the Aldine *Boys' Own Library*, which started about 1907, appeared a highly imaginative story (No. 44) entitled 'The Aerial War, A Tale of What Might Be', heralding a clash between a scientifically armed Germany and a Great Britain left in the lurch. Doubtless it was digested, like all the others, by German Intelligence, and filed away in the Wilhelmstrasse with a black mark against the author, John G. Rowe.

The story began with a welter of Nihilist plotting in Ireland, where a secret aerial battleship, 'Hope of Russia', was almost ready to set off on a lethal mission, as a result of which 'the name of the Czar would be spoken no longer by the sons of men'. Somehow the Nihilists faded out of the story, and the scene was switched to an aerial dockyard in the South of England where two aeronefs were almost completed. The plans of these had been stolen some time previously by the Germans.

Then the bombshell came.

Long threatened had been the war which had just been declared with our old medieval foe, Germany. Our relations with that country had been strained to breaking-point for months on account of the high-handed treatment of English interests and British-owned property in Germany, by the German Government, and the inflexible attitude adopted by the latter.

Hostilities opened with the arrival of five 'aeroplanic battleships' described as 'huge-winged monsters unlike any bird that ever flew with their wide spread and com-

plex arrangement of aeroplanes [wings] sailing up from
the south-east at a speed that was annihilating distance'.
Halting over our aerial dockyards, the Germans chival-
rously, if rashly, offered to fight duels with our new vessels
ship for ship.

The challenge was accepted, and scores of gunners of
the Royal Artillery were rushed on board the British aeronefs, which rose to do battle with a great buzzing of 'typho-
noids'. There followed an aerial slogging match, rather
in the style of a naval battle, but with a greater variety of
weapons, including 'dynamite torpedoes' and 'liquid
bombs'.

When one of our aeronefs went down crippled, the
Germans unexpectedly forbore to fire on her.

It was the one redeeming point about their behaviour, which
otherwise looked almost like treachery, though everything is
fair in war.

Despite the loss of this vessel, the British won the en-
gagement and captured three enemy craft. 'So ended the
first aerial battle between two great Powers on earth.' But
while the country began to maffick over this 'second Trafalgar' came the news that the German battleships which
had escaped had bombed and wrecked Woolwich Arsenal
on the way home. Also one of the vessels had made a
determined effort to kidnap the King at Windsor, hovering above the window of the Royal bedroom and landing
boarders. In the nick of time the Royal Family had been
smuggled out and removed to unknown destinations.

Public Enemy No 1 was now Aeroduce Swaffenbach
(the rank was the equivalent of Admiral). Operating their
new fog-dispeller (a wireless wave of great intensity) Aeroduce Blundell and Vice-Aeroduce Thorpe cruised the
skies over London looking for him. They found him only
after he had flattened St Paul's and Westminster Abbey.
During a temporary truce, called for by the British, Swaffenbach explained that he had destroyed the cathedrals
not out of malice but only as an object lesson. He ex-

pressed surprise at his moderation. 'The whole of the metropolis was at our mercy, but we have contented ourselves with destroying those two buildings. We spared the Houses of Parliament as they were sitting.'

There was a lot more thrilling action, including a battle staged over the Thames (to avoid damage to property!), a German raid on Tilbury and Shoeburyness, and a big naval battle off Margate, where the German Fleet was easily routed by the doughty British blue-jackets. But this success was not enough. The enemy's aerial strength had to be destroyed at its source. So was carried out the first British air raid on Berlin, where nine aeroplanic battleships were on the stocks. It was so successful that not only were the aerial dockyards burned out but the German Government, in panic, capitulated and undertook to defray the expense of rebuilding St Paul's and Westminster Abbey.

A little later a conference of all the chief powers met at Geneva and signed a treaty by which they mutually agreed to preserve the peace of the world and to submit every international dispute to arbitration by the other neutral powers and abide by the decision arrived at if this were agreed by two-thirds of the arbitrators.

Lord Blundell (as he became) was to be regarded as a benefactor of the human race, since 'by his great victory he probably made war impossible between civilized nations and opened the way for universal peace'.

He was a long way before his time, was Mr Rowe. Technically, he was inclined to be on the defensive, to judge by frequent footnotes quoting scientific justification for his aeronautical detail. In one chapter he tells how the windows of an aeronef iced over, in spite of which the navigators could tell where they were by the ice patterns on the glass. Says the footnote:

Grand, the founder of the Copenhagen Academy of Science, vouches for a case where frost traced upon windows of a coach an accurate outline of the surrounding scenes. No satisfactory theory has yet been advanced to account for this curious phenomenon; but it is well known that lightning has also the singular power of tracing the outline of distant objects on the surface of the bodies through which it passes.

The long-prophesied war with Germany duly arrived, and proved to be a very different proposition from what had been forecast. Four years after it was over, the Amalgamated Press *Champion* (1922) ran a serial describing Germany's 'War of Revenge'.

The author, Leslie Beresford, seems to have underestimated Germany's power of recovery, for he placed World War Two in 1962. He declared in his preamble that in the 'next war' navies and armies would have a small part to play beside the chemists and the scientists.

Powerful wireless will control the most terrible weapons of death, flattening out cities and wiping out whole communities without a single man moving more than to press a button.

The 'war of revenge' was not an undeclared war. Posters had mysteriously appeared all over Britain reading:

In retaliation for the humiliating Peace Treaty of 1919 which the German Government was forced to sign the hour has come when German honour must be avenged. Ignored by the signatories of the Washington Conference of forty years ago and therefore not pledged to peace, the Imperial Government considers itself fully justified in announcing that on and from the morning of Tuesday, April 13, 1962, a State of War will exist between Germany and Great Britain, unless the conditions imposed by the Imperial German Government and handed to the British Ambassador at Berlin a week ago – namely on April 1, 1962 – have been accepted by Great Britain.

(sgd) Johern von Kreutz.

Von Kreutz was described as 'the sabre-rattling Imperial Chancellor' who had come into power when the Republic was replaced by a new Emperor Wilhelm.

The British newspapers and public laughed at this

threat and at the accompanying demand for a
£10,000,000,000 indemnity. After all, Germany had an
inadequate army, no navy whatever and an air fleet in-
ferior to ours. But those who held the British nation's
secrets knew that Germany had elaborate plans for bombarding England by radio-controlled aerial torpedoes from
the Frisian Islands (and if that wasn't V2, what was it?).

The cover of the *Champion* containing instalment
number two of this story showed a crowd in Ludgate
Circus staring at a vast information board which read:

LATEST NEWS

Liverpool and Manchester were bombarded for two hours
after daylight this morning.

Bombardment of Birmingham reported just begun.

London meanwhile was taking it in a big way. The
news was grave enough to bring the King – King Albert –
back from the North.

After the bombardment the Germans invaded. Their
chief secret weapon was the walking machine, a robot-like
tower on mechanical legs, armed with machine guns and
poison gas, which patrolled English cities spreading havoc.
There were also 'flaming balls' – 'a new form of spherical
explosive', and such chromatic novelties as a green ray
and a red gas.

It must not be supposed that the Germans had a
monopoly of inventions. The British leaders, with the
fortifying names of General Duff-Cavan and General Sir
Francis Drake, were able to counter with some very effective triphibians. The winning weapon proved to be a ray
before which all metal vanished – navies dissolved at sea,
aeroplanes disintegrated in the sky, spilling their human
freight, and guns, tanks and even the trouser buttons of
the infantry disappeared into nothingness.

It was a novel illustration of the old principle of
catching your adversary with his trousers down.

CHAPTER XII

PLANETS AND LOST CITIES

AFTER the atom bomb had been dropped on Hiroshima and a dubious world had been invited to hail the birth of the Atomic Age, someone rang up the editor of a science fiction magazine in New York and suggested that Fact had at last caught up with Fiction. Somewhat austerely the editor replied that for a considerable time past his contributors had been writing about the state of affairs which would exist after the world had been destroyed.

Authors of scientific romances in the British blood-and-thunder market were never in quite the same hurry to polish off the world. One or two of them destroyed civilization, but usually gave it a second chance – leaving the moss-grown ruins of the London Underground as an example of what their forefathers could do when they applied their energies to peaceful progress. Blowing up the world or throwing it off its orbit into outer darkness were considered bad form.

Possibly it was the *Champion's* futuristic vision of a German war of revenge which inspired the Allied Newspapers' *Boys' Magazine* to go a step farther. In 1923 it described the war which destroyed civilization in 1934. The story was Michael Poole's 'Emperor of the World'. It had a memorable title picture showing the Emperor, clothed in the skin of a wild beast, presiding at a savage Olympiad amid the ruins of a great city, in the skyline of which stood the reproachful outline of one half of the Tower Bridge.

The nations which initiated this death struggle were not individually specified, but were cloaked under names like the Quadruple Alliance. No details were given of the fighting, but the weapons were chemical. It was 'sufficient that man had created something more powerful than himself and against which he could devise no protection'. Professor Marckstein, the mad scientist who had done more than a little to precipitate the war, locked himself and a chosen few in an underground laboratory, and drugged everybody, including himself, with a serum which would keep them quiet for 200 years, or long enough to let the gases disperse. He was careful to ensure that he himself would be the first to wake. And he kept a few ray pistols handy, just in case.

By August 1934 the earth was 'much as it was at the morning of time'. By the year 2134, when the party came out of suspended animation, it had progressed little. The few descendants of those who had survived the world war in caves and remote places were wandering round in skins, carrying clubs. It was not difficult for anybody with the evil of genius of a Marckstein equipped with a ray pistol to make himself emperor of the world. The youths of the party, however, did not care for the professor's leadership and fled to America, which again was in the possession of Red Indians. One of the tribal ancestors had left a message foretelling some such invasion as this and urging a policy of Isolation:

They will come again by sea and by air, but never again shall America join with Europe, though they speak fair words and utter many promises. There is but one thing to do when Europe comes to America again.

That one thing was to slay the invaders, who were promptly tied to the stake in the old-fashioned manner.

Hereabouts the story seems to have come rather precipitately to an end. In the space of a couple of hundred words or so the heroes toured the world, rallied the vestigial tribes everywhere, fostered the spread of knowledge, the rebirth of radio and aircraft, the formation of Parliaments and the welding together of the peoples of the world, ruled by the Council of Three (the three youthful adventurers).

It was in the *Boys' Magazine* of about the same time that

there appeared an exciting serial, 'The Raiding Planet', describing the war between the Earth and the planet Thor in 1987. Wrote the author, Brian Cameron:

The years between 1923 and 1987 were remarkable by virtue of the colossal forward march made by the world's scientists. There had been extraordinary discoveries; extraordinary inventions were incorporated in the common life of the people.

The tides were harnessed and made to furnish power for the huge mills which thundered day and night along the coast. The sun's rays were captured by day and the electricity manufactured by their heat lighted whole countries at night. A means of transmitting power by wireless had been invented and the huge aeroplanes which plied the world's trade routes were propelled by small electric motors fed from tall steel towers set near the generating stations. The danger of fire in the air was thus practically eliminated and the only disaster which ever befell this method of locomotion occurred when the world's electrical workers came out on strike suddenly and cut off the current. Every machine flying at the time was immediately forced to descend.

Commercial shipping was a thing of the past and the only vessels to be seen upon the seas were the pleasure yachts of men of wealth or else vessels of the gigantic navies of the greater powers.

Among the novelties in the armaments line were the Wilkinson double-explosion gun, which fired a shell for eighty miles, at which point a second explosion in the shell propelled another projectile for sixty or seventy miles; and Flamvior's Gaz de Mort, one canister of which could destroy Paris.

In 1987 astronomers began to get excited about the new planet Thor, 'named after the great push Britain made in the European war of 60 years ago' – i.e. 1927. One professor announced that it was heading towards the earth at 40,000 miles an hour.

'That means,' said the professor, 'that unless something occurs to divert Thor from the course it is taking the event which is popularly known as the end of the world will be an accomplished fact in three weeks from now.'

The earth seemed to know what was coming to it. Quakes were frequent and mysterious fissures appeared everywhere. An epidemic of Fear ran round the world. In Trafalgar Square a speaker attracted an enormous crowd by proclaiming: 'Woe to the people of London, for death is upon them!' Another prophet tried the same game in Paris, but the crowd, showing more spirit – or more fright – hanged him on the spot.

When Thor had grown very big indeed in the sky the last bastion of Britain collapsed: the Stock Exchange closed. Looting began in the big cities. Downing Street crumbled under earth stresses, and the Houses of Parliament were choked by hundreds of refugees from the tidal wave which had engulfed Southwark. Suddenly Thor stopped and began to circle the earth like a moon. This looked like a respite, until Thor began to send out raiding battleships, packed with thousands of men. The invasion was on. Soon the air was full of Thorians in chain mail, each descending individually with the aid of a small propeller behind his shoulders.

London by now was badly bruised. Whitehall and the Houses of Parliament were in ruins. A 'caterpillar machine' had reared itself in the air and fallen smack on the Marble Arch, where the Cabinet were suspected of hiding. An eighty-foot tidal wave caused by a burst dam swept down Bayswater Road. Towers of Terror, each bowling along on a huge ball, were stretching out giant grabs to pick up cars and shake out their occupants. Ray guns were being erected by the invaders right across the Midlands. And a Thorian plan was afoot to create a vast magnetic field to embrace every division of the British Army, causing all items of metal equipment to stick together – an even more embarrassing stratagem than depriving the enemy of his trouser buttons. Meanwhile, lashed by Thorian foremen, slave gangs of Englishmen were digging a gigantic circular pit for some unguessable purpose in Huntingdonshire.

The rest of the world was being savaged too. Berlin and

Vienna had been destroyed, though Paris – as usual – had got off with an occupation. England – as usual – was the one hope of the world. And the one hope of England was the 'atom-destroyer', a powerful disintegrator which operated on the ray principle. It could bisect an aerial battleship or a skyscraper considerably more quickly than an oxy-acetylene flame could bisect a safe. The Thorians were unable to counter it or to capture it.

Why had the Thorians invaded, anyway? The answer was that theirs was a dying planet, and it was a question of finding new living room or perishing. From the outer void Earth had seemed as good as anywhere. But unrealized by the Thorians the moving of their planet from its orbit had solved their problem for them. The axis had been altered and the poles had begun to melt. This meant – as any reader of science fiction knows – the unfreezing of brontosauri and mastodons and sabre-toothed tigers which had been locked for centuries in their remote caverns of ice. These were a thorough nuisance for a while, but you can't have a new world without new (or rather, very old) problems.

The Thorians evacuated Earth in space-ships fired from the great pit of Huntingdonshire. They made a final vengeful effort to destroy Earth by moving up closer to fry everybody, but this attempt was frustrated by Earth's schoolboy delegates on Thor. At the end it seemed probable that the few Thorians remaining on Thor would settle down and make the most of the revived world left to them.

This was only the start of inter-planetary skullduggery. A later story in *Boys' Magazine* – 'Buccaneers of the Sky' – chronicled the departure of a fleet of spaceships, commanded by Lord Harkness, to the Moon in order to foil a plot by the emissaries of Venus. Having discovered the secret of moving heavenly bodies, the people of Venus, who had long wanted a moon of their own, had decided to divert our moon from its orbit and set it spinning round Venus. That a 'have-not' planet should seek to help itself to bits of the Universe like this occasioned great indignation on Earth.

This attempt by Venus to steal the Moon was only one illustration of a failing which characterized the inhabitants of other planets: they were not sporting. Time after time, in stories of planetary adventure, this deficiency was stressed. The dwellers on alien stars might be, and usually were, ahead of us technically; they might have robots working for them as slaves; they might have attained the twin goals of perpetual motion and perpetual life; but they had no more sense of fair play than Neanderthal Man.

In 'The Raiding Planet', for example, the two lads who were kidnapped from Earth and transported to Thor found themselves set down in a mighty arena to entertain the Emperor of Thor and his assembled subjects. Resigned to face bull, bear or lion, they were shocked to find that their adversary was a fighting machine:

It was a thing of steel which moved on a whirling ball at its base, in the manner of the Thorian tower. Above this ball was a square box-like structure, at each corner of which was a moveable arm holding a revolving knife. On the top of this was a smaller box of the same shape as the lower one, and in this was the brain of the machine. The thing was about the same height as a Thorian and as it moved across the sanded floor of the arena it gave a horrible impression of intelligence and grimness of purpose.

The robot was able to judge its distance from its opponents by electrically nerved feelers (presumably a form of radar) and to frame its approaches accordingly. Very soon it had its human adversaries at a disadvantage.

The Thorians were cheering wildly, anxious to see their mechanical idol – so synonymous with progress – slash its victims with its revolving knives and spill their blood about the arena. Their wish would have been gratified had not the boys' guardian professor arrived unexpectedly and yanked the machine's head off, to the crowd's fury.

Not only were the men of other worlds unsporting, they were humourless and void of all ordinary human emotions except the lust for power and the lust for revenge. They were too highly mechanized – that was the plain truth of it. Oddly enough there never seemed to be any women or children; the populace were apparently bred in laboratories. As fighters they lacked initiative and could be swatted in hundreds by any British schoolboy (especially as the lowered force of gravity on an alien planet gave schoolboys ten times their normal agility). In their civil wars – one group were always trying to become a Master Race – experience showed that whichever side could first call in the aid of a British schoolboy would win. One planet even sent a spaceship to fetch an Earth scientist to ascertain the cause of a mysterious plague among the people of the planet. The scientist rapidly diagnosed the complaint and prescribed lime juice.

Not that the inhabitants of other planets were necessarily human or even approximately human. In a *Union Jack* story entitled 'In Trackless Space' (1902) the Moon was found to be occupied by giant spiders fitted, for no very adequate reason, with electromagnets. A trip to Venus revealed only giant centipedes and scorpions. There was gold in vast quantities on the Moon, but the hero declined to allow it to be exploited for the admirable reason that there was enough gold causing trouble on Earth already.

The method of propulsion of a space-ship was left vague in those days.[1] Someone would discover the secret of overcoming the force of gravity, just as someone else would trip across the secret of invisibility, and that was that. An anti-gravitational device would be incorporated in the sky-ship. You turned it one way to start and the other way to stop. As you were liable to be travelling at

1. In the first recorded story of an interplanetary voyage – Bishop Godwin's *Man in the Moone* (1638) – the hero was carried to the Moon in twelve days by birds called 'gansas', harnessed to an intricate framework.

more than a million miles an hour you had to be careful how you handled it. The crook who had stowed away on board usually chose the difficult moment of deceleration to emerge from his hiding-place with a flame pistol.

There had to be a reason for inter-planetary travel. Mere lust for scientific knowledge was not enough. Sometimes (as has been seen) it was necessary to prevent the theft of the Moon or the wanton destruction of, say, the Pole Star. Sometimes it was necessary to check up on what another planet was doing in the Milky Way, or to forestall an attempt at colonizing useful nebulae, or to protect trade routes through Space. Or it might be necessary to do battle with a Space Emperor.

Those who today devour stories of inter-planetary adventure in American-style magazines like *Astounding Science Fiction* may find the details more plausibly worked out, but the basic plots are not necessarily more ingenious or audacious. The space-ship Llanvabon in one of these stories was introduced when she was decelerating at full force because she was 'a bare half light-year from the Crab Nebula' (itself six light-years long) and a matter of 4,000 light-years from the Earth. Experts on board the atompowered, radar-equipped Llanvabon had been photographing the Nebula on the journey 'by the light which had left it from 40 centuries since to a bare six months ago'. The space-ship's speed had been stepped up to seven times the speed of light by an over-drive. She was equipped with blasters

... those beams of ravening destruction which take care of recalcitrant meteorites in a spaceship's course when the deflectors can't handle them. They are not designed as weapons, but they can serve as pretty good ones. They can go into action at 5,000 miles, and draw on the entire power output of a whole ship. With automatic aim and a traverse of five degrees, a ship like the Llanvabon can come very close to blasting a hole through a small-sized asteroid which gets in its way. But not on overdrive, of course.

That 'of course' points the difference between the super-confident science fiction of today and that of fifty or sixty years ago, with its defensive footnotes. Another extract from a latter-day story in *Astounding Science Fiction* will show how the language and the mood have changed:

He was looking into a long, severely utilitarian room, lit only by flickering glows reflecting from the grouped scanner videos and the moving centre strip of the Ro-Eye Relay.

Standing back a few feet from the disks and frames and the fluxing panels was a lean man in Tech overalls, a knob micro adjuster in his hand. He was curiously rigid.

Lodner clawed at his belt, failed to find his disciplinary stun gun, turned to Horovic, who was entering behind him, and yanked the cruel stud-nosed electronic clubber from the chief guard's waist clip.

The Tech man said, 'Sir, I've done nothing.'

Lodner threw the gun on him. The Tech man tried to dodge. But the bolts sledged the quick-turning shoulder and head. The Tech man was slapped over. He lay huddled on the floor.

Lodner tossed the stun gun on a flange between the stills and the fluxing panels. 'I'll teach you to stand and gawk at me, you swine,' said Lodner coldly....

While British authors always sought to teach Thorians and Plutons to play a straight bat, some American authors used the universe as just another place to play cowboys and Indians. S. J. Perelman in his *Crazy Like a Fox* quotes this science-story description of the main street in Jungletown, a stop-over town full of clip joints somewhere in the Cosmos:

Here were husky prospectors in stained zipper-suits, furtive, unshaven space-bums begging, cool-eyed interplanetary gamblers, gaunt engineers in high boots with flare pistols at their belts, bronzed space-sailors up from Jovopolis for a carousal in the wildest new frontier-town in the System.

The hero of this story, 'Captain Future, Wizard of Science', had a bodyguard which Mr Perelman considers one of the most paralysing in modern fiction. It consisted of a white-faced, green-eyed, rubbery android, or synthetic

'The thing curled itself round the space ship and its weight
nearly pulled the machine to the ground ...'—The Hotspur

man, and a giant metal robot with a pair of photo-electric
eyes who carried a transparent box in which was housed a
living brain, with two glittering lens-eyes.

Against this, an extravaganza in a recent British thriller,
in which a hovering space-ship is encircled and dragged to
the ground by a giant earth-worm is a trifle of the imagination. Or is it?

Closely akin to the inhabitants of other planets in that
they lacked the sporting instinct and a sense of humour,
and were too easily exploited by Master Races, were the
inhabitants of Atlantis. This fabled land – first hinted at
by Plato – was rarely discovered in the same place twice.
Sometimes it appeared mysteriously as an island right in
the middle of the shipping lanes; sometimes it rose and
sank at the whim of the Lord of Atlantis; sometimes it was
to be found snarled up in the Sargasso Sea; and once at
least it was found flourishing in a gigantic air-lock at the
bottom of the Atlantic. Ferrers Lord discovered a rival to
Atlantis in Mysteria (*Boys' Friend*, 1905). This was a
rising-and-sinking island which surrounded itself usually
with a mysterious rosy glow but was capable of changing
hue – in fact, it seemed to have most of the properties of
a mighty Wurlitzer. It was an over-lush and over-odorous
isle, full of armoured crabs and black owls as bigs as rocs.
Ferrers Lord did well to blow it to smithereens.

As unpredictable in location as Atlantis was the City of
El Dorado, which shifted between the Peru of the Incas
and the Upper Amazon. The natives of El Dorado were
rarely friendly, which is not surprising in view of the
numerous attempts made by syndicates of crooks to rob
them of their basic raw material. Those inveterate dis-
coverers of lost civilizations, the boys of St Frank's, once
chanced upon El Dorado (in Brazil) when it was being
administered by the master crook, Professor Zingrave.
Their flying machine disabled, the boys found themselves
marooned on an island of molten gold, from which they
were eventually rescued in a giant chariot drawn by tri-
ceratops. The flying machine became airworthy again, and

it only remained to beat off an attack by pterodactyls before returning to England, home and school. Short of a love interest, it is hard to think what other ingredients could have been introduced in that memorable story.

But others may remember the lost England discovered by the boys of St Frank's in the Antarctic. Warmed by a hot stream flowing below an unexplored part of the ice cap, this Kingdom of Wonder was inhabited by settlers of English descent, who had strayed there three centuries before. They wore olde Englishe smocks, their architecture was neo-Elizabethan and they talked prithee English. As usual, the explorers arrived just in time to take part in a civil war; this time between the subjects of King Arthur and King Jasper, whose territories were separated by a mighty wall beside which the Great Wall of China was a trench in the ground.

That elusive temperate land beyond the Antarctic ice-cap had been cropping up for years. It had figured in Sidney Drew's serial 'Wings of Gold' in the first *Boys' Herald*, a story which began with the killing of a mysterious bird-lizard in far southern latitudes and continued, week by week, with the shooting of pterodactyls (these always came first), labyrinthodons, plesiosauri, giant crustaceans, mastodons, dog-apes and ape-men; with fitting accompaniments in the way of volcanic eruptions, meteor showers and sub-aqueous explosions.

In a serial by Reginal Wray in the *Boys' Friend* (1915) the lost land with its full range of prehistoric monsters was located under the Yorkshire moors – a vast world complete with sea and sky buried beneath the earth's crust.

A lost civilization story – whether set in the Antarctic, the Himalayas, the Amazon or the high lands of Africa – was always a good excuse for trotting out the prehistoric zoo.[1] The reader soon grew to know the warning signs. If it wasn't a strayed bird-lizard or a sea-serpent, it was an obscene smell rising from the primal mists in a valley

1. Conan Doyle's *The Lost World*, which possibly inspired some of these stories, was published in 1912.

where no man had trodden before. The explorer-hero would say, 'We are on the edge of the oldest things.' An author who worked affectionately through the Book of Evolution was John Hunter. Not content to leave his saurians in their lost valleys he must needs bring them to Britain. In 'The Menace of the Monsters' in an early issue of the *Boys' Magazine* he described the return of a vessel known as No. 913, 'homeward bound from a place that lay beyond the dark curtain of one of the world's unknown places, her open hatches emitting a sickening odour of musk and foulness, a slow steam of hot and monstrous living creatures'. Behind glass shot with wire two serpents lay, thicker than the body of a bull and 120 feet in length.

They stood, the two boys and the Big Game Hunter, in a hallway of the world that was before man trod the heated earth, in the presence of the things that waded in the stinking marshes of the forming world, that sunned themselves on the steaming mudflats, that fought and tore and ravened across this cooling universe aeons and aeons ago.

How the big game hunter proposed to off-load this old-fashioned cargo was not made clear. The point is of no consequence because the ship was wrecked and the animals made their way ashore. It was the invasion pattern all over again, with prehistoric monsters instead of German armies. Pterodactyls clawed down aircraft, stegosauri derailed the Royal Scot and invaded packed football grounds. A giant ape clung to one side of Tower Bridge and plucked a taxi from the opposite bascule. A dryptosaurus measured its length on Brighton pier, crushing it into the water. One motoring party found themselves driving into the jaws of a pelagosaurus, which had cunningly opened its mouth where a bridge had once been.

But the monsters did not have everything their own way. The wastage was considerable. One was torpedoed by a naval craft, another was bisected by the *Bremen*. Some killed each other, and some were slain by the most formidable foe of all – the English climate. What the mon-

sters really missed was the good white mist they had been
accustomed to. Nature played into their hands and sent
a London fog. So the monsters, having concluded a trium-
phant provincial tour (with special attention to Newcastle), concentrated on long-suffering London. St Paul's
for once was spared, but before the last creature had been
accounted for Nelson had been lashed from his monument. There was some satisfaction in the fact that the
Admiralty Arch resisted all efforts by a dryptosaurus to
overthrow it. It is one of the few London landmarks which
have not been gutted by fire, wrecked by gunfire or sapped
by earthquake.

CHAPTER XIII

MAGNET AND *GEM*

The year is 1910 – or 1940, but it is all the same. You are at Greyfriars, a rosy-cheeked boy of fourteen in posh tailor-made clothes, sitting down to tea in your study on the Remove passage after an exciting game of football which was won by the odd goal in the last half-minute. There is a cosy fire in the study and outside the wind is whistling. The ivy clusters thickly round the old grey stones. The King is on his throne and the pound is worth a pound. Over in Europe the comic foreigners are jabbering and gesticulating, but the grim grey battleships of the British Fleet are steaming up the Channel and at the outposts of Empire the monocled Englishmen are holding the niggers at bay. Lord Mauleverer has just got another fiver and we are settling down to a tremendous tea of sausages, sardines, crumpets, potted meat, jam and doughnuts. After tea we shall sit round the study fire having a good laugh at Billy Bunter, and discussing the team for next week's match against Rookwood. Everything is safe, solid and unquestionable. Everything will be the same for ever and ever. That approximately is the atmosphere.

In those words the late George Orwell summed up the world of Billy Bunter's Greyfriars. The passage quoted is from an article published in the literary magazine *Horizon* in 1940. It was one of a series in which Orwell sought to assess the social significance of sundry neglected art forms, including the comic postcards of Donald McGill and the hard-boiled novels of James Hadley Chase.

The author of the Greyfriars stories, then in his seventies, found the article in *Horizon* 'entertaining' but misconceived. His name was Charles Hamilton, though he preferred to call himself Frank Richards. At various times he had written under the names of Martin Clifford, Owen Conquest, Ralph Redway, Winston Cardew and Hilda Richards. For thirty years his schoolboy characters had delighted the readers of the *Magnet* and the *Gem*. To his publishers he was a prodigy; they paid him some £2,500 a year for his annual stint of one-and-a-half million words. At this time – 1940 – few people knew the range of his activities and his aliases.

Charles Harold St John Hamilton, to give him his full name, was born in 1876 in a small house in Oak Street, Ealing, the sixth child in the family. Though his journalist father was hardly a rock of stability, he was able to attend a succession of private schools and emerge with a strong taste for the classics. By the age of seventeen he had begun to make money by his pen. It was a time when school stories had grown markedly more popular. The writers of them steered clear of the excesses of Jack Harkaway even as they avoided the anguish and mawkishness of *Eric, or Little By Little*. Hamilton's light and easy approach was welcomed in a variety of markets. By his own account one of his first publishers, after meeting him, cut his rate for a short story from five guineas to four, a more suitable fee for one of immature years. The first of the famous schools Hamilton created was St Jim's, in *Pluck* in 1906. The earliest boys there were Jack Blake, Herries and Digby of the School House and Figgins & Co. of the New House. Later arrived the monocled Arthur Augustus d'Arcy ('Bai jove, deah boy!'), second son of Lord Eastwood, whose passion in life was the study of trouserings. Many an opportune fiver he screwed out of his 'governor'; many a topper he lost in the rough-and-tumble of St Jim's. He is said to have been based on an unusually elegant sub-editor (a profession not usually remarkable for immaculacy).

In 1907 Charles Hamilton was asked to turn out a series of fortnightly school stories for a new magazine to be called the *Gem*, edited by Percy Griffith, a voluble talker with large ideas, of whom Hamilton writes amusingly in his *Autobiography*. Griffith invited the young author to find himself a suitable *nom-de-plume*, and eventually the choice fell on Martin Clifford.

But Martin Clifford did not open the *Gem*. The cover of the first number showed a bulldog bloodily at grips with a python – an incident in an adventure story called 'Scuttled'. Clifford did not make his début until No. 3 with 'Tom Merry's Schooldays'. The school was Clavering College. Newly arrived Tom was considerably embarrassed by the attentions of his nurse, Miss Priscilla Fawcett. He found himself in a study with Harry Manners, Lowther and Gore. But all was not well at Clavering. One day there was much speculation because a stout gentleman with a fur-lined coat called to see the Head. All too soon 'the grip of the money-lender fell on Clavering, and the fine old buildings came down to make room for a newly discovered coal seam'. Tom Merry was consoled by the news that he would be transferred to St Jim's.

Behind this outrage on a venerable seat of learning (who said that harsh reality never impinged on a school story?) the astute reader of the day may have deduced an editorial merger. Henceforth the St Jim's stories from *Pluck* were to be amalgamated with the Tom Merry yarns in the *Gem*. In succeeding stories Merry, Manners and Lowther all made their several ways to St Jim's, there to be known for the next thirty years as the Terrible Three of the Shell.

The change of schools was a bit hard on Tom Merry, who had been well ragged already on joining Clavering. This was the scene when he arrived at St Jim's:

Jack Blake of St Jim's fell into the arms of Herries, while Digby collapsed into the embrace of Arthur Augustus d'Arcy.

The chums of Study No. 6 in School House seemed completely overcome.

'What is it?' murmured Blake in tones of exaggerated faintness. 'What can it be? I wonder if it has a name?'

'It is something new,' said Digby. 'I have never seen anything like it before off a Christmas tree. Fancy meeting that!'

'It is weally too extwaordinary,' said d'Arcy. He pushed Digby into a sitting position on the step and solemnly adjusted his eyeglass, and through it took a survey of the wrathful Tom

Merry. 'It is alive. I can see its features move. What a stwange object!'

This elaborate display was conducted in full presence of Tom Merry's nurse, who was chaperoning her charge. Not surprisingly she began to wonder whether St Jim's was all it was cracked up to be. However, Merry was strong enough to stand up for himself and soon he earned more suitable recognition. His stock rose after he had helped Ferrers Locke, the detective (of Baker Street), to investigate some nefarious activity in the vicinity of St Jim's. Said the detective afterwards:

'You've been a lot of help to me in this case. I am deeply obliged to you and I shan't forget it. I do not know what you will be when you leave school, my boy. But if you want a start in life as a detective there'd be a place for you as assistant to Ferrers Locke. You can bear that in mind. Good-bye.'

Thus Tom Merry might easily have become a Tinker or a Nipper, but he seems to have preferred to be the leader of the Terrible Three. Ferrers Locke, a relative of Dr Locke of Greyfriars, grew tired of waiting and acquired the services of Jack Drake, who was to masquerade when occasion demanded as the duffer James Duck; a cynical example of playing ducks and drakes.

The *Gem* was by now prospering. It became a weekly, which meant twice as much work for Hamilton. Then the restless schemers of Amalgamated Press, quick to distinguish a steady demand from a passing craze, had the idea of launching a companion paper to the *Gem*. They looked speculatively at Charles Hamilton. He was wasting a good deal of his time on music and art. Obviously he ought to be properly harnessed. They pressed him to do the same for the new paper, the *Magnet*, as he was doing for *Gem*. Hamilton, with only slight misgivings, agreed. He ceased composing songs. After all, this demand might not last long, and he was well able to satisfy it.

The demand, however, was clamant and perennial. For more than thirty years Charles Hamilton 'never failed to maintain his million and a half words a year and often exceeded that quota'.[1] (A million and a half words represents nearly twenty ordinary novels.) He did not, of course, write every story in the *Gem* and *Magnet* – the feat would have been utterly impossible. A number of stand-ins wrote under Charles Hamilton's pen-names, mostly in the *Gem*; and, as the years went by, old stories were re-published.

It was on the *Magnet* that Charles Hamilton chose to lavish most of his talent. For this paper, under his best-known pseudonym of Frank Richards, he invented a new school, Greyfriars. Here he launched his most famous character, Billy Bunter – 'a really first-rate character', as even Mr Orwell has testified; a character who was to become a household word not only in Britain but in the more improbable parts of Empire.

The first story in the *Magnet* was entitled 'The Making of Harry Wharton'. It started with Colonel Wharton draining a glass of port at Wharton Lodge and, saying, with an air of decision, 'Send Harry Wharton to me.' His nephew entered with a bad grace. He was wilful and headstrong, completely wild and given to insulting his tutor. There was but one solution: Greyfriars.

On the train Wharton met Frank Nugent and fought with him, unsuccessfully. Wharton at this stage did not know how to scrap and that was fatal. Nugent, the bloodshed over, offered a gift of toffee, which was spurned. Soon Wharton found himself in the same study in the Remove as Nugent, Bunter and the bully Bulstrode. The problem now was to learn how to master Bulstrode. Wharton's stock rose when he saved Nugent from drowning; so that was one firm ally ...

The two juniors – friends now and for life henceforth – shook hands upon the compact. And so Harry Wharton faced his difficulties again to fight his battles out with a true chum by his side to help him win.

Gradually he triumphed – rescuing a lad from drown-

1. Frank Richards: *Autobiography*.

ing or a maid from burning – until he became the established leader of the Famous Five (Harry Wharton, Bob Cherry, Frank Nugent, Johnny Bull and Hurree Jamset Ram Singh).

William George Bunter, of Bunter Court, the Fat Owl of the Remove, leading keyholer and tuck fancier of Greyfriars, was meanwhile being groomed for stardom. In his *Autobiography* Charles Hamilton reveals that, back in the nineties, he offered Bunter to an editor (unnamed) who pooh-poohed the idea. Sensitive to criticism, he relegated Bunter to the far recesses of his mind. He has said that the Bunter who finally emerged was derived from four persons – one a fat sub-editor (the staff of Amalgamated Press again), another an acquaintance who was always blinking over his spectacles, another a person who was always expecting but never receiving a postal order, and an unnamed Victorian statesman of more than ordinary fatuousness. The owner of 'the tightest trousers in Greyfriars' (for some reason they were striped horizontally and vertically, instead of just vertically) was the perfect butt. He had few praiseworthy qualities, other than the power to incite mirth. He would borrow money with no intention of paying it back; he would pirate another boy's tuck without a qualm; he would unscrupulously feign afflictions, not omitting blindness, deafness and dumbness, to further his ends; he would spend infinite guile trying to persuade others to be his catspaws; and indefatigably he would seek popularity by claiming the credit for other fellows' acts of bravado – like throwing missiles at masters. Therefore no one felt markedly sorry when dogs ran away with his sausages, when he sank his teeth into decoy pies filled with pepper, when pins punctured his hide or when he slipped or was thrown into stream, fountain, barrel or horse trough. Withal he was never really unpopular – a fat boy never can be. Although he was supposed to be 'the guest nobody wants at Christmas', everybody would have been disappointed if he had failed to crash the party. His machinations were so bare-faced and his *bonhomie* so sus-

Scene from an earlier Greyfriars – 'Tom Torment, or The Lads of Laughington School'

pect that it was a fellow's own fault if he was taken in. His eager, 'I say, you fellows ...' generally earned an exasperated 'Kick him, somebody.' Doomed to be the object of everybody else's japes, Bunter devised retaliatory ones and was the victim of those too.

Bunter never walked anywhere; he rolled. He did not possess hands, but paws. He did not speak, he bleated. Where other boys laughed 'Ha! Ha! Ha!' Bunter laughed 'He! He! He!' Under the simplest cross-examination he was a total loss. Here he is accused of playing pranks with a pin:

'No, sir! Nothing of the kind,' stuttered the confused fat Owl. 'I never had a pin, sir. Besides, fellows are allowed to have pins, sir. I – I – I – was going to pin a page into my Latin grammar, sir. Not that I had a pin, sir!' added Bunter cautiously. 'You can ask Skinner, sir. He knows – he gave it to me.'

From a modest début, Bunter grew steadily in popu-

larity until in due course the cover of the *Magnet* carried
as a sub-title 'Billy Bunter's Own Paper'. For good
measure, he was given a heavyweight sister, Bessie, who
shared all his unlovely traits, adding to them the female
vice of vanity. Sometimes Bessie rolled into the stories of
Greyfriars, but ordinarily she was to be found at Cliff
House School in the schoolgirls' paper, *School Friend*.
Charles Hamilton (as 'Hilda Richards') launched her, but
other masculine pens took over. Gradually Bessie (or
Elizabeth Gertrude, to give her her real name) acquired
rather more amiable qualities than her brother.[1]

After Bunter, one of the best-remembered characters of
Greyfriars is the Nawob of Bhanipur, Hurree Jamset Ram
Singh:

His complexion, of the deepest, richest olive showed him to
be a native of some Oriental clime, and though clad in the
ordinary Eton garb of the schoolboy there was a grace and
suppleness about his figure that betrayed the Hindoo. Slim
and graceful as he was, however, there was strength in the
slight form, and although the lips and the dark eyes were smiling there was resolution about the chin and a keen observer
would have seen that the Indian was no mean antagonist if
put upon his defence.

The newcomer's greeting from Bulstrode was slightly
less than cordial:

'My only pyjama hat! You should have taken the other turn
to the lunatic asylum.'
'If I have made mistake the apologize is terrific. But if this is
not the lunatic asylum what are you doing here, my esteemed
friend?'

This stung Bulstrode to cry 'Nigger!' whereupon
'Inky' (as the Nawob was nicknamed) speedily showed that
he had the necessary basic training to hold his own at
Greyfriars.

If he had one ambition, it was

1. There is a theory that the lesser success of Bessie Bunter was due
to the fact that girls recoil from the idea of fatness.

'to induce my esteemed and ludicrous chums ceasefully to stop talking slangfully and to use speakfully only the pureful and honoured English language as taught by my learned and preposterous native tutors in Bhanipur.'

Charles Hamilton did not mind saddling himself with a character who spoke Babu English, or for that matter with characters who spoke pidgin English ('Me tellee whoppee. Me solly. Only jokee'); German ('Vell, Bulstrode, I tink you vas vun pully and a prute'); French ('Nom d'un nom d'un nom – I am smozzer viz somezing!'); or American ('I'm allowing those guys are sure loco'). At some early stage Hamilton (or his editors) decided to standardize all exclamations. 'Oh crikey!' 'Oh scissors!' 'Oh my hat!' and 'What the thump –' were suitable comments on almost any irregular happening. More picturesque phrases were inspired by Lewis Carroll's 'Jabberwocky' – 'you frabjous fathead!' and 'you blithering bandersnatch!' Bunter's yells were rendered as 'Yarooh!' or 'Yaroop!' the number of 'o's' depending on the intensity of the anguish. Spluttering, as on a mouthful of soot, was denoted by variations on 'Gurrrrgh.'

There can have been few readers of the *Magnet* and the *Gem* – in the humblest or the highest schools of London or Glasgow, Calcutta or Singapore – who could not find one character with whom to identify themselves, or their playmates. Periodically were published character studies of all the leading figures, with pen and ink drawings. In these potted biographies it was to be noted that no one was insufferably good or irredeemably bad. Even Vernon-Smith, the Bounder of Greyfriars, son of a *nouveau riche*, was by no means without virtue. It was recklessness, not viciousness, which impelled him to break out of school at night to hobnob with rough company in the Cross Keys public-house.

Other well-remembered denizens of Greyfriars are bumptious Horace Coker, the fool of the Fifth, who was always trying to 'whop' one or other of the Famous Five; Gerald Loder, prefect of the Sixth, given to tormenting

fags; the languid Lord Mauleverer (Mauly to his friends),
who, if his creator had allowed him to grow up, would
doubtless have become one of those heroic silly asses;
Fisher T. Fish, the boastful moneygrubber with all the
vices of the New World, and Putnam van Duck, his more
likeable fellow countryman; and of course those long-
suffering pedagogues, Dr Herbert Locke (headmaster),
Mr Henry Samuel Quelch (Remove) and Mr Paul Prout
(Fifth).

The boys of St Jim's and Greyfriars, like those of St
Frank's were for ever touring the globe on their holidays,
though their creator seems to have drawn the line at El
Dorados and Lost Valleys. On a treasure hunt in wildest
Africa Bunter became king of a fierce cannibal tribe and
narrowly escaped the pot. Once, Christmas overtook the
boys of St Jim's as they were travelling by airship over the
Rockies. The airship crashed and there was a free-for-all
with a party of Crees. St Jim's suffered casualties, 'but
there was not one of them so badly hurt that he could not
take part in the huge Christmas dinner that was held on
Christmas Day, some little time later, at the new Sioux
camp'.

Refreshed by travel, back the lads would come for a
new round of priceless japes, dropping soot-bags from
windows, squirting ink through keyholes, filling toppers
with treacle, upturning the desks of swots, ragging new
masters, breaking up love affairs, clashing with suffra-
gettes, capturing spies, tracking down ghosts, rescuing each
other's sisters from gypsies, and confounding the plans of
those mufflered, unshaven, simple-minded roughs who in-
fested the purlieus of Greyfriars and St Jim's. Once the
Fourth Form at St Jim's suffered the excruciating ordeal
of being taught by a woman, who called the boys by their
Christian names. Sooner or later every boy in the school
would be accused, and later acquitted, of theft. Sometimes
a fellow would allow himself to be expelled in order to
shield someone else, perhaps a young brother. Another
time an old boy who had been drummed out in disgrace

would return to plot a cunning revenge. One such committed a 'standing offence to Greyfriars' by erecting a sign near the school stating that he, late of Greyfriars, was prepared to repair boots and shoes with efficiency and dispatch. Periodically some too-enterprising youth would be dunned by bookmakers. Periodically some boy's father would lose all his money, through trying to pay off liabilities incurred by dishonest fellow-directors, and the boy would be threatened with a transfer to a more modest establishment. When this calamity loomed the editor would never fail to invite the sympathy of all his elementary school readers. Tom Merry had a bad spell. He spent his Christmas holidays down and out in London, too proud to tell his pals of his plight. The Head of St Jim's heard about it and offered him a job as temporary form master – a job he was gratified to accept. But if Merry thought the boys' sympathy was such that they would refrain from japing him in his new role, he was disappointed.

Not all the boys at Greyfriars and St Jim's were boarders. St Jim's had Dick Brooke, a day boy who (according to the editor of the *Gem*) won the admiration of his schoolfellows by 'his grand fight to keep his end up'. Day boys were not numerous, and, explained Martin Clifford, 'the other fellows regarded them with a good-natured tolerance, as if they really were not quite St Jim's fellows'. The Terrible Three generously allowed Dick Brooke the use of their study to swot for a scholarship. One day Brooke's father, drunk, arrived at St Jim's, looking for his son, 'surrounded and followed by a laughing crowd'. But the Terrible Three did not laugh. D'Arcy summed up their view: 'Bai Jove. This is fwightfully wuff on Brooke.' They sallied out in time to prevent the cad Levison from inciting Brooke senior to perform a song and dance, and d'Arcy averted further embarrassment by inviting the noisy visitor to tea in his study. Eventually Dick Brooke, deeply grateful for this lesson in *noblesse oblige*, steered his contrite father home. The honour of St Jim's was saved. Dick Brooke may have been introduced as a sop to working boys, but it is likely that they preferred d'Arcy for their hero.

New boys from the outposts of Empire were constantly arriving at Greyfriars and St Jim's. If it wasn't an Australian bringing his own kangaroo it was a young cowboy riding a horse bareback. These Dominion recruits were always well received and soon conformed to pattern.

It would be ungallant as well as misleading to omit mention of Cousin Ethel, who at one time (*c.* 1911) cropped up in almost every story in the *Gem*. D'Arcy, whose relative she was, used to invite her to St Jim's whenever he could. She was a great favourite with the Terrible Three, who were prepared to scratch from a football match in order to entertain her, even if it meant losing the match. And well might they be loyal to her, for did she not once personally intervene to save them from a flogging, herself receiving a sharp cut on the arm in the process?

According to the illustrations, Cousin Ethel had a pretty face, a smart feather in her hat, and a skirt only a few inches from the ground. Figgins, of the New School, had an especial weakness for her. In the story 'Figgy's Folly' he ran away from school in order to see her safely to Paris, where she was to attend finishing school. Ethel was travelling with an elderly female relative who, Figgins felt, was an inadequate protection against the attentions of Frenchmen. In the train to Paris the lovesick youth became furiously jealous of an elderly Frenchman who entered the compartment and started to make conversation. Figgins' feelings towards Frenchmen were those of all right-thinking fellows at St Jim's:

That a man old enough to be the father of a big family should take such minute care of his personal appearance offended Figgins' notion of the fitness of things ... that a man of elderly years should cram his feet into boots too small for them filled Figgins with disgust ... that an elderly gentleman should have no better business than to get himself up as a

young fellow and go about making himself obnoxious to
decent and sensible people seemed an outrage to Figgins . . .

But that was not the full indictment against this unseemly foreigner:

The elderly Frenchman moved with grace and elegance but
at the same time with a slight suspicion of stiffness, and once
or twice Figgins thought he heard a slight creak – which confirmed him in his suspicion that the Frenchman wore stays.
Figgins had heard that Frenchmen wore corsets to improve the
elegance of the figure. Words could not adequately express
Figgins' opinion on the subject.

Cousin Ethel had preserved a certain coolness towards
Figgins so far. Their fingers had overlapped for a second
or two on the boat, but she still called him 'Figgins'. When
the train was wrecked, as it was bound to be on a French
railway, and Figgins distinguished himself in rescue operations, Ethel went so far as to catch both his hands and
press them to her lips. Figgins came back with 'Ethel,
dearest!' which made her blush and turn away. Later
when he apologized for his jealousy in the train, Ethel
'pressed her hand to his lips', though whether to silence
him or to let him kiss her fingers is not clear. Finally
Figgins expressed the wish that someone would punch his
head, but all that happened was that Ethel pressed his
hand. Figgins, of course, returned to St Jim's a hero, instead of a disgraced runaway.

Girl cousins and sisters caused a number of embarrassing moments in these stories. 'Ashamed of His Sister'
(*Gem*) told of the ordeal of the poser Valentine Bishop
when he learned that his sister was going to visit him at
St Jim's:

Maud with her sweet and patient face, her plain dress of
materials cheaper than those worn by the maids at St Jim's,
and her long fingers showing only too plainly signs of long,
long sewing which she did partly that her brother might have
pocket money in his pockets . . .
Ashamed of his people!

To what lower depths of meanness could he have descended? Ashamed of the sister, the kind patient sister who worked for him and who regarded him as the finest and the grandest fellow the earth held!

Oh hang! Oh dash it!

There were other boys who were ashamed of their brothers, or ashamed of their fathers. One had the mortification of seeing his convict brother in handcuffs at the local railway station. The ending to this story does not read like vintage Hamilton:

Strangely enough the shout [that the convict was innocent] rings through the stone wall to the convict. But Convict 79 does not shout. The tears are thick upon his eyelashes and he sinks upon his knees on the stone floor, his hands clasped together, to render thanks for his freedom to the Giver of all good. And Lynn, after a moment's silence, joins him there. In that moment all is atoned for; it is light – light and happiness – after long darkness, for the man who has been pent in the convict cell shunned by his friends and disowned by his brother.

There was a third academy created and maintained by Charles Hamilton under the name of Owen Conquest: Rookwood, in the *Boys' Friend*. While St Jim's boasted the Terrible Three and Greyfriars the Famous Five, Rookwood offered the Fistical Four (Jimmy Silver & Co.). Yet three schools were not enough for the indefatigable Charles Hamilton. As Ralph Redway he wrote Wild West stories about the Rio Kid for the *Popular*, and he also turned out schoolboy detective stories in the *Modern Boy*, another Amalgamated Press paper.

The secret of the common identity of Frank Richards, Martin Clifford and Owen Conquest was artfully, and most successfully, preserved. Indeed, 'the artfulness was terrific', as Hurree Jamset Ram Singh would surely have testified. Many a false trail was laid. At one time Martin Clifford had a series describing the schooldays of 'Frank Richards and Co.' at a backwoods school at Cedar Creek. Occasionally there would be stories describing visits by Frank Richards and Martin Clifford to the schools of their creation. Those double Christmas numbers were the occasion for some remarkable flights of fancy. It was by no means unusual for the boys of Greyfriars, St Jim's and Rookwood to celebrate Christmas under the same aristocratic roof; one such story was boldly proclaimed as 'by OWEN CONQUEST in collaboration with those worldfamous authors FRANK RICHARDS and MARTIN CLIFFORD'. There was another story about a Christmas party at which Frank Richards, Martin Clifford and Owen Conquest playing billiards, with Hilda Richards marking up the score. One editor is said to have written a piece of whimsy about meeting Richards, Clifford and Conquest together in the flesh.

A certain tendency to repetition is to be seen in the Hamilton style. At times a sub-editor surgically disposed could have cut out every other sentence without impairing continuity; it would have been a futile labour, however, because indignant readers would at once have exclaimed, 'This is not the genuine article.' They revelled in the repetitious style. Here is a characteristic passage:

Argument was waxing warm among the Famous Five of the Greyfriars Remove.

Four members of the famous Co. were trying to dissuade the other member – Bob Cherry! Bob was not to be dissuaded.

Bob's face, generally as bright and cheery as the spring sunshine, was clouded. It was grim with wrath. For once, the best temper in the Remove had failed its owner!

Bob seldom, or never, remembered offences for long. But it was not ten minutes since a heavy hand had boxed his ear! That ear was still scarlet, and had a pain in it!

Not that Bob was a fellow to make a fuss about a spot of pain. But ears were not boxed at Greyfriars School. It was an indignity. It was one of the things that were not done ...

Defenders of the Hamilton style point to the classical allusions with which it is punctuated. So-and-so would choose, like Agag, to tread delicately ... 'The glory had departed from the House of Israel, so to speak ...' 'Contempt, the Oriental proverb says, will pierce the hide of the tortoise.' But how many readers were able to relish the enormity of the howlers which d'Arcy and the others perpetrated when construing Latin?

Now to the Orwell article. Any *Horizon* readers who themselves took *Magnet* and *Gem* in their youth – and they were probably more numerous than might be supposed – doubtless took a guilty pleasure in Charles Hamilton's spirited defence of himself and of his schoolboy creations.

What, asked Hamilton, was life like in 1910 – the period which George Orwell appeared to hold in peculiar horror?

I can tell him the world went very well then. It had not been improved by the Great War, the General Strike, the outburst of sex-chatter, by make-up or lipstick, by the present discontents or by Mr Orwell's thoughts upon the present discontents.

Young readers ought not to be allowed to worry over the instability of life, he said; a sense of security was good for them and made for happiness and peace of mind.

Orwell had been disappointed that sex was never mentioned in *Magnet* and *Gem*.[1] These journals, pointed out Charles Hamilton, were intended for readers up to the age of sixteen. 'If Mr Orwell supposes that the average Sixth Form boy cuddles a parlour maid as often as he handles a cricket bat, Mr Orwell is in error.'

On the charge of snobbishness, Charles Hamilton felt he had no need to apologize:

1. Sir Noel Coward registered the same complaint. In his autobiography *Present Indicative* he claims to have derived great enjoyment in youth from reading *Magnet* and *Gem*, but adds: 'They were awfully manly, decent fellows, Harry Wharton and Co., and no suggestion of sex, even in its lighter forms, ever sullied their conversation. Considering their ages, their healthy-mindedness was almost frightening.' Re-reading one of the later *Magnets* (*c.* 1937) he was conscious of a 'tender emotion'. 'There they all were, Harry Wharton, Frank Nugent and Billy Bunter, still "Ha-Ha-Ha-ing" and "He-He-He-ing" and still, after twenty-four years, hovering merrily on the verge of puberty.'

It is an actual fact that in this country at least noblemen generally are better fellows than commoners. My own acquaintance with titled Nobs is strictly limited; but it is my experience, and I believe everybody's, that – excepting the peasant-on-the-land class, which is the salt of the earth – the higher you go up in the social scale the better you find the manners and the more fixed the principles. The fact that old families almost invariably die out is proof of this; they cannot and will not do the things necessary for survival.

In any event, he claimed that a working-class boy at Greyfriars or St Jim's was represented in a popular light.

Mr Orwell would have told him that he is a shabby little blighter, his father an ill-used serf, his world a dirty, muddled, rotten sort of show. I don't think it would be fair play to take his 2d. for telling him that!

Accused of habitually representing foreigners as funny, Charles Hamilton was content to point out that foreigners *were* funny. They lacked our sense of humour.

Doubtless it was galling for Charles Hamilton to read that the Greyfriars and St Jim's stories were derived from the school stories of Desmond Coke and Gunby Hadath, authors to whom he owed nothing; and that the slang was inspired by Kipling's *Stalky and Co*. But what perhaps irritated him most was Orwell's statement that, since the stories which had filled *Magnet* and *Gem* for a generation could not all have been the work of one man, they were written in a style easily imitated. In the view of Charles Hamilton and of his more discriminating admirers, the stand-ins had failed to catch the master's style. It was not enough for an imitator to borrow the familiar standardizations and stylizations. Only Charles Hamilton could bring full credibility to the academies of Greyfriars and St Jim's. (The *Magnet Companion*, compiled with the aid of W. O. Lofts and published by the Howard Baker Press, lists all the *Magnet* stories and the names of their writers. The most prolific substitute writer seems to have been G. R. Samways. From 1931 Hamilton wrote all the *Magnet*

*The Greyfriars games master deals with the cad who came
back to disgrace his alma mater* – The Magnet

stories. This handbook also gives biographical information on the *Magnet* editors: Percy Griffith, Herbert Allan
Hinton, John Nix Pentelow and Charles Maurice Down.)

The *Horizon* controversy died down, but a bigger jolt
was waiting for the creator of Billy Bunter. Already the
Gem had died, in late 1939; now, in the early summer of
1940, the *Magnet* and a score of other boys' papers were
discontinued, on the grounds of paper shortage. Charles
Hamilton was left with his typewriter and his characters.

But it took more than Hitler's war to kill off Billy
Bunter. In 1947 he turned up as plump and unabashed as
ever in Sparshott School, in a shilling series published by
William Merritt. Soon Charles Skilton started publishing
Bunter in seven-and-sixpenny volumes, with oustanding
success. Subsequently Bunter achieved the dignity of being
published by Cassell. As a further measure of his status,
his adventures became available in Braille.

In 1952 Bunter achieved a new notoriety: he made the

first of many appearances on BBC television. The search
for a suitable actor received a good deal of delighted attention in the press and fat boys from far and wide were
trotted out for audition. Mere fatness and a passion for
jam tarts were not enough, however; eventually the choice
fell on the actor Gerald Campion. The least of his quali-
fications was that he was a married man; but his portrayal
of Bunter found favour, in the main, with the old guard,
even as it did with the post-*Magnet* generation.

Visitors to Charles Hamilton in his bungalow at Kings-
gate-on-Sea, near Broadstairs, found a reserved old
bachelor in skull cap and dressing-gown, with trousers
cycle-clipped against the cold. Nobody seems to remember
him as the young man who, on his own admission, gam-
bled away his hard-earned money on the green-clothed
tables of Europe (and what would Harry Wharton and
Co. have said about that?). In his *Who's Who* entry, under
Frank Richards, he said nothing about the *Magnet* and
the *Gem* but described himself as the 'author of the Billy
Bunter books and plays – over 30 books and about 45
plays on television'. It was as if he regarded all the rest
as ephemera. His recreations appeared as 'chess; the
classics, especially Horace and Lucretius'. He was at his
typewriter until the end, which came on Christmas Eve,
1961.

Since then, the ephemera have been accorded hard-
back status. A series of volumes composed of facsimiles of
vintage *Magnets* has been issued by W. Howard Baker,
the author-publisher who came to the rescue of Sexton
Blake. Reviewers wondered why nobody had thought of it
before.

St Frank's School has already been touched upon in the
chapter dealing with Nelson Lee, the detective who became a schoolmaster there. In many ways it was modelled
on Greyfriars and St Jim's; its admirers claim that it has
been unfairly overshadowed by the other two. The characters included such derived types as Hussi Rangit Lal

Khan, 'a dusky son of India with typical, characteristic features' (lacking more specific information than this, the artist was hardly to be blamed for representing him as an English boy with a dark complexion); Yung Ching, 'a typical Chinese boy of the upper class, thoroughly westernized, very tricky, although pretending to be innocent. Good-natured, but difficult to understand; very deep'; the Hon. Douglas Singleton, 'languid by nature, generous and easy-going and a slacker in form'; Sir Montie Tregellis-West, out of the same stable; Timothy Tucker – 'speaks in a peculiar shrill voice and uses grotesque and exaggerated language. A crank in every way. Is popularly believed to be "touched", but is really well aware of all he is doing. Is a bold agitator ...'; and a remarkably unattractive character called Enoch Snipe – 'slightly hunch backed, long neck, protruding head, habitual foxy expression, protruding red-rimmed watery eyes, scanty hair, a crawly cringing nature, will take a blow from a fag and creep away, but is cunning, vindictive and venomous ... an out-and-out worm'. St Frank's, of course, had its hearty manly characters too. Edwy Searles Brooks, who turned out the St Frank's yarns in the *Nelson Lee Library*, wrote a brisk and always readable story.

One of the more memorable episodes at St Frank's was the Communist revolt of 1921, when the school was divided into Rebels and Loyalists. The revolt was the work of agitators, of course, and behind the agitators was Mr Trenton, one of the masters. Smooth-tongued but a 'black-hearted scoundrel', he was trying to cause the downfall of Dr Stafford, 'the dear old Head'. He had succeeded in secretly doping the Head with a drug, each dose of which resulted in an exhibition of terrible violence and savagery. These outbursts had an unfortunate effect on the less disciplined members of St Frank's. There were meetings of protest. Then at the close of the Christmas holidays some of the dissidents, arriving a day or two earlier, stormed the Ancient House and refused to leave it until their demands for reform were granted. Timothy Tucker

was the ringleader. When Nelson Lee expostulated with
him he retorted:

'You do not seem to realize that the regime of tyranny and
bloated autocracy is over. In fact the time has now arrived
when the humble slaves come into their own. Hitherto the
modern schoolboy has been downtrodden and enslaved. We
have decided to end this state of affairs. This great blow has
been struck with the intention of setting an example for every
other school in the kingdom to follow.'

At this Nelson Lee 'laughed outright', and the Loyalists,
lacking his sense of humour, 'yelled with anger and shook
their fists'.

Tucker and three of his confederates put their heads
together and called themselves the Supreme Council of
the Revolution. Their word was law. They issued a mani-
festo entitled 'For the Cause of Liberty', which read:

'The Rebels in our command are all members of the new
schoolboy union, a body which has been organized and invented
for the good of every British schoolboy ... Masters must un-
conditionally surrender all control to the boys. Form councils
will be inaugurated and we, the Supreme Council, will undertake to supervise the whole work of propaganda and organization ...'

Surprised – very surprised – were the Rebels when a
notice was posted up in the Head's name stating that he
had seriously considered the proposals advanced, and had
agreed to the formation of Form Councils as an experiment. This notice, like most notices at St Frank's, was a
hoax. Nelson Lee, who knew that the Head had not issued
it, nevertheless advised the Head not to disown it. Far
better, he argued in his new role of political ádviser, to
let the Communists come a cropper of their own accord,
rather than to try to suppress them by force, and thus
breed the sense of injustice in which Communism would
thrive.

The cover of the next number – 'The Communist
School' – showed a class of boys going through the motions

'Ow! Ooooogh! Aytishoo! Grooooogh!' gurgled Bunter –
The Magnet

of what they supposed to be Communism. One was out in
front arguing with the master, two others were half-sitting
on their desks chatting, and a fat boy was scoffing a tray
of jam tarts on a small table beside him. The desks were
in irregular rows. Only the Loyalists sat to attention.

But the blackest hour was yet to come. One of the
Head's more unfortunate outbreaks coincided with a visit
of the heavily-titled Board of Directors, on whom he committed grave assault and battery. Shortly afterwards he
and Nelson Lee were removed from office for their in-
competent handling of the situation, and the rascally
Trenton was appointed headmaster.

St Frank's was not the only school in the grip of Communism. Explained one of the conspirators to his associates:

'It is in the great public schools of England the young mind
receives its education. And if we can only commence our
propaganda at school and thoroughly get our doctrines fixed

in the minds of the coming generation the results of our efforts will be far-reaching and abundant. It will be a long process, but that is only to be expected.'

'Too long,' said one of the plotters, who wanted to see bloodshed.

It turned out that Nelson Lee was right. The schoolboy Communists and the crooks exploiting them overplayed their hand. At the end Lee was able to explain to the juniors:

'The whole thing is an insidious propaganda among the youth of this country. Quite a number of people may laugh at the whole thing and say that it is an absurd scare. They will declare that the boys of Britain are too sensible to listen to such rubbish. But people who talk in that way are all wrong. When the mind is young it is liable to get wrong ideas fixed. And such ideas stick ... The boys grow up with these notions firmly instilled, and although they may not actually know it they have a certain secret sympathy with this revolutionary movement.'

Luckily next week there was a great flood at St Frank's, which had already been ravaged by a great fire, and the whole unfortunate episode was rapidly forgotten. Except, perhaps, by George Orwell.

When their school was not in the throes of revolution or being harried by master-crooks the boys of St Frank's had friendly contacts with Irene & Co. of a neighbouring girls' school. Edward Oswald Handforth, who was affluent enough, and old enough, to run an Austin Seven, was at an advantage here. Such fraternization, however, was too much for Master T. E. Pattinson, of Walthamstow, who wrote in to protest. He was in a minority. Shortly afterwards the author of the offending story wrote:

In the November 22nd issue I had occasion to point out to Master Pattinson that his dislike of Irene & Co. in the stories was a little selfish and unfair ... But it now gives me the greatest pleasure to report that Master Pattinson has acted like the real sportsman I always hoped him to be ... He agrees that Irene & Co. have a perfect right in the St Frank's district and that any girls have an equal right to be readers of the Old Paper.

It was in 1933, when the boys of St Frank's were cruising on the yacht of Lord Dorrimore, the biggest schoolboy of them all, in the China Sea, that the announcement was made:

Last Issue of *Nelson Lee*.

But our chums of St Frank's and our editor invite you to meet them again in the *Gem*. From now on *Nelson Lee* and the *Gem* are one paper.

That kind of merger (this was for 'policy reasons') usually bodes ill for one or other party. The stories of St Frank's now went to the back of the magazine. In the winter of 1933 Lee found himself in charge of the flying section of St Frank's touring the unknown Amazon in an airship. Parents had in all cases been consulted and an examination had been held to select the lucky lads. From these far-flung operations all our schoolboys returned. But in 1934 the jaunts ended. Nothing more was heard of St Frank's – except in reprints in the *School-Boy's Own Library*.

A feature of the Greyfriars, St Jim's and St Frank's weeklies was the incorporation of a 'school magazine' purporting to give latest news and gossip, and to be edited by a different boy each week. Here solemn arguments went on over 'Should tuck shops be abolished?' Here tables of fictitious sports fixtures were meticulously kept. And here, in response to repeated demands, were printed the names of all the fellows in the Remove, the Fourth or the Shell, sometimes study by study.

In World War One there was a separate publication called the *Greyfriars Herald*, which tempted its readers with offers of 'monster tuck hampers', the kind which in normal times were broached nightly in the dormitories of Greyfriars and St Jim's. To William Bunter this open-handedness with foodstuffs must have seemed the final injustice, for already he had been paraded by his more patriotic chums with a notice on his chest reading: 'The Prize Hog. This animal has been caught helping the Germans by wasting food supplies.'

The *Greyfriars Herald* was 'edited by Harry Wharton', and listed as 'fighting editor' Bob Cherry. One early issue advised schoolboys not to read it under the desk but to 'show it to your schoolmaster'. It added:

Schoolmasters are sometimes regarded as preoccupied, narrow-minded individuals who take no personal interest in the fellows committed to their charge; but I know that such is not the case. As a general rule a master is also a friend and a jolly good friend.

The 'Pen Pals' pages gave an illuminating picture of where the *Magnet* and the *Gem* circulated. Readers were invited to state with whom they wished to correspond and on what subjects. Here are typical entries:

Abu Baker bin Ali Bashah, Kampong Kuchai, Ipoh, Perak, F.M.S., Malaya: age 14–17; photography, fretwork, cycling.

Miss B. Srini, 20, Pulau Tikus Lane, Penang; girl correspondents, age 15–18; views, autographs, books, film stars and films. America, England, Australia, Egypt, Persia and Honolulu.

Miss R. Cheater, 171, Upper Newtonards Road, Belfast, Northern Ireland; girl correspondents, age 16–18; any topic; anywhere except British Empire.

G. Hershkovitz, 18, Beit Hasheva Street, Tel-Aviv, Palestine; age 14–16; stamps, sports, postcards; Eire, Australia, Canada, South Africa, British West Indies and Pacific Islands.

It was noteworthy that girls usually wished to correspond only with girls. Other readers, by design or accident, gave no hint of their sex.

Finally, let no one go away under the delusion that the kind of things which happened in school stories never happen in real life. The newspaper files of early 1947 contain a report of a court case in which one headmaster was alleged to have banded his boys together to storm and seize another headmaster's school.

CHAPTER XIV

DUNDEE SCHOOL

THE Amalgamated Press were still seated firmly in the saddle after World War One. Paper shortage had had surprisingly little effect on their boys' publications. True, the *Boys' Realm* had been forced into suspended animation in 1916, and the *Dreadnought* had been merged with the *Boys' Friend*. On the other hand new publications had been launched during the war – among them the *Sexton Blake Library*, the *Nelson Lee Library* and the *Greyfriars Herald*. Towards the end of the war the *Magnet* and *Gem* had carried urgent appeals to 'Eat Less Bread' and even Bunter had been forced in the national interest to curb his consumption of tarts and doughnuts. But no one in Greyfriars or St Jim's emerged noticeably emaciated. It had been a jolly war.

There was little time for self-congratulation, however. Another kind of war was brewing. Soon the first shots of a broadside fired from nearly 500 miles away began ranging on Fleetway House. This was the half-expected assault from Scotland. For once the Scots were attacking Fleet Street from their native heath instead of from Fleet Street itself. In the van of the assault was the *Adventure* (1921), the first of a string of new weeklies which the publishers were to describe – on occasion – as the 'Big Five'. All had vigour unhampered by tradition and imagination which knew no fetters.

In 1922 the Amalgamated Press launched the astonishingly successful *Champion*, which speedily reached a half-million sale. Its first editor, F. Addington Symonds, modelled it, not on the *Adventure*, but on Pearson's *Big Budget* (1897), which had run for a decade under A. C. Marshall. Only later did the *Champion* begin to resemble its Scots rivals. Also in 1922 the Scots, undaunted, pro-

duced the *Rover* and the *Wizard.* Two years later Amalgamated Press put out the *Champion*'s companion paper,
the *Triumph.* Not till 1930 did the newcomers launch the
Skipper; three years later came the last of the five – the
Hotspur.

The headquarters of the 'Big Five' was in Dundee, tra-
ditional centre of jute, jam and journalism. Over many
years the firm of D. C. Thomson & Company had acquired
a reputation for shrewdness, hard-headedness and giving
the public what it wanted. Its newspapers and weekly
journals had a down-to-earth, forthright quality; they
made no pretence at aiming at a highbrow public.

Similarly, the boys' papers now launched by this firm
had no false airs about them. They were produced by
young men of fertile mind, some of whom had undergone
a course of indoctrination. From the irruption of these
weeklies dates the modern period of boys' thrillers; already there is a generation which remembers them with
affection, in some cases to the exclusion of all others.

Perhaps the editors of the *Adventure*, the *Rover*, the
Wizard, the *Skipper* and the *Hotspur* might have been
able to point to differences between their journals, but
the boys who bought them almost certainly could not. All
five carried sport, adventure, school, historical and futuristic stories (possibly the *Hotspur* ran more school stories
than the others). All five had a similar format, the same
type of coloured cover and line illustrations which always seemed to have been drawn by the same hand, with
everything – particularly shoulders, chests and biceps – a
little larger than life.

Whereas the journals of the Amalgamated Press were
frequently produced with an eye not merely on boys, but
on old boys, the Thomson 'Big Five' appeared to be aimed
exclusively at boys – and rather younger ones at that, if
such lures as 'A hundred biff balls free' are any guide. To
judge by the illustrations, the schoolboy heroes of the
Dundee magazines were a year or so younger than the boys
of Greyfriars and St Jim's, and the general get-up and

presentation of the stories was just that shade nearer to
the 'comics' which the readers had begun to outgrow. Incidentally, the drawing of 'The Editor' at the head of the
Editor's Chat usually showed a smooth, handsome young
man who could not have been using a razor for more
than five years, even though he might claim an impressive
knowledge of the odd corners of the world.

The Thomson papers were – and are – a curious mixture of inhibitions and lack of inhibitions. The problem
of sex was very simply solved: girls did not exist. Occasionally, but very occasionally, there might be a reference to some fellow's sister being rescued from a fire, but
it could just as easily have been a tame goat or a sack of
flour. This ban on females was probably the most absolute
in the history of boys' magazines. The existence of an opposite sex was admitted only in the advertisements of
magazines which catered for a fellow's sister: 'Famous
Perfumes Free – This week Phul Nana.'

Though they refused to admit that girls had any part in
the daydreams of adolescence, the Dundee School recognized such innocuous aspirations in a boy's subconscious
as the desire to fly with bird-like wings, or to make himself
invisible. It was a bad week when not one of the Big Five
had a story about a boy who could walk about unseen.
These were not the first invisible boy stories by a long
way, but hitherto the exploitation of this idea had been
left to the 'comics'. In Dundee they recognized the ever-
green appeal of the invisible boy and promoted him from
the comic strip to the adventure columns. One week it
was a boy who sniffed at a mysterious phial from the East
and dissolved into thin air. The next it was a lad who
rubbed himself with a literal brand of vanishing cream.
Happily this cloak of invisibility was employed as a rule
only for the discomfiture of the pompous and oppressive;
bad boys and Peeping Toms never got access to it, though
sometimes master crooks did. Closely allied was the kind
of story in which a lad got possession of a 'magic box' or
a 'magic mixture' which would allow him to shrink ob-

jects to a fraction of their real size, thus giving him a tremendous pull over objectionable relatives and interfering policemen. There was another kind of magic box which contained the antidote to the law of gravity. Not only could the hero ascend vertically to escape from embarrassing situations, but he could suspend an unpopular form master in mid air, with his feet trying desperately to reach the ground. There were also X-ray spectacles (already encountered in Sexton Blake stories and elsewhere) enabling a person to look through opaque objects; an embarrassing device which once again happily never got into the hands of Peeping Toms.

Thus did the *Adventure, Rover, Hotspur, Skipper* and *Wizard* dream their readers' dreams for them. The Amalgamated Press had tended on the whole to respect the laws of Nature; but plausibility and probability never worried the writers from beyond the Tweed. Their chief concern seems to have been to avoid any charge of conventionality.

None the less, certain very marked fashions are to be noted in the Thomson stories. For example, there was the vogue for the short series of stories based on the recovery of a specified number of objects, all of which are necessary to provide the solution to some puzzle. The first number of *Adventure* in 1922 carried a story of this kind. Next time it would be a story of twelve seaports scattered all over the world in which were twelve sailors each with different portions of a map tattooed on their backs; all would have to be traced before the sunken galleon with the gold aboard could be located. Another time it would be a casket which could be opened only by seven keys, all of which were distributed in hidden cities and lost temples. To the obvious objection: 'Why not break open the casket?' would be furnished an answer: 'Because any attempt to force the casket will release powerful acids which will at once destroy the contents.' A variation was the story in which Chief Sitting Bull would distribute seven feathers from his headdress to each of his seven sons, with the proviso that war might not be declared until all seven feathers were brought together again. It did not follow that a series involving seven feathers or twelve pieces of map would necessarily run for seven or twelve instalments. If the series was a flop the hero could recover two or more keys or pieces of map in one instalment; if it was a success he could be tricked out of the whole lot and have to start again. Quick success on the part of a hero is always a suspicious sign; the most popular performers receive the most set-backs.

Another favourite seam was that of a boy, or a pair of boys, travelling the world (and making a comfortable living) with some ingenious and improbable machine. Perhaps a super-bulldozer, which would help explorers to excavate for hidden treasure, or dig a river bed to prevent a town being engulfed by flood; perhaps an out-of-date and battered double-decker bus pressed into commission in a gold rush; perhaps a desert yacht, towed in calm weather by camels; perhaps a new type of amphibian or a soundless helicopter (useful for rescuing chums from eagles' nests); perhaps an undersea tractor, just the thing for recovering five silver ikons from five sunken ships. None of these youthful adventurers seemed to have any difficulty in raising capital to launch their highly speculative enterprises. Any promising pair of 14-year-olds could acquire a streamlined motor cycle combination (and a licence to drive it), a movie camera (and the ability to operate it), and then tour the world taking photographs of assassinations and revolutions which the film companies fell over each other to buy.

They were a godsend, the film companies. Thus a 'strange car crawling up the steep slopes of the mountains of Hawaii' turned out to be the property of a daredevil who toured the world collecting noises for film and broadcasting companies – anything from the song of a nightingale to the roar of a Hawaiian volcano.

Another adventurer who seemed to have no difficulty in finding clients, even in the heart of the jungle, was

Crispin Gaunt, who ran a portable light railway for the benefit of members of eclipse-viewing expeditions stranded with their heavy equipment, or zoo-stocking parties anxious for assistance in transporting their heavier and more obstreperous mammals. The portions of his locomotive and track were carried by indefatigable natives of the highest morale. Gaunt, who personally carried no portion of the railway, strode in front, a powerful figure wearing speckless silk jacket and shorts, a monocle and (in rotation) the ties of the twelve schools which he had been asked to leave, but for which he still cherished a loyal affection. To keep up morale, Gaunt's retinue argued incessantly about First Division football.

Gaunt, it will have been observed, wore the usual jungle monocle. The natives were invariably distrustful of any white lord who did not carry a window in his eye. Even jungle animals accepted this convention. There was an illustration in one of the 'Big Five' showing an ape proudly wearing a monocle.

Which leads to another favourite seam – the animal story. Caligula may have made his horse a consul; in Thomson's Wild West they made horses into sheriffs and dogs into deputy sheriffs. Husky stories seemed especially popular; there were dogs which did everything but talk; there were dogs which wrote their own first-person stories of their adventures; there were dogs which became king of all the other dogs, and organized dog revolutions against savage masters, and raids upon their masters' towns. Running dogs a close second in popularity were kangaroos. Not only were they required to fight human beings, but they had to put on the gloves to fight goats, ostriches, apes and anything on two feet or four which could be persuaded into a boxing ring. But standing head and shoulders above boxing kangaroos, sacred ostriches, wild bulls and super-sagacious horses was O'Neil, the Six-Gun Gorilla. O'Neil's master, a Colorado prospector, had taught him to dig, fetch firewood, haul up buckets of water from the mine shaft and generally make himself useful about the shack. Unfortunately he had also taught the gorilla how to load and fire a revolver. All went well until O'Neil's master was murdered. Then the gorilla strapped on pistol and bandolier and set off on the trail of vengeance. For a hundred miles he followed the murderers, picking them off one by one. He discovered a quite remarkable talent for holding up stage-coaches, and his hairy presence filled the occupants with more alarm than the descent of any Spring-Heeled Jack. On one occasion he held up a coach, mounted the driver's box and drove the terrified horses on the heels of a flying gunman. It was the highwayman story brought up to date.

In school stories the *Hotspur* and its companion papers strove hard to be different. The schools were boarding establishments without the aristocratic pretensions of Greyfriars and St Jim's. They were 'tough' schools and on the whole they produced tougher pupils; but the boisterous extroverts they bred had no vice in them. The usual crooked ex-pupils came back to ruin the name of their *alma mater*: outbreaks of ventriloquism and invisibility were chronic; and no school was without its terrible twins or tricky triplets. One journal even produced a headmaster who was twins: the clever one conducted the classwork and the athletic one organized sport, and whichever one was not on duty hid in a cottage in the woods. Burwood College, where this neat piece of integration went on, must have been a much smoother-running place than St Jude's, where the Head turned out to be a savage who suffered from attacks of atavism, during which he dressed up in a leopard skin and swung about the roofs.[1]

Beachcomber's Narkover and Dickens's Dotheboys Hall were saintly seminaries compared with some of these schools; but discipline caught up with them all. There was a school in which not merely one master, but every master, was a wanted man. There were schools in which

1. For an amusing dissertation on the popularity of twins in juvenile literature, see Geoffrey Trease's *Tales Out of School*.

both masters and boys were starved. There was one school – especially got together, regardless of expense, by a tyrannous father anxious to discourage his son from being a schoolmaster – in which cretinous boys tried out Spanish Inquisition practices on such masters as were rash enough to go about unarmed by clubs and red-hot pokers. The masters appeared to be less interested in achieving a state of discipline than in wreaking their personal revenge. To such schools would be sent new masters, clean-limbed young men with a straight left, who would try to fight everybody single-handed. They would be lucky if, additionally, they did not have to fight sixteen Tibetan priests looking for a jewel stolen from a monastery. Small wonder that the new teacher at one inordinately tough school resorted to the ever-popular device of making himself invisible.

The trick of introducing eccentric pupils was not overlooked. There was the remarkable academy in which the boy king of Manavia was installed with a £5-a-week whipping boy to take his punishment for him. Pug, the whipping boy, had got the job by walloping all the other applicants. When the boy king misbehaved the Headmaster flogged Pug, and Pug in due course took it out of the 'dratted monarch'.

Nor was the vogue for schools in strange places forgotten; rather was it extended. There was, for instance, an international school in France, with English boys, Eskimos and Red Indians, and there was a treetops school run primarily for the study of wild animals, with precarious catwalks running all over the roof of the forest.

The next chapter tells how the *Rover* introduced the Sweeney Todd disappearing chair motiff into a story of the Wild West, and brought Red Indians from their happy hunting-grounds to act as fighter pilots on the Western Front or as sleuths in New York's underworld. The Thomson five had no hesitation in combining two or three kinds of story in one. If readers could swallow a serial about a huge stone statue which came to life and

Dirk Reid balances the Rocking Stone – and starts a war in in Africa – The Rover

strode about the mountain passes of India, why should they jib at the statue being called upon to fight a prehistoric animal in a lake? The Dundee School saw no objection to winning World War One with sensational inventions which had never been invented, or if they had, had been kept remarkably quiet. One of these was the Snatcher, a super tank with an enormous grab which could as easily pick up a German staff car, complete with occupants, as lift a hundred tanks from an enemy laager and drop them one by one into a lake, or bring down a viaduct by nibbling away at the centre arch. To get through a forest it pulled up trees by means of its grab or felled them with its rotary saw.

Nor did the 'Big Five' turn up their noses at tales of Roman legions, of Red Macgregors or of Robin Hood. The latter stories were calculated to shock the traditionalists; they were possibly the first Robin Hood stories which did not make a feature of atrocious ballads. Quite often, by breaking with tradition and mixing one type of story with another, the 'Big Five' hit on an adventure series which could stand comparison with the best of boys' stories.

Dixon Hawke, the Thomson detective, proved to be fairly conventional in his methods. His exploits were chronicled in the *Adventure* and also in occasional 'case-books'. He conformed to the orthodox pattern in that he was tall, aquiline, wore a dressing-gown and smoked a 'blackened briar'. His rooms in Dover Street were run by Mrs Benvie. His assistant was Tommy Burke and his bloodhound was called Solomon. In general his cases called for a minimum of deduction and a maximum of action. As with Falcon Swift, sporting mysteries occupied a great deal of his time. Why did the winning team fall asleep after half time? Why did so many horses mysteriously fall at the fourteenth jump in the Grand National? And so on.

The firm of Hawke and Burke were never happier than when chasing round the world picking up a ruby in

each country. On one of these jewel hunts by way of
New York, San Francisco, Yokohama, Tibet and the usual
Hidden City the detective and his assistant got off to a
good start, recovering four jewels in as many instalments.
Then Hawke was confronted with a cruel choice: the
master crook who was chasing round the world as fast as
he was, and often faster, offered him the alternative of
handing over the four jewels or letting Hawke's Japanese
assistant freeze to death. There was the boy pathetically
curled up unconscious inside a block of ice the size of a
tea chest. Hawke handed over the rubies, then angrily
smashed the block of ice open. The Japanese, a hardy
youth, survived this ordeal by frost and sledge hammer.

Hawke was unlucky in his assistants during this world
tour. He had discovered almost all the jewels when
Tommy obligingly told the arch-crook, who was made
up to look like Hawke, where they were. But Hawke recovered them all in one swoop on the last instalment.

Dixon Hawke rarely expressed surprise at the kind of
adversary he was called upon to face – whether it was a
white-washed orang-utang or a levitational crook like
Marko the Miracle Man. Modestly described as 'a rather
amazing type of criminal', Marko had equipped himself
not only with a device which enabled him to defy gravity
but with X-ray spectacles as well.

With a man like that around, it was not surprising that
Hawke should try an old Baker Street dodge and leave
his dummy in the window seat; though why Marko should
have wasted ammunition on the dummy when he ought
to have been able to see Hawke lurking in a corner is not
clear. That Marko was a determined fellow is shown by
the fact that even when handcuffed by Hawke to an area
railing, and tugged upside down by his anti-gravitational
device, with all the money falling out of his pockets, his
attempt to harpoon the detective with a concealed knife
missed by only an inch.

The style of writing in the Dundee stories was starkly
simple. There was no attempt to explain or justify im-

probable situations; the facts were stated and the reader could take it or leave it. Usually he took it. A certain amount of slang went into the presentation of the stories – 'a beezer yarn next week, boys' – but the stories themselves largely avoided slang and avoided also the stylized exclamations of the *Magnet* and *Gem*. No one cried 'Oh haddocks!' The characters in the 'Big Five' managed to get along with hardly any expletives. In all the stories the grammar was vastly better than in the boys' magazines of fifty years ago. It is difficult for a student of style to say that a story in the *Adventure* was written by such-and-such a person, and a story in the *Rover* by another. All seem to have been written by the one person – which is not so surprising when one learns that certain anonymous prodigies sometimes wrote almost entire issues single-handed.

In a survey of children's reading by A. J. Jenkinson,[1] published in 1940, the Thomson 'Big Five' headed the lists of favourite papers read by boys in a group of elementary and secondary schools. Among elementary boys the order of popularity was identical in the 12-year, 13-year and 14-year groups: namely, the *Wizard, Hotspur, Rover, Skipper* and *Adventure*. Among secondary schoolboys in the same age groups the order varied a little, but the same five held their supremacy, except that the *Champion* dislodged the *Adventure* from fifth place among the 14-year-olds. The survey as a whole was a rousing success for the *Wizard*, which led in five out of the six groups, and even topped the poll among secondary school 15-year-olds. This paper, as Mr Jenkinson pointed out, was read by one in two of the top boys in the secondary school and two in three of the top boys in elementary school.

World War Two put an end to the *Skipper*, a casualty of paper rationing, but the other four continued unabashed. The war stories they published came in for criticism in the *Library Assistant* (1941) by a writer who

1. *What Do Boys and Girls Read?*

felt it was undesirable that the up-and-coming generation should be encouraged to believe that one resolute youth aided by a comic Indian with a cricket bat could rout an Axis division in Libya week after week, throwing tanks off the road by the simple expedient of laying ice-cream in front of them. Was this the kind of fancy to be implanted in the minds of the lads whose brothers had gone through the bloody ordeal of Dunkirk and Crete?

Almost every boys' yarn penned is open to the same objection. The impeachment does not appear to have caused any heart-searching in Dundee, for fantastic war stories continued to appear – as they do to this day. The young have their own peculiar standards in these matters. Whether a Lockheed Hudson aircraft can be landed on a vast sea monster (on which an asdic team have already erected steel masts, believing it to be an island), matters less to the boy reader than that the aircraft shall be accurately portrayed as a Lockheed Hudson. It is fair to say that 'straight' war stories also appear in some profusion, even featuring such forgotten excitements as the Omdurman Expedition, Rorke's Drift and the Mahratta Wars.

Collectors of old-style 'penny dreadfuls' shake their heads sadly at the *Hotspur* and the *Wizard*, but already there is an adult generation which talks wistfully of Morgyn the Mighty, Strang the Terrible, Thick-Ear Donovan, the Wolf of Kabul and even Sergeant Matt Braddock V.C., who is periodically 'busted' for cheeking officers who are not V.C.s. In the *Spectator* of 26 December 1970 Benny Green describes the lasting influence on himself and his contemporaries of the amazing Wilson, that hardy centenarian-plus who emerges, barefoot and chewing grass, from his Pennine fastness to win the world's sporting records one after another. Beside Wilson, Tarzan was a hopeless also ran.

CHAPTER XV

WILD WEST

SOONER or later, a fictional hero had to pit his wits against Red Indians. The only exception to this rule seems to have been Jack Sheppard. Dick Turpin was shipped to America by the Blue Dwarf and found himself caught up in some stirring adventures with the Mohicans. Jack Harkaway had numerous bloodthirsty encounters with redskins, and was fortunate perhaps to be able to fight them with the aid of a balloon. Jack, Sam and Pete were as happy and self-possessed in an Indian reservation as in a Hidden City or at Margate. And the boys of Greyfriars were as certain to be embroiled with Apaches on their trips to North America as they were on their trips to Paris.

To put the fictional Wild West into perspective it is worth tracing the growth of the dime novel in America. This phenomenon of popular literature was the achievement of the Beadle brothers, Erastus and Irwin. Erastus was a printer who began his career, humbly enough, by cutting type from hardwood, at one penny a letter, for labelling flour bags. Among his first publications were dime song books and collections of jokes; from these it was a fairly easy step to dime romances. The Beadles, as their latest historian[1] has pointed out, were not the first to issue cheap novels; they were the first to issue them in a continuous series. Some of the credit must go to Orville J. Victor, who appears to have laid down the general pattern of the dime novel and recruited its authors. The Beadles' first story was *Malaeska, The Indian Wife of the White Hunter* (1860), a romance of the utmost respectability, which had already been published in the *Ladies' Companion*. A great many of the later Beadle titles were

1. A. Johannsen: *The House of Beadle and Adams.*

by Edward Sylvester Ellis, author of the Deerfoot series. His *Seth Jones*, which was advertised with something of the Barnum touch and sold 400,000 copies, was the first big money-spinner of the House of Beadle. Another notable contributor, though less prolific than Ellis, was that Irish soldier of fortune, Captain Mayne Reid. Soon Beadle novels were being published in Britain, from Paternoster Row, the reproduction of the 'dime' on the orange cover being replaced by a sixpence.

The favourite theme of Beadle's early authors was the frontier of fifty or even a hundred years before. Almost always there was a heroine – witness titles like *The Backwoods Bride*, *The Maid of Esopus*, *Myrtle, Child of the Prairie*, and *The Indian Princess*. All the tales were clean to the point of inhibition. Beadle was fond of quoting from the *North American Review* which, in 1864, said that his novels 'did not even obscurely pander to vice or excite the passions'. No backwoods maid was called upon to suffer the fate worse than death, though sometimes that fate was discreetly hinted at. Thus, in Edward Sylvester Ellis's *The Frontier Angel* Marian's father said he had heard a dark story about her former suitor, now a renegade assisting the Indians to lure white men to destruction.

'What does he do with his prisoners?' asked Marian, breathlessly. The reply came:

'He has never been known to give quarter to anyone. All are consigned to the tomahawk and the women perhaps to a still more dreadful fate.'

If Marian knew what her father meant, she was too well-bred to make any comment. Her next question was:

'What induced him to turn traitor?'

Her father, who was not a man to probe for hidden motives, replied: 'His own devilish disposition, I suppose.'

Although Ellis could paint a horrifying picture of a

man burned at the stake, there were scenes on which he forebore to dwell; lovers' meetings, for example. 'They' (the lovers) 'had arrived at an understanding – exactly what and in what words concerns us not,' he wrote in *The Mystic Canoe*. The story ended with the hero realizing an unexceptional ambition:

Home, with its charms and sacred joys – a place where to lay his head; a gentle form, with the love-light beaming in her eyes, waiting to welcome his return; the sweet word 'Father' uttered by infantile lips; the days of wandering ended, and rest – peace – repose.

The dime novel flourished greatly during the Civil War; it was one addiction of the 'damn Yankees' in which the Southerners were not too proud to indulge. If reports are true, dime novels were swopped surreptitiously by sentries on opposing outposts. After the war the type of story began to change; its heroes were no longer the old-time guides and trappers but the scouts and cowboys of the Western plains. Perhaps the most notable date in the history of popular Western fiction was 1869, when the legend of Buffalo Bill was born.

The man responsible for this feat of transfiguration was Edward Zane Carroll Judson, otherwise known as Ned Buntline, whose career had been considerably more colourful and turbulent than that of 23-year-old William F. Cody. Buntline, a self-created colonel, had been sailor, soldier and rolling stone; he was supposed to have earned himself $600 by pursuing three men wanted for murder and capturing two of them; he had killed a jealous hus-band and been strung up by a lynching mob, but cut down uninjured; he had done for New York what Eugene Sue and G. W. M. Reynolds had done for Paris and London – that is, he had written a highly moral exposure of its vice spots (*The Mysteries and Miseries of New York*, 1848); and at one stage he had earned enough by writing cheap fiction to run a steam yacht on the Hudson.

By 1869, however, his own life had ceased to afford him

sufficient inspiration and, like many other writers of paper-back literature, he began to seek out Western adventurers whose achievements he could embellish. The answer to his search was William F. Cody, who had been a rider for the Pony Express and had since built up a reputation as a scout and an unusually skilful buffalo slayer. Cody was impecunious; he was also vain, ambitious and a 'line shooter'. Almost overnight, Buntline's first tale about Cody – 'Buffalo Bill, the King of the Border Men', in the *New York Weekly* made Cody a popular figure. Realizing that in the Scout he had a valuable property, Buntline induced him to appear in stage shows which, though of a staggering naïveté, nevertheless served to nourish the legend. Before long the two men quarrelled about profits and Cody, who had seen where his future lay, found other pens to tell his praise. He is supposed to have written a number of dime novels about himself, but it is likely that he received considerable assistance. Henceforth the bulk of the Buffalo Bill tales were turned out by Colonel Prentiss Ingraham, a soldier of fortune who had served in Mexico, Austria, Crete, Africa and Cuba. Ingraham is credited with writing at least 200 dime novels about Cody, yet that was less than a third of his total output of popular fiction. It is said that, on one occasion, to meet an emergency, he wrote 35,000 words in a day and a night, in longhand, locking himself in his room until the task was done.[1]

The Beadle organization did not remain long unchallenged. Irwin Beadle was edged out of the business and teamed up with George Munro, a former clerk of his brother Erastus. The two were prevented by legal action from using the name Beadle, but Munro's dime novels had no need to trade on anyone else's reputation. Munro was the driving force. His huge success roused more ad-

1. Edgar Wallace, with the aid of a dictaphone, produced a novel of 80,000 words between a Friday night and a Monday morning. See Margaret Lane's *Edgar Wallace: The Biography of a Phenomenon*.

miration in the university he loaded with professorships than among the English authors whose works he pirated.

As competition increased, so the high-mindedness of the dime novel began to dwindle. After the seventies, Western heroes underwent a temporary eclipse in favour of stories about big-city crime. It was George Munro who introduced those pioneer popular detectives, Old Sleuth and Old Cap Collier. By this time the dime novels, which sold at anything from five cents to thirty cents, were incurring from teachers and preachers the same odium which in Britain was being visited on the 'penny dreadful'. By the end of the century the dime novel was dying, but the cowboy hero – strangely enough – was not. He was destined for an ever-growing popularity in the pulp magazines. At the same time, thanks in some measure to Buffalo Bill's famous Wild West show, he was being absorbed into the popular mythology of European countries.

Some of the first Buffalo Bill tales to reach Britain were by no means easy reading. The dialogue was full of words like pizen, ginuwine, purty, p'ticklerly, animile and so on. With a little practice the reader would be able to take passages like this in his stride:

Buffler. Come ter wonst. Injuns thet is said ter be Aztecs has hooked onter Little Cayuse and kerried him away. I follers em immejutly, on ther trail leading south from Eagle Pass. This I sens ter you by the hand of a red what belonged to ther band which his name is Ilhuat, er something like et; he's ther clear quill, I b'lieve, an he'll get this ter ye at Calumet Wells quick's he kin, tho he's hoofin' et. – Yer ole pard in trouble, Nomad.

It was of considerable assistance that correspondents like Nomad usually spelled place names correctly.

When he grew really proficient the reader might even be able to translate the following, from *The Tribunal of Ten, a Tale of Mystery and Love on the Rolling Prairie, Washington Territory*:

'I want ye to understand I'm Lion Lije, the vigilant

chief of this burg, and I'm bizness. Thet, corpus-going ter whoop out who war the Capting's Tribunal of Ten only he were shet off, an bein's he couldn't let us know no other way his sperit helped ter pint ye out.'

There was a foolish sort of competition between publishers to claim the only genuine, or ginuwine, Buffalo Bill stories. Foolish, because nobody really cared whether the tales bore even a fleeting resemblance to the exploits of 'Colonel' W. F. Cody. It would have been more sensible if there had been a common agreement to regard Buffalo Bill as a free-for-all legend like Dick Turpin or Robin Hood.

The Aldine Company ran some of the liveliest Buffalo Bill stories in the late nineties – including stories 'by' Buffalo Bill and such unexpectedly literary pards of his as 'Colonel Sutliffe, United States Army'. One which appeared in the *O'er Land and Sea Library* under the title 'Oath-Bound to Custer' showed the 'Hon.' W. F. Cody, knife in hand, waving aloft the scalp of Yellow Hand who lay on the ground beside him. Cover pictures were often deliberately misleading, but the text in this case supported the artist:

Buffalo Bill, dragging off the Chief's war bonnet, scalped him in the twinkling of an eye, and waving the red trophy and its attachment of feathers and head-dress in the air, shouted in ringing tones, 'The first scalp for Custer!'

An apologetic footnote explained:

It was not the custom of Buffalo Bill to scalp redskins, but knowing how highly Indians prize their scalp lock, and embittered by the Custer massacre, he determined to do so on his trail of revenge. – Author.

In the last chapter Buffalo Bill rode in triumph into the camp of a United States general who looked inquiringly at the 'string of ghastly souvenirs of death' hanging from the Scout's belt.

'Oh, these are the dead roofs of the braves who felt my grip, general. I intended to have a rope made of them to hang Bill

Bevins with, but he persuaded me with a knife to give him a soldier's death.'

'You killed him?'

'Yes, general, I had to do it, so I'll have the scalp locks made into a bridle for you.'

The reader who expected the general to wave aside the offer with a depreciating gesture did not know his United States generals. The answer came:

'Thank you. Bill. It will be a unique present and one most highly prized.'

Another story in this series portrayed Buffalo Bill and his comrades in a more mellow mood, yarning around the camp-fire. Their yarns were less remarkable than the language they employed. Buffalo Bill said that he once knew of a snake being used as an instrument of murder, and Wild Bill Hickok begged for further information:

'In Hayti and Martinique,' said Cody, 'the venom of the terrible serpent indigenous to those islands, the formidable *fer-de-lance*, which is far more deadly than the rattlesnake, has been often employed by the Negroes in disposing of their enemies.'

Wild Bill showed no surprise, so Buffalo Bill continued in the same vein:

'A horrible but well authenticated instance of Negro ingenuity and malevolence is told in Martinique ...'

He went on like this for column after column. His whole speech could have been lifted out of the story and used with hardly a word of editing as an article in a magazine. Wild Bill had to cap his comrade's tales of snakes with some personal reminiscences of scorpions, and he too chose to speak in the same language.

After alleging that scorpions, failing to achieve their objective, often sting themselves to death in disgust, he said:

'Brandy taken till stupefaction follows is a favourite

remedy for scorpion bites in Mexico, and ammonia has also given very good results.'

Buffalo Bill came back with a story about a tarantula-versus-rattlesnake encounter described in the language of a provincial football report, and eventually the two men fell asleep. Perhaps the strain of talking old-fashioned journalese had been too much for them; or perhaps they had bored each other stiff.

Just how that kind of padded story crept into the Aldine series will never be known. It would be charitable to assume that the mails were held up, with the result that an inexperienced pen had to vamp up a story at short notice. Most of the Aldine Wild West stories were good value for money. The scarcity of copies today tells its own story.

Occasionally there was a dying flicker of Gothic in the early Buffalo Bill tales. There were hags in haunted canyons, and spectral riders ranged like the riders of Apocalypse, with phosphorescent hounds at heel. It was surprising how eerie an effect could be worked up against a background of wide open spaces, with no aid from clammy ruins or ancient burial grounds. The Things which appeared on the prairie usually had a satisfactory physical explanation in the end – they were, in fact, the work of the villain.

Guaranteed not to shock 'the most fastidious', the Aldine *New Buffalo Bill Library* which began in 1899 started off with a story in which the heroine in the opening chapter received a parcel containing her lover's scalp and eyeballs. On the coloured cover of each number appeared the King of Scouts, looking like an arrogant Stuart courtier in Wild West dress – pointed beard, pointed moustache and a long mane of hair which must have been a standing temptation to every brave with a scalping knife. Wild Bill Hickok wore his hair even longer – it hung below his shoulders uncombed and uncouth.

These, too, were full-blooded stories. It was a dull day on which the Scout did not come across one of his old pards being crushed to death by a b'ar, or strapped Mazeppa-fashion to a wild mustang and burning like a torch; or catch a glimpse of a train of covered wagons, likewise flaming, racing into a petroleum-covered lake. An editorial footnote pointed out that petroleum was so plentiful in North America that hundreds of lakes were oil-logged with the fuel which ran to waste.

He was no sentimentalist, this Buffalo Bill. *Pour encourager les autres,* he had Cunning Fox tied to a sapling and flogged with buffalo hide whips, Surgeon Frank Powell in attendance. His aides were no amateurs:

They laid their stripes in a beautiful regular way, crossing each other's strokes until the redskin's back was a mass of bruised and quivering flesh.

From time to time Frank Powell felt the redskin's pulse but always found it steady and strong. The man had a huge capacity for taking punishment.

Excess bravery in a brave had its drawbacks, however. Indian admiration was apt to take an embarrassing form:

'Take him alive! Take him alive! He must die by the torture; we must eat his heart hot, for he is a brave chief!'

So often was Buffalo Bill called upon to undergo the knife-throwing torture that he developed an almost sure technique to deal with it. He looked at the eyes of the brave who was at the head of the queue, and if he saw the death lust in the man's eyes he jerked his head to one side at the last second. If not, he stayed still and put his faith in the warrior's fear of the ridicule which was reserved for those who threw clumsily enough to maim. Occasionally he would be rescued at the eleventh hour by an Indian maid with a delightful name like Picture Eyes or Feather Feet. They had a weak spot for a white man, these Indian maidens; and the braves never seemed to bear any grudge.

Every now and again the editor came gallantly to the rescue when the author seemed to stretch the probabilities. At one point, after a man fell into a vitriol pit and died instantly and unpleasantly, it was found that a previous victim's body, already in the vitriol, was excellently preserved. Said the editor:

The properties of vitriol are such as to render it a terribly corrosive agent when brought suddenly into contact with a living body; while at the same time it will arrest decay in a corpse. Captain Wolverton's body was slowly permeated and so preserved; whereas his enemy, falling alive into the vitriol, met a terrible end.

A rather more restrained Buffalo Bill appeared in *Buffalo Bill Stories, a Weekly Devoted to Border Life*, which reached this country about 1909 under the auspices of Street and Smith. In these tales the Scout rode the Border like a knight-errant, concluding peace treaties with Indian chiefs and confounding the knavish tricks of renegade whites. He shot to wing, not to kill. He would break up a lynching party by firing two guns simultaneously, hitting each of about seven gunmen in the wrist or arm, causing them to drop their weapons, and inflicting wounds which, the reader was assured, 'would heal in a few weeks' time'.

Buffalo Bill's pard was perhaps the more colourful character of the two, even though his conversation was largely limited to 'Er, waugh!' Probably it was a habit he had picked up from the Indians, who were always saying 'Wah!' The phrase served for all occasions. If they found a dead man hanging from a tree he would say 'Er, waugh!' If they lost their way he would say 'Er, waugh!' As he sank his teeth into a juicy steak he would say 'Er, waugh!' When greatly moved he would exclaim 'Hallelujer! Gleeory! Er, waugh!' His terms of opprobrium, when he could be bothered voicing them, were drawn straight from Nature: coyotes, skunks, tarant'lers, warty toads.

Another hard-working but hardly more articulate aide

of Buffalo Bill was Little Cayuse, who had been a bugler
in Uncle Sam's Army. His speech was complicated by an
admixture of pidgin. Thus, his comment on seeing an
intermittent flash away in the plain was, 'Mebbyso um
horse soldier have um light box.'

Another 'pard' who assisted Buffalo Bill, besides Nick
Nomad, Wild Bill Hickok and Little Cayuse, was a Baron
von Schitzenhauser. This meant grafting a German-Dutch
accent on to the Western original. The result was 'Py
yiminy!'

'Aber I ain't afraidt uff Inchuns. I tondt vandt any such
exberiences ag'in as vot I haf had. Nodt in dot vay, eenhow.'

Before they buried him in the solid rock of Lookout
Mountain, William F. Cody had enjoyed the by no means
distasteful experience of seeing himself become a schoolboy's legend. Whether or not he read all the dime novel
outpourings about himself, we do not know. At the end,
he must have been in almost as much doubt over what
constituted fact and fiction in his annals as are his bio-
graphers. He took no strenuous steps to dispel the more
extravagant fancies spun about his name, and a good
many to increase them. More honest, perhaps, was old
Kit Carson who, when confronted with a dime novel
cover showing him slaying seven Indians with one hand
and holding a fainting girl with the other, studied it
gravely for a few moments and then said: 'That there
may have happened, but I ain't got no recollection of it.'

For blood-thirstiness and lurid adventure the Deadwood Dick stories tended to outshine those of Buffalo
Bill. Mostly, they were the work of Edward L. Wheeler,
who began to turn them out for Beadle in the 1880s. He
was a prolific young man whose style was in no way
cramped by the fact that he had no personal acquaintance
with the West. A one-time Pony Express rider called William Clark claimed to be the original of Deadwood Dick.
He rode in a pageant attended by President Coolidge at
Deadwood in 1927. It may be assumed that any resem-

blance between his life and the Deadwood Dick of Wheeler's creation was negligible.

The Aldine company imported Deadwood Dicks by the score from the nineties onwards. In a foreword readers were assured:

Trappers and Scouts are prone to the use of emphatic expletives, most of them racy with humour, all of them harmless; but there will not be found here or in any of the Aldine world-renowned libraries a single unchaste episode – and this latter is of great importance.

There was an insatiable thirst for alliteration on the part of the Deadwood Dick editors which extended far beyond the hero's name: 'Deadwood Dick's Dozen', 'Deadwood Dick's Ducats', 'Deadwood Dick's Diamonds', 'Deadwood Dick's Danger Ducks', 'Deadwood Dick at Danger Divide', and so on for scores of titles.

The fictional Deadwood Dick had many phases: he was outlawed, he was reinstated, he married at least twice, he sought vainly to settle down, and finally he was killed, in an adventure called 'Deadwood Dick's Dust'.

In the Aldine illustrations Deadwood Dick did not greatly differ in appearance from Buffalo Bill or any of the other Western heroes. But much more handsome and dashing was Calamity Jane. She wore men's breeches, a saucy jacket buttoned with ten-dollar gold pieces, a boiled shirt and collar, and a belt containing 'self-cocking five-shooters'. The pair of them were described as 'two wild spirits who have learned each other's faults and each other's worth, in lives branded with commingled shame and honour'.

It was a long time before Jane was able to bring her true love to the altar. She would be referred to as 'poor, sore-hearted, but brave and true Calamity Jane'. Sometimes she was not very quick in the uptake. For instance, she suffered herself to be rescued by the masked Unknown and rode beside him for two days before he removed his mask and announced that he was Deadwood Dick, and reminded her that he held a 'mortgage of betrothal' against her.

Decapitation, or the threat of it, or the false report 'of it was a favourite theme in the Deadwood Dick series. One cover showed Calamity Jane intervening to protect a gambler who had rashly wagered his head and lost. The winner was approaching with his knife at the ready. It was characteristic of Calamity Jane that she kept her head when others were about to lose theirs. Then there was the time a showman put up a placard:

Startling Curiosity

The Wonder of the World

The Genuine Head of Deadwood Dick

Preserved in spirits.   On exhibition within this pavilion

The head of the greatest road ranger that ever lived!

Come one!   Come all!

Admission only 30 cents

Dick knew of this fraudulent display but took no action; he was masquerading at the time under the not inappropriate name of Hard Cheek.

In the Aldine *Boys' First-Rate Pocket Library* Calamity Jane was killed at least twice. Number 64 had Deadwood Dick kneeling beside her grave – she had been slain trying to cut down the enemy flag. Number 68 had Calamity Jane being hanged at the end of a rope by a group of desperadoes, in company with Mormon Bill; surely the first time in this type of fiction that a good-looking, God-fearing heroine ever came to such an ignominious end. Deadwood Dick, after cutting her down, swore a great oath to destroy the camp in which dwelt her murderers. This he did at the cost of his life. No undue sentiment was expended on his passing, which was described in no more than 150 words. He was buried in a quiet valley beside Calamity Jane, whose tombstone said, 'Frank with friends, fearless of foes.' His own said, 'Brave, honourable and kind in peace, cool, daring and fearless in war.' There

were no editorial crocodile tears; somebody had decided
that both characters were to be dispatched, and dispatched they were. The next issue started off with a tale
of Deadwood Dick, Junior.

The Aldine *Boys' Own Library*, which started in 1909,
had Deadwood Dick, senior, married to a girl-wife called
Leone:

Deadwood Dick, the Prince of Outlaws once, was now a
reformed man, leading the life of a cattle herder with his loved
and loving wife and boy, and servants enough to do the work
in the house and upon the stock lands; for Dick was annually
receiving handsome profits from a gold mine in the Black
Hills and could afford to live luxuriously.

Leone, who frequently called him Prince, could not
believe that this placid, well-regulated life would last;
nor could the reader. Though she adored him, Leone
was worried about the other women in her husband's life,
though not about Calamity Jane:

'Ah, Eddie, you know not what moment that Edith Stone
may come, for she is your lifelong enemy. Do you really believe
that she is crazy, dear?'

Edith came back, and she was crazy all right. Deadwood
Dick, from a hidden position, watched her hang a dead
man from a tree. She had always wanted this man's blood,
but someone had beaten her to it, so she was getting what
satisfaction she could by stringing up a corpse.

The call came to Deadwood Dick to clean up his old
stamping-grounds. He returned with his Eagles, whose
names only he himself knew. The war was bitter. Came
the day when Edith laid hands on Dick. She had him tied
to a stake, and then made this memorable proposal of
marriage:

'Deadwood Dick, I have come to give you one more chance
for life. Wed me and take me East to live and we will omit
this burning at the stake and ever live happily together. What
shall it be – will you accept me, or what you will find ten
times more unendurable, a horrible death?'

Edith must have entertained some doubts about her charms, since she assessed death by burning as only ten times worse than marriage. Deadwood Dick's answer not only dispelled all hopes of marriage but put a more realistic rating on the proposition:

'Death, a thousand times death, in preference to linking myself with you! Go ahead, you will find I am not afraid.'

As Edith, who knew when she was beaten, turned away to help the Indians gather some more tinder, Leone arrived. She had been reported dead, so by rejecting Edith's offer Dick had also saved himself from committing bigamy. Leone's relief at finding her husband, who had also been reported dead, was equalled by her fury at the other woman.

'Stand, you fiend!' cried the wife of Deadwood Dick, hurling a long narrow sword at the feet of Edith, and retaining a similar one in her own hand. 'Pick up your sword and stand on your guard, for it shall be your life or mine.'

Leone knew her own strength, or she would hardly have put this encounter on a duelling basis. In no time her sword was 'deep in Edith's black heart'.

Deadwood Dick, junior, was not the son of the outlaw, but a young and rather whey-faced namesake who arrived with his dying mother thrown over the saddle at the still-fresh graves of Deadwood Dick and Calamity Jane. There, taking brief respite from his pursuers, he swore to be worthy of the man whose name he thereupon assumed; a more exciting name than his own, which was R. M. Bristol. The adventures in which he was involved were not at first very different from those of his distinguished namesake; but in the Aldine *Life and Adventure Library*, many years later, he had become just another detective. No demon lovers lay in wait for him. The West was settling down. And just as Sexton Blake was required to undertake assignments from time to time in provincial cities of Britain, so Deadwood Dick, junior, tackled cases in

Blue Blaze and Eagle Eye leap to attack the crook's convoy – The Rover

Detroit, Cincinnati, Boston and even Coney Island. One of his adventures ended on a particularly unromantic note:

Dear reader, this is not a love story; consequently there are no heroes or heroines to be married off in the stereotyped manner, and therefore there is little left to add.

Ben Brice was buried at Dick's expense, while the expenses of Mrs Redfern's funeral were borne by the Coroner ...

In their heyday the Deadwood Dick stories were good value. The arts of suspense were well studied, even if the rules of grammar were neglected.

Early numbers of the Harmsworth magazines carried a variety of Western tales, sometimes about Buffalo Bill, sometimes about Deadwood Dick, occasionally both in the one story, but there were no early Amalgamated Press publications which were specifically Western in appeal. Detection had become the obsession. In 'Trapper Dan' (*Boys' Her-*

ald, 1903), George Manville Fenn shed some light on the great puzzle: is scalping always fatal? Old Dan, the grizzled trapper, was seeking to impress his young assistant with the ruthless ways of redskins. Suddenly he decided to give a practical demonstration:

... he snatched off his square skin cap, making the boy spring to his feet aghast with horror, while the dog started back glaring at the visitor and bursting forth into a deep angry bay.

Horrible! came from Wat Waring's lips – one word only but meaning so much, for the sight he gazed upon was terrible indeed, his visitor standing transformed into a hideous object as with one quick motion he laid bare the trace of a frightful act of triumph of the savage redskin over his defeated enemy, the trapper's head, with its long-healed scars looking strangely white above his sun-bronzed face, telling the tale in its frightful bareness of the rapid placing round of the savage's knife and the tearing away of the scalp.

In 1938 Amalgamated Press put out a short-lived *Wild West Weekly*. The cover was as colourful as the contents. Promised the editor:

'... We will put a hot rifle in your hands and make the sweat run down your face. You shall look down the long smooth barrel of a gun and, with nerves strung tight as a bow-string, you shall feel a bullet spatter the dry earth into your face.'

After that it seemed something of an anti-climax that the free gift selected for permanent subscribers should have consisted of a shove-ha'penny board.

It was left to the Dundee School to break all traditions and work out some really original angles on the Wild West. Deerfoot padding through the undergrowth was no use to them. The *Rover* produced Hawkeye, the redskin detective, padding up Fifth Avenue in all the glory of his native costume, seeking to do battle with the Black Bat, King of the New York underworld. The *Rover* also took pleasure in presenting Blue Blaze, Demon of the Air, who in company with Hawkeye did much to win World War One in a phantom aeroplane. An illustration showed him half out of the cockpit, pointing downwards. The artist had been to some trouble to indicate, by means of the usual striations, that the plane was swooping rapidly, but the eagle feather in Blue Blaze's hair remained miraculously vertical, and his pigtail drooped in a dead calm. After the Great War Blue Blaze and Hawkeye brought their phantom plane home to their native hunting-grounds in the Great Barrier Mountains, complete with machine-guns and apparently limitless ammunition, and there found plenty of gainful and spectacular employment.

But the *Rover*'s masterpiece was probably the Demon Barber of Six Trails, in which the sinister apparatus of the disappearing chair was used, probably for the first time, as an instrument of high purpose. Crooks were lured into the barber's shop and then dropped on to a pile of straw in the cellar for subsequent removal to the town jail. And who was the Demon Barber? The evidence was strong that it was Wild Bill Hickok himself.

CHAPTER XVI

VIVE LE SPORT!

ANY historian of the remote future relying exclusively on old volumes of boys' magazines for his knowledge of the British way of life in the early twentieth century – notably the nineteen-twenties and the nineteen-thirties – will record that the country was the battleground of an unending civil war between a small vigorous race known as Sportsmen and a large, sluggish and corrupt race known as Slackers. The Slackers had a great deal in their favour – wealth, cunning, ruthlessness and an unlimited supply of secret drugs. The Sportsmen had nothing but a clean pair of fists. Yet the Sportsmen always won. They would have won in half the time and at less injury to themselves if they had used knuckle-dusters, but then they would have forfeited their status as Sportsmen.

Readers either enjoyed sporting stories or they hated them. To some, sport was nothing but a creeping blight which overtook and paralysed many a long-established magazine, driving well-loved authors into retirement.

It is hard to trace just when the preoccupation with sport began. Desmond Coke in his chapter on 'Penny Dreadfuls' in *Confessions of an Incurable Collector*, quotes exultingly from *The Oxford and Cambridge Eights*, published by Brett, in which a punters' plot to poison the entire Cambridge crew miscarries and Oxford is poisoned instead. This admirable story appears to have been ahead of its time.

Edwin Brett's *Boys of England* described itself as 'A Magazine of Sport, Travel, Fun and Adventure', but the reader would require to do a good deal of researching to find a story which, by any standards, could be called a sporting story. *Boys of England* was launched in the same year that the Queensberry Rules were drawn up in an attempt to purge professional pugilism of some of its more scandalous abuses. Three years previously the Football Association had been formed with the object of cleaning up contemporary football, in which hitherto hands and feet had been used impartially, and hacking and tripping were normal tactics. Bracebridge Hemyng, who contributed the first Jack Harkaway stories to *Boys of England*, would seem to have overlooked the Queensberry Rules; the reader has already read a description of a fight under the Harkaway rules.

In one of his later publications – *Jack Harkaway's Journal for Boys* – Brett set out to encourage what he called 'The Manly Sports of Britain', which included football, cricket, sculling, fencing, cycling and even golf. He sponsored Jack Harkaway Cycling Clubs. In italics he emphasized that his encouragement was extended only to participants in amateur sports. Presented free with his *Journal* were large coloured plates showing boys playing football – a bigger bargain, it might seem, than those small 'real glossy' photos of players which the next generation were to be stampeded into collecting. The most interesting development, perhaps, was the offer of £20 to the next-of-kin of any boy killed playing football or cricket, or riding a bicycle. If this could not make the youth of the country sport-minded, what could?

But the stories in *Jack Harkaway's Journal for Boys* were in the old pattern. There is little doubt that most of the authors who wrote for Brett and his rivals knew nothing about sport and cared less. When it came to describing a schoolboy fight there was no talk of hooks and uppercuts, only of blacked eyes and bleeding noses. One popular author of school stories would content himself, though perhaps not his readers, by saying, 'With the details of the fight we need not concern ourselves.' Again, the Old Guard could no more describe a football match than they could describe the Otto Cycle. They had been reared on, and many of them had helped to write, 'penny dreadfuls', and the gulf between the Gothic obsession and the Sport-

ing obsession was an almost impossible one to bridge. It
may be that somewhere in the archives is a story in which
the rightful heir to a haunted castle turns out to be the
crack centre-forward of Mountjoye Wanderers; if so, the
present writer would be happy to hear of it. Certainly
such a plot would be not nearly as extravagant as some of
those which were later encountered in sporting fiction.

The *Boy's Own Paper*, launched in 1879, was determined to strike a sporting note from the outset. The first
item in the opening number was entitled 'My First Football Match'. It was an excited, breathless description of
the sensations of a youngster chosen to play for the first
time in an important match; of his apprehensions lest he
should commit some unfortunate act which would cost his
side the match; and of the glow he felt at the end in having contributed to 'the glorious victory of the Old School'.
A few months later the *Boy's Own Paper* repeated this
article in terms of cricket, with eleven boys riding home in
ecstasy because they had won a good clean game.

But simple enthusiasm for sport was not enough to hold
the attention of boy readers avid for thrills, and the editor
of the *Boy's Own Paper* must speedily have realized as
much. He was up against the hard fact, unquestioningly
accepted by editors of a later day, that a sporting story
pure and simple is unreadable. A sporting encounter became interesting only when an element of crookedness or
comedy was injected into it.

The paradoxical result was that while real life sport was
only moderately dirty, fictional sport – in which boys were
encouraged to revel for their health's sake – was vastly
dirtier than in real life. No one is likely to forget the long
and unflagging sequence of stories about football matches
in which the lemons were poisoned at half-time, in which
rascally backs hacked the home forwards with boots containing poisoned nails, and bogus referees blew poison
darts at the star players. There was the goalkeeper who
had to lose the match or lose £1,000, and the centre-
forward who had to score a hundred goals in the season

or lose his life. There was the forward who turned out to be a convict, and the player arrested at half-time on a trumped-up charge. There were the spectators who loosed mad dogs, snakes and even menagerie lions on to the pitch.

If a club was winning it was because a crook had got control and was bribing down all opposition. If a club was losing it was because a crook had got control and did not want it to win. The only honest men among the directors were those who were being blackmailed or threatened with foreclosure of mortgage. The one honest player in the team spent the week shaking off kidnappers and trying to clear his own or his father's name. It was all he could do every Saturday afternoon to break through the crooks' blockade and reach the football ground in time to score the winning goal.

The theme of the 'wonder player' or the 'mystery player' was ever-popular. The masked forward took the field with unfailing regularity, and the Football Association never seemed to mind, nor did they take any exception to the fielding of blind forwards, forwards who had lost their memory, hypnotized players, Red Indians, Hottentots or Boy Tarzans. The Empire was always contributing brilliant players who had learned to play in peculiar circumstances – such as boys who had been shipwrecked for years on a desert island with a party of footballers, and had had nothing else to do except to perfect their technique among the palm trees. Far-fetched these stories may have been; yet on 20 April 1949, according to press reports, the Leicestershire club of Hinckley Athletic fielded a hypnotized eleven and lost 2–1.

When World War One arrived, players with Teutonic antecedents were drummed out of the team and were later convicted of espionage. Teams joined up wholesale in Footballers' Battalions, and were promptly moved to key positions in the line, where they earned the personal thanks of Kitchener and Foch. As soon as they had hurled back the Big Push they would celebrate with a rousing game of football on the fringe of no-man's-land, watched by the men of half a dozen Allied divisions. 'Ach, those English sportsmen,' Hindenburg would say as he licked his wounds, 'they do not take war seriously.'

Some of the writers of sport stories had no inhibitions about introducing real-life characters into their narratives. A bizarre story of this type in the *Boys' Friend Library*, entitled 'Good Enough For England', was 'reviewed' by Sir John Squire in *The Observer* in 1927. Hobbs, Strudwick, Jupp, Tate and other leading characters of the day figured in the narrative and were mostly outshone by the young hero, the kind of virtuoso who could go in ninth wicket down and achieve a three-figure score. Young Tom might have been an even better cricketer if he had not been under the necessity of fighting off a gang, led by a wicked cousin from Australia, which 'attempted Tom's life about twice a week or once per match'. At various times the crooks kidnapped him, dropped Mills bombs into his punt from bridge parapets and tried to prick him with a poisoned needle. Then his villainous cousin, disguised as a clergyman, hurled a dagger at him outside Old Trafford; it was caught when only three inches from Tom's chest by Gregory, as smart a piece of fielding as he had ever performed. Not all the eminent cricketers would have been as flattered as Gregory on reading the references to themselves in this story. Thus, when Tom bowled out Strudwick, he took no great pride in the feat, because it was 'only Strudwick'. Sir John Squire wondered how leading barristers would react if they found themselves introduced into crime stories in a similar manner – 'Sir Patrick Hastings put up a much worse show than we expected.' We do not know whether Lord Roberts objected to being appointed by the *Boys' Friend* to lead that expeditionary force against France; but the *Boys' Friend* knew better than to have Lord Roberts thrown back into the sea.

No master crooks in all boys' literature went to more tortuous lengths than those whose depraved purpose it was to kidnap star footballers. In the *Boys' Realm* of the

nineteen-twenties Professor Cyrus Zingrave, hypnotic
head of the League of the Green Triangle, harried for his
own inscrutable reasons the Blue Crusaders Football Club,
which 'as every schoolboy knew', was owned by Lionel
Corcoran, a boy at St Frank's. A typical Zingrave move
was to plant an agent at St Frank's and by means of this
creature – 'a sort of relay station for the Professor's hypnotic power' – coerce the owner of the club into getting
rid of loyal footballers or officials. The Professor would
think nothing of sending up a smoke-writing aeroplane,
with his green triangle markings, over the Crusaders'
football ground to trace in the sky a triangle with the
word 'Remember' (this presented the cover artist with a
nasty problem since the only colours available to him were
red and blue). Zingrave's ruffians lay in the branches of
trees waiting to snatch footballers from the tops of open
double-decker buses. Once he sent a threatening note to
the team inside a football which exploded on being
kicked, thus liberating the message. This was a change
from footballs which merely exploded.

It was left to the Dundee School to take the sporting
story and throw into it everything on the shelf. A story
entitled 'The One-Man Forward Line' in the *Wizard*
started with the team of Prestfield United going out to
West Africa to prevent a massacre, the Africans believing
the team to be a powerful ju-ju worshipped by the people
of Britain. In Africa the team recruited the exiled son of
the Earl of Kilblane, who turned out to be a talented foot-
baller. The Earl declined to have his son back in England,
and his rascally lawyer Kripp blew up the United ground
as a mark of aristocratic displeasure. That was only a
minor upset; the real fun started when the throb of war
drums began to be heard at Prestfield, and it was remembered that the Earl's son, in a weak moment in Africa, had
carved his initials on the Golden Chair of Seremba, the
penalty for which was death. Whatever this story may
have lacked, it did not lack plot.

In Dundee they had a weakness for sporting ju-jus.

Outstanding among these was the cricket bat, which natives venerated even to the point of seeking to do human sacrifice in front of it. In any clash with cannibals a cricket bat in the hero's strong right hand rated half a dozen Excaliburs or a hundred Maxim guns.

Boxing stories tended to follow the same fictional pattern as football stories. Crooked managers were the rule, and dope, drugs and poison were their weapons. The towel wafted in front of the flagging hero had been steeped in a debilitating drug, the sponge was alive with germs. A man was lucky to leave the ring suffering from simple concussion, and not from anthrax, infantile paralysis and the Black Death.

A common trick in boxing stories was to make one's fighter a member of an improbable profession. Arthur S. Hardy ran a long series of boxing stories of this type in the closing days of the *Marvel*. One week he had the boxing parson hanging up his surplice in the vestry and rolling his sleeves ready to do battle with a Sykes-like intruder; the next he had a boxing editor forsaking pen, paste-pot and proofs to do likewise. Boxing dockers, boxing Chinamen, boxing farmers, boxing millionaires, boxing plumbers, boxing taximen and boxing barmen – the author was nearly as hard put to it to find new occupations for his boxers as the Sexton Blake authors were to find new disguises for their hero. As an editorial device for tapping new fields of readers it was perhaps just as successful as moving the hero to a new provincial city each week.

By the nineteen-twenties the *Marvel* – in the pages of which such notable characters had been born – had become a sporting magazine. Its title was *Marvel and Sports Stories*. Many of its older readers were not happy about this change of policy, and were disappointed without being surprised when, in 1922, they were informed that the *Marvel* was ending and that henceforth they must ask for *Sport and Adventure*.

The editor of the new magazine indulged in no lamen-

tation for the old *Marvel*. In his first issue, addressing
readers, as he hoped, of from ten to seventy, he said:

To those who do not greatly care for footer this may seem
the wrong time of the year for giving away counterfeit present-
ments of Buchan, Clay, Meredith and the rest of the League
heroes. But we believe that those who do not care much for
footer are in a small minority among our readers; and we
know that to the true enthusiast there is no close season of
interest.

Those former *Marvel* readers who continued to take
Sport and Adventure through the summer of 1922 may
have smiled cynically when in October they were again
promised a 'big surprise' and then found themselves being
invited to ask, not for *Sport and Adventure*, but for
'Number One of a Great New Paper' with a name almost
as old as that of the *Marvel – Pluck*. There were no fewer
than ten separate announcements of the new *Pluck* in the
final issue. It was to be a companion paper to the 'tre-
mendously successful' *Champion*, and was to carry a
detachable 'long complete' story. The short life of *Sport
and Adventure* did not mean that the policy of running
sport had proved unsuccessful, or was to be abandoned.
Meanwhile the pink *Boys' Realm*, revived from suspended animation, was carrying as many as six sporting
stories in each issue – boxing, football, horse racing, motor
racing and sometimes cricket. It was a leading protagonist
in the competition to see who could give away the largest
and glossiest photographs. First it had been a single matt-
finished black-and-white photograph; then a 'real glossy
photo'; then two glossy photos; then two coloured photos;
then two glossy photos in an envelope, and so on. Collecting of these photographs eventually came to rival the collecting of cigarette cards. Stimulation came from the firm
of Thomsons who took hero-worship a stage further and
published stories bearing the signatures of famous footballers. The giants of sport did not hesitate to perform in
even the humblest of literary arenas.

'Jimmy the Dodger's training was amazing to watch. With one hand strapped to his side he took on two sparring partners at once' – The Wizard

All this time the Aldine firm was putting out one sporting library after another; notably a racing library, most of the tales being written by Bat Masters, a football library and a boxing library, to which Sydney Horler contributed.

Motor racing does not appear to have been honoured with any notable library of its own, though in America a 'Motor Matt' Library had enjoyed a considerable vogue in the early years of this century. Here again was a sport in which the deeps of criminality were plumbed. Revolutionary new carburettors had to be invented almost weekly to make up for those which were stolen. A new alloy was hardly cold before the formula was being scrutinized in Berlin and Barcelona. The hero's home-made racer was a target for saboteurs: the stub axles would be filed three-quarters through, or an infernal machine fitted to the accelerator pedal. At the very least his petrol would be sugared. Even if these hazards were circumvented and the car started to circle the track there would be a concerted effort to side-swipe it over the banking; the standard of track discipline was akin to that displayed in a New York taxi cab 'war'. The same practices were liable to crop up in tales of dirt-track racing.

In the *Champion*, just before World War Two, sport grew from a fetish to a frenzy. Through the eighties and nineties the editor of the *Boy's Own Paper* had tried his hardest to sell his readers the idea of a daily cold bath. The *Champion* played up almost impossibly hearty types who were always scrubbing themselves under icy showers. Take the frightening case of Smudger Smith, the Cruiser Bruiser:

Big, brawny and powerful, and the heftiest middleweight aboard the *Turbulent*, Smudger bore down like a battleship upon the fellows who were racing to beat him.

He tackled them like a rugger half-back, slinging them aside as he waded into their ranks, and chuckling with glee as he was the first to sluice himself down in icy water.

Smudger Smith was always the first dressed, the first tidied up and the first to fall in; in spite of which he was the most popular man on board his man-o'-war.

He was no isolated case. On board the S.S. *Carolia* was 'Sporty' Dawson, whose day started just as explosively:

'Scrape my barnacles. This is great!'

'Sporty' Dawson, late of the Royal Navy, bounded from his bunk and inhaled the fresh morning air from his open porthole. Then he started punching away at a punchball fixed between the ceiling and the floor of his cabin.

The walls of the cabin were covered with sporting pictures and a stack of sports gear stood in one corner.

As he thumped violently at the punchball Sporty Dawson grinned.

Tall, splendidly muscled, square-chinned and determined looking; he was a perfect specimen of physical fitness.

Sporty had been a schoolmaster before going to sea and, on leaving the Navy, he had found a good job. He was to be Fourth Form master aboard the s.s. *Carolia*, the mighty cruising liner which had been commissioned to take two hundred schoolboys on a tour round the world.

Warmed up by his morning exercise, Sporty quickly changed

into shorts and sweater, tucked an old Rugby football under one arm, and picked up a battered muffin bell.

'Bet none of the scalliwags are up yet,' he chuckled. 'I'll soon rouse 'em.'

Bounding out of his cabin, Sporty raced along the Fourth Form cabin passage, ringing his muffin bell.

'Show a leg! Show a leg, you young landlubbers! You're at sea, and it's a fine morning for a game of rugger on the main deck!'

'Gosh, it's Sporty Dawson, our new Form master!' cried Chirpy Morgan, one of the Fourth Form. 'I didn't think we were going to have much sport on board ship. But rugger on the main deck's a good idea. Come on, chaps, let's join in.'

And Sporty Dawson kept up this tempo right through the day, increasing it if anything towards nightfall. Even the fat boy was co-opted in the cult of heartiness. There were Slackers, of course, but their opposition was mown down like corn before a whirlwind.

In the other *Champion* stories someone was always trying to suppress Sport, and coming off second best. Assistant Commissioner Macnab, wearing his monocle in the jungle, spent much of his time trying to teach the natives to play Rugby, to the unaccountable annoyance of the Commissioner. In the Royal Flying Corps Rockfist Rogan's major was always putting obstacles in the way of holding boxing matches, especially the kind which involved two men slogging it out in an open cockpit in mid-air while the Richthofen Circus banked for the kill. Other sportsmen in unexpected places were Q9, the Boxing Spy, who introduced a touch of clean fighting into a notoriously dirty profession; Bulldog Blade, the 'biggest sport in the Foreign Legion'; the Boxing Boss of the Convict Castaways, who ruled an island of convicts with his fists; Serjeant Dunn and his Fighting Sportsmen in the Flanders trenches; and Square-Deal Samson, the Strong-Man Sheriff, who upturned caravans with one hand and brought in desperadoes two at a time lashed to a pole across his shoulders.

Always the heroes punched hard and clean. Only a cad would wish to conjecture how many would-be heroes in real life have been needlessly maimed through trying to dispatch ruffianly assailants with a clean right to the jaw rather than to the stomach.

CHAPTER XVII

DICK BARTON – AND AFTER

WORLD War Two killed off a score of legendary heroes who had survived the Kaiser's war, and one at least who had come through the Boer War. When the publishers, faced with crippling paper cuts, issued their first casualty lists, the names of the boys' thrillers were high up on the page. It was the old problem of throwing the least essential passengers from the raft; sentiment did not determine the order of sacrifice. Conceivably the opportunity was taken to jettison a few old friends who probably would not have lasted much longer anyway.

Thus, it was a meagre offering of romance that awaited the schoolboy when Hitler's war was ended. In this partial vacuum, however, was born in October 1946 a new mythical hero of scarcely credible dimensions, a superman whose popularity was unaffected by paper rationing: the BBC's Dick Barton, Special Agent. Conceived as a phantasy figure for adults, Dick was taken over by the juvenile population. At the height of his fame Dick's adventures, prefaced by the exciting signature tune 'The Devil's Gallop', were followed by an audience variously estimated at between one in five and one in three of the population.

With his two resourceful assistants, Jock and Snowy, Dick Barton pitted his wits freely against smugglers, black marketeers and bullion robbers, mostly with foreign names. He defeated a Sexton Blake-style crook who sought to establish a reign of terror over London – one of those exhibitionist, super-confident crooks who publicly announce the time and place of their next outrage. He was ready to confound the plans of those who sought the green eyes of little yellow gods. He tackled a super-smuggler who, profiting by the tactless disclosure of World War Two secrets, had built himself a synthetic, gun-defended

iceberg on the Habakkuk plan out in the Atlantic. Another of his adversaries was a mad scientist who sought to
wield a radio-active secret weapon against the population
of Britain. No Gothic horrors beset the path of Barton.
Radio-active rays, yes; vampires, no. Barton was firmly
planted in the twentieth century.

The clergymen and teachers who were horrified at the
rake's progress of Charley Wag would have found it uncommonly hard to frame an indictment against Barton on
moral grounds; and yet, here and there, incredibly, were
found people in public life willing to blame Dick Barton
for the misdemeanours of youth. Once it was realized that
Dick had a huge juvenile following the BBC went to extreme lengths to ensure that their hero should be *sans
reproche* as well as *sans peur*. His personal life was soon
seen to be ascetic to a degree – even the odd glass of beer
was cut out. His vocabulary did not contain even the
words they use at Girton. His sex life was wholly subli-
mated in the war on evil; so much so that a psychologist
forecast that, some day, he would break out spectacularly
in a way that would have startled Krafft-Ebing. Dick did
not lie. In no circumstances did he break the law of the
land. He did not call on nervous citizens for help in his
headlong pursuit of crooks, even though failure might
mean destruction of half the population. Unlike Jack
Harkaway, he did not slice off his adversary's ears to teach
him a lesson in manners. His methods, though forceful
and forthright when required, were less forceful than
those which they taught him in No. 20 Commando. The
clean blow to the jaw was his only weapon. All that Dick
was allowed to remember from his Commando days was
that one resolute man need never fear being outnumbered.
Indeed, Barton authorities will maintain that he never
entered a rough-and-tumble without being outnumbered,
or at least physically matched. Thus, nobody could accuse
Dick of being a fist-proud bully.

On what grounds, then, could the cult of Barton be
attacked? This was the question which worried those who

knew that anyone so popular with the rising generation must be an unhealthy influence. In due course Dick was called everything: a stimulant, a relaxation, a drug, a safety valve, a social menace, an imperfect catharsis, a source of xenophobia, a crypto-Fascist, and a pattern for parasites. One of the first accusations was contained in a letter to *The Times*. The writer said that Barton was distracting the youth of the nation from that stern assessment of the post-war world and a realization of their function in it which alone constituted the country's hope of salvation. Moreover, children had come to regard parents who expected them to continue with their homework during the Barton programme as 'insensate and tyrannical giants'. A reader of *Picture Post* described Dick as a lower middle class spiv; and a reader of *Illustrated* said that children had no right to be listening to the adventures of Dick Barton 'and other characters leading abnormal lives'. (But in the history books in which this reader wished schoolboys to bury their heads how many characters lived normal lives?)

Defenders of Barton were not lacking, however. In the *Daily Telegraph* a correspondent rejoiced that Dick set an example of 'initiative, quick decision and private enterprise' ... 'Can anyone see Barton referring any matter to a committee?' A Cabinet Minister, Herbert Morrison, said in a speech: 'I like Dick Barton and listen to him when I get the chance. I listen because I like it, which seems a good reason for doing a thing provided you don't get yourself into trouble. There are too many people going round publicly trying to psycho-analyse other people.'

The BBC tired of Dick Barton and put him into suspended animation in 1951. For the record, those associated with his brief, meteoric career were Norman Collins, then in charge of the Light Programme; John McMillan, who laid down the lines on which the character was to be developed; Edward J. Mason and Geoffrey Webb, the two principal script-writers; Neil Tuson, the producer; and Noel Johnson and Duncan Carse, the actors who played

Dick (and were assumed to carry his characteristics into private life).

In the early 1950s were heard the first rumblings inspired by the so-called horror comics which were being imported in growing quantities from America – partly to satisfy the demands of American Servicemen in Britain. The horror comics fell into three main categories: the pornographic, the sadistic and the necrophilous. Some of them contrived to combine all three appeals. The stories were told in strip form, with the minimum of legend, thus enabling the horrors to be laid on more thickly.

It was the necrophilous comics that attracted most attention. More than a century before, the mock-Gothic writers had been obsessed with graves, skeletons and vampires, but their imaginations were not actively diseased. There was also this difference, that the old-time reader had to plough through many columns of small print to reach the gruesome episodes. In the new comics the horrors were scrupulously and often lewdly delineated, half a dozen to a page.

From time to time shocked Members of Parliament read out in the House extracts from horror comics which had come into their hands. One of them was entitled 'Born In The Grave' – 'the incredible story of a man who was born five years after his mother died':

One night in the damp heat a strange activity takes place at the lonely grave. Dirt is flying! The mound is moving! A foul stench pervades the air. Loud groans break the silence. A deep-throated chuckle and then the cry of an infant!

Another tale was about a mad scientist who dug up from the grave the body of a woman electrocuted that day for murder. He brought her back to life, by means of further electrical treatment, and she rewarded his efforts by developing into a criminal lunatic who went about tearing up animals and people for fun. Eventually the scientist destroyed the monster and himself with the aid of a doll containing a time bomb in its stomach.

Probably the bottom was reached in a horror comic a scene from which is reproduced in Dr Frederic Wertham's *Seduction of the Innocent*. It shows a midnight baseball game played with portions of a murdered man, the head (with gouged-out eyes) being the ball and a leg serving as bat. The legend begins: 'Look closely. See this strange baseball game. See the long lines of pulpy intestines that mark the base lines. See the two lungs and liver that is home plate ...'

Some of the publishers of this literary offal tried to make a joke of their trade:

Imagine — you are selling a nice line in Komfy Kiddies' Komics and Dainty Dailies when a parcel of putrid patter slithers slimily in at the back door. You hold your nose and cut the string and your reeking ration of horror has arrived.

Others fell back on the irresistible appeal of 'definitely not for the squeamish and should be kept away from the kiddies'.

Whether the worst of this stuff reached Britain from America is open to doubt, but what did arrive was enough to alarm the school teachers who daily confiscated it. Like the 'penny dreadfuls' of old these sheets were sold in mean shops anxious to turn a quick profit. They were to be had even in fish and chips shops. That the horror comics were not without effect on the young is suggested by a curious episode in Glasgow in September 1954. After a Gorbals school had closed for the day a rumour went round that a vampire was at large in a near-by cemetery. It had iron teeth and had eaten two children. Arming themselves with sticks and stones, the children surged through the cemetery, seeking the Thing. Some of them, apparently, were not too clear whether they were looking for a vampire or a space man. The police had difficulty in breaking up the hunt. It would be easy to make too much of this affair; no doubt most of the participants thoroughly enjoyed it.

The graveyard comics were only part of the problem. There were crime comics, stamped 'Crime Does Not Pay', in which were plentiful scenes of mutilation, gouging, eye-pricking, face-treading, flogging and preparation for rape. The heroines' skirts were usually riding up their thighs and all had pumpkin breasts (according to Dr Wertham the papers in which these females appeared were known to the young of America as 'headlight comics').

J. B. Priestley summed up the nature of the new cult with discernment and precision:

This new violence, with its sadistic overtones, is ... not simply coarse, brutal from a want of refinement and nerves, but genuinely corrupt, fundamentally unhealthy and evil. It does not suggest the fair-ground, the cattle market, the boxing booth, the horseplay of exuberant young males. It smells of concentration camps and the basements of secret police. There are screaming nerves in it. Its father is not an animal maleness but some sort of diseased manhood, perverted and rotten.[1]

The writers of it, he said, 'give the game away by their gloating eagerness, the sudden heightening of their descriptive powers'.

Eventually, after Members of Parliament had been suitably stirred by displays of horror comics in the Palace of Westminster (whence three specimens mysteriously disappeared), a Bill was introduced with the object of putting the publishers and importers out of business: the Children and Young Persons (Harmful Publications) Bill. Its purpose was to ban the portrayal of 'acts of violence or cruelty or incidents of a horrible or repulsive nature' in publications which consisted 'wholly or mainly of stories told in pictures'. The existing laws against obscenity in print, it was pointed out, could not be stretched to cover those publications which specialized in the cruel and the repulsive.

There was much opposition, a great deal of it silly, from self-appointed fighters for literary freedom. The Bill, some said, would make it an offence to publish a picture story of 'Three Blind Mice' or Struwwelpeter. Earl Jowitt

1. *New Statesman and Nation*, 24 July 1954.

told the Lords that when his secretary went out to buy a copy of Struwwelpeter he found that it was in heavy demand in all bookshops. 'This rush is on because many people imagine that the publication of Struwwelpeter will be stopped after this Bill becomes an Act.'

The Bill, its application limited to publications 'of a kind likely to fall into the hands of children or young persons', was passed in 1955. Little or nothing has been heard of horror comics in Britain since. It would be wrong to suppose that the passing of this Act was the sole cause of their disappearance. Some of the credit must go to the new native 'comics' (as all types of boys' paper were now called) launched in the post-war years.

The most auspicious of these newcomers was *Eagle*, which elevated the picture-strip technique to something very like an art form. First published in 1950 by Hulton Press, with an initial sale of almost a million, it was the brainchild of the Rev. Marcus Morris, vicar of a Lancashire parish. To him it seemed that many of the existing British comics were tired and tawdry, incapable of fighting the American challenge. Why not hit back with the aid of the picture-strip technique?

Mr Morris had little more experience of journalism than that which he had acquired in popularizing a parish magazine. With the aid of a young artist fresh from art school, Frank Hampson, he prepared a dummy of what was to be *Eagle* and began to hawk it round London. For many weeks he was unlucky. Fleet Street often displays a parochial suspicion of projects which are not hatched within its own narrow confines. Here was a country vicar asking the press lords to sink a fortune in a comic which contained, among other things, a picture story about St Paul ('The Great Adventurer'); surely this was the costliest evangelical proposition yet? The vicar from Lancashire had lost a good deal of money and a certain amount of hope by the time that Edward (later Sir Edward) Hulton decided to back *Eagle*. Not for the first time, it turned out that Fleet Street had waved away a gold mine.

Number One of Eagle – the challenger of 1950

Eagle's front-page attraction was Dan Dare, Pilot of the Future, as resourceful a young colonel as ever roamed a rogue planet with a paralysing pistol or forced warring spacemen to diet their way to peace. His exploits were shown in imaginative, meticulous and beautifully printed detail. Other characters included P.C. 49, taken over from the radio, and Jeff Arnold, the cowboy. There were picture biographies of famous men and there were fascinating exploded drawings of mechanical devices. In the main, *Eagle*'s triumph was one of technique and treatment. It did not pioneer any new type of story (if, indeed, there are any left to pioneer); but with the aid of its picture strips it brilliantly re-told many of the old ones. Its success was sufficient to induce its creator, who had now said good-bye to his parish, to produce *Girl, Swift* (for younger readers) and *Robin* (for the very young).

The amount of 'straight' reading in *Eagle* was possibly only one-twentieth of that which the old *Marvel* provided for only one-eighth of the price; but the modern boy, if he could compare the *Marvel's* cramped pages of minute type with the polychromatic splendours of *Eagle* would hardly consider himself cheated. It is doubtful whether there is any boy living who would be prepared to sit down and read the old *Marvel*.

It was not long before the founder of *Eagle* was rebutting charges that his papers were having deleterious effects on the young. Strip pictures, the critics said, were robbing children of the incentive to read; the artists were doing the boy's imagining for him; and there was too much emphasis on action and violence. To which Mr Morris replied, heretically, that there was no virtue in reading *per se*; it was just one of numerous ways of absorbing information. In a sterile and stereotyped urban world picture strips helped to stock the young mind with visual images. Moreover, he argued, they led the inquiring child into new fields of interest which otherwise he would not have been tempted to explore. So long as imagination was fired and curiosity quickened, what did it matter

whether the stimulus came from print or pictures? As for
the portrayal of violence, Mr Morris contended that to
exclude it would merely give children a false picture of
life. The thing to be avoided was violence as an end in
itself. The debate continues.

Eagle lasted only two decades. The Amalgamated Press
challenged it with a new picture-strip paper *Lion* (1952),
followed by *Tiger* (1954). It was now the war of the birds
and beasts. *Lion* gobbled up the sport-crazy *Champion*,
leaving Rockfist Rogan, who had slogged his way through
three decades, to perform in *Tiger*. *Eagle* passed into the
hands of the International Publishing Corporation, which
absorbed the Amalgamated Press, and by 1970 *Lion* had
gobbled up *Eagle*.

Among old-timers to fall by the wayside were several
comic comics (to distinguish them from adventure comics).
In 1953 the guileless readers of *Comic Cuts* and *Chips*
read that their editors had Important and Exciting News
for them. Hoping, perhaps, to read of an attractive free
gift, they turned to the indicated page and found that
henceforth they would be expected to read *Knock-Out*
and *Film Fun*. Thus (or thusly, as *Comic Cuts* would have
said) perished the two papers which had been foundation-
stones in Alfred Harmsworth's publishing empire. Viewed
beside the new Hulton papers, or such robust rivals from
Dundee as *Beano, Dandy* and, latterly, *Topper*, they had
presented a curiously old-fashioned appearance, and the
reaction of many an old addict, on hearing of their demise,
was 'I thought they had been killed off long ago'. On the
front page of the last issue of *Chips* Weary Willie and
Tired Tim appeared to have fallen on their feet at last –
they were invited to be the guests for life of Murgatroyd
Mump, millionaire. At the same time died the *Wonder*,
merged in *Radio Fun*; it dated from 1912 but it could
prove an irregular descent from the *Wonder* of 1892. It
was significant that two of these old-timers were absorbed
by comics which accepted their characters ready-made
from radio and screen. An entertainer is hardly a success

today unless he can point to a weekly comic which shows him being hit in the face with custard pies, rolled up in giant snowballs or plunged into water-butts.

In April 1956 there was Exciting News for the readers of *Rainbow*, the doyen of coloured comics, which had been running since 1914: henceforth they were to ask for *Tiny Tots*. In better days children of the Royal House (so rumour said) had written letters to *Rainbow*. From first to last issue its front page featured the anthropomorphic antics of the Bruin Boys: Tiger Tim, Jumbo the Elephant, Joey the Parrot, Fido the Dog, Bobby Bear, Georgie Giraffe and Jacko the Monkey. There were elders who remembered *Rainbow* equally for Marzipan the Magician and Suzie Sunshine, others for Sing Hi and Sing Lo. Here and there a leader writer tried to squeeze a tear for the Bruin Boys, and the *Spectator* offered prizes for graceful elegiacs, but on the whole the passing of the comics roused curiously few pangs. It is the blood-tingling tales of boyhood which men remember.

Among heroes imported from America was the heavily exploited Batman, who enjoyed a run on television. Intellectuals began to make a cult of him, and, being intellectuals, questioned the nature of his relationship with his boy assistant, Robin. In the annals of British boys' papers batmen and birdmen were, of course, no novelty. In the mid-1960s Batman was all but submerged in a new American invasion of ultra-fantastic heroes. They reached Britain in a sudden explosion of 'Power Comics' with names like *Wham!*, *Smash!*, *Pow!* and *Fantastic*. Soon old friends like Iron Man and Invisible Man were left gasping at the exploits of the newcomers: Spider Man, Sandman, Iceman, Flame Man, Stone Man, Smoke Man and Rubber Man, not to mention the Incredible Hulk and the Missing Link. Their united capabilities were not to be minimized. Sandman poured himself under a locked door and restructured himself into human shape on the other side. Iceman made a shield of his frozen breath; anyone who shook his hand was left holding ice cubes. Flame Man, crying 'Flame on', turned himself into a torch, shrivelling everything except his own briefs. Stone Man, apparently put together from builders' waste, could take anything on the chin or anywhere else. The body of Rubber Man served as a catapult and his arms were infinitely extensible. Smoke Man dissolved when cornered. This new style of hero called for something special in villains who could give the freaks a run for their money. What can Sandman do when pitted against Tomorrow Man, who can vanish at any time into the next century?

These fantastic comics were put out by the International Publishing Corporation, into which the Amalgamated Press was now absorbed. *Fantastic* called itself the comic with the mid-Atlantic accent, but the accent was a good bit west of mid. Its reincarnated Thor swung his hammer amid skyscrapers in which men stole each other's 'greenbacks'. The fan pages had letters from British readers who had learned to say, 'Who, dey?' and 'Howzabout?'

As these lines are written, most of the freaks seem to have transferred to the Marvel Comics Group, still with a London address. In *Spider-Man Comics* 'Spidey' is battling Kingpin, a master crook with a disintegrator cane. Thor is up against the Absorbing Man, who runs his hands along a brick wall to absorb its strength. In *The Mighty World of Marvel* the Incredible Hulk is hard-stretched against an evil Galaxy Master; only the 'indescribable gamma rays' inside him sustain him through orgies of *bam*, *splat* and *thpoom*.

Which of the boys' heroes of today will be remembered in A D 2000? Will detectives and cowboys still form part of our folklore? Will Sexton Blake achieve his centenary? Will early copies of *Eagle* ever become collectors' items? Will old men gather in the chimney corner to listen to recordings of Dick Barton?

Pessimists have suggested that the boys' magazine will decline in status and become a poor relation of coloured television. That seems extravagantly unlikely. Television will serve a useful purpose, however, by keeping the boys' editors on their toes.

One thing at least is sure. There will be many another inquest on the state of juvenile literature and wise men who have forgotten their youth will continue to talk deprecatingly about blood and thunder.

Let G. K. Chesterton have the last word:

The vast mass of humanity, with their vast mass of idle books and idle words, have never doubted and never will doubt that courage is splendid, that fidelity is noble, that distressed ladies should be rescued and vanquished enemies spared ... [Their literature] will always be a blood and thunder literature, as simple as the thunder of heaven and the blood of man.

INDEX